1995

Adult
Personality
Development

To Allan and Karen

Adult Personality Development

Applications

Lawrence S.
Wrightsman

volume 2

SAGE Publications
International Educational and Professional Publisher
Thousand Oaks   London   New Delhi

For information address:

SAGE Publications, Inc.
2455 Teller Road
Thousand Oaks, California 91320

SAGE Publications Ltd.
6 Bonhill Street
London EC2A 4PU
United Kingdom

SAGE Publications India Pvt. Ltd.
M-32 Market
Greater Kailash I
New Delhi 110 048 India

Printed in the United States of America

Library of Congress Cataloging-in-Publication Data

Wrightsman, Lawrence S.
    Adult personality development / author: Lawrence S. Wrightsman.
      p. cm.
    Contents: v. 1. Theories and concepts – v. 2. Applications.
    Includes bibliographical references and indexes.
    ISBN 0-8039-4399-7 (v. 1). – ISBN 0-8039-4401-2 (v. 2). – ISBN
0-8039-4400-4 (pbk. : v. 1). – ISBN 0-8039-4402-0 (pbk. : v. 2)
    1. Personality. 2. Adulthood–Psychological aspects. 3. Aging–
Psychological aspects. I. Title.
BF724.85.P47W74 1994   93-43076
155.6–dc20   CIP

94 95 96 97 98 10 9 8 7 6 5 4 3 2 1

Sage Production Editor: Yvonne Könneker

Contents

Preface

The publication of the original version of *Personality Development in Adulthood* in 1988 reflected my long-standing interest in the ways that personality characteristics form and change. That book was organized into 12 chapters, with the first half presenting different theories as explanations, and the second half applying these theories to different aspects of adulthood.

In the intervening years my own quest for understanding this phenomenon has led me to further reading and study. I have benefited from participating in workshops led by Daniel J. Levinson and by James Birren, and I have taught a course on this topic several times.

This book and its companion volume (*Adult Personality Development, Volume 1: Theories and Concepts*) reflect an expansion of the coverage of the initial book. The structure has been maintained but the coverage has been doubled, through the addition of examples as well as more recent findings. The luxury of a greater length has permitted me to explore new topics, including the use of biographies and case studies; increased attention is devoted to creativity in adulthood, to learning and memory, to marriage stability, and to other topics.

A major goal has been to provide a readable survey of ideas and findings on different manifestations of personality development during adulthood. The book is selective, not exhaustive; the proliferation of material since the renewed interest in midlife in the mid-1970s prevents complete coverage. In my desire to stimulate thought, I have used a wide variety of sources: scholarly articles and books, but also newspaper and magazine articles and selections from autobiographies and biographies. The number of new references exceeds the number retained from the earlier book.

This book, along with the companion volume, may provide the focus for a Psychology of Adulthood course that encourages students to look at the evolving nature of their own lives. Particular attention has been given to developing an extensive set of references (almost 700 in this volume) as an aid to scholars.

Of all the books I have completed, this one and its companion volume are the most personal, in the sense that they reflect my mission as a psychologist and an educator to help others learn about themselves, while I learn about myself in the process. It has been a pleasure to write, and I hope it is a pleasure to read.

–Lawrence S. Wrightsman

Acknowledgments

More than most books in the field, perhaps, this is a book of ideas. My role has been to transmit the ideas of others, and thus my first acknowledgment is to those psychologists, educators, philosophers, and writers whose thoughts I have reproduced in this book. On many occasions I have quoted them at length, because the topic of personality development is one in which the content of ideas cannot be separated from the style of expression and the values behind the ideas expressed.

The staff at Sage Publications has given me unconditional support in my desire to reframe my earlier work in an expanded, updated version. It is a pleasure to work with a congenial staff in achieving a goal we all share.

Preparation of this book was also facilitated by the efforts of Tamara Bryan, who tracked down elusive references, and Katia Silva, whose word processor provided a magic transformation of my messy manuscript.

To all, my appreciation.

–Lawrence S. Wrightsman

1

Recurring Issues in the
Development of Personality in Adulthood

*I have made a ceaseless effort not to ridicule, not to bewail,
nor to scorn human actions, but to understand them.*

Spinoza

During a long weekend in the fall of 1991, the American public was
riveted to the television set, watching a U.S. Senate committee
evaluate the claims of Professor Anita Hill that she had been sexually
harassed by Supreme Court justice nominee Clarence Thomas. Reactions of the public, just like those of the Senate committee members,
were divided, but Clarence Thomas was later confirmed (barely)
by the full U.S. Senate, making him one of the nine justices of the
U.S. Supreme Court.

Who *is* Clarence Thomas? You would think that we would have
a clear, agreed-on portrait of his personality, given the intense
scrutiny allocated to him by the media, the earlier confirmation
hearings by the Senate Judiciary Committee, and all the testimony
by Professor Hill, Judge Thomas, her advocates, and his, during that
long weekend. But any emerging picture is at best a complex one,

1

BOX 1.1

The Personality of Clarence Thomas

"In one universe, there is the compassionate, even-tempered, curious and independent Thomas, the quintessence of old-fashioned hard work and self-help. This is the Black Horatio Alger for our time: a humble individual who has lifted himself up and out from punishing Southern poverty to the peaks of power, never forgetting those who paved the path along the way. He knew the names of all the women who toiled behind the steam counters in the Senate cafeteria, he stays in touch with the Roman Catholic nuns who taught him, he takes time to talk to Washington's homeless. This Thomas can't wait to open his mind on a new subject; once he learned of the lore of Lincoln, he scoured stores and bought shelves of books. . . . This Thomas understands racism and bigotry the way an owl knows the night; he stared down the Reagan administration when he thought his principles required it. This Thomas even reads psalms every day.

"In the other, darker universe exists the bitter, impulsive, hot-headed and opportunistic Thomas. Here is the family man who publicly skewered his own sister as an example of welfare addiction. And the 33-year-old civil rights chief at the Department of Education who bellowed to an aide, 'You could fill books with what you don't know.' And the boss at the Equal Employment Opportunity Commission who tried to transfer an employee 2,500 miles away for making critical remarks. . . . Here is the Thomas who vowed not to take any job involving racial issues, only to accept two from Ronald Reagan. Here is the Thomas who logs obsessive hours at a desk and in a gym, had his kid doing pushups at the age of 3, and confided to a friend that he idolized 'Darth Vader.' "

---

and at worst, ambiguous. A writer for *Newsweek* magazine perhaps sums it up best, in Box 1.1.

As Kaplan (1991) observes, conflict and confusion have been characteristic in assessments of Justice Thomas's personality. He once advocated the Black-nationalism movement, including the writings of Malcolm X, and he showed bitterness toward Whites;

he now lives with his White wife in a predominantly White Virginia suburb. Born a Baptist, he enrolled at a Catholic seminary and now attends an Episcopal church. In the mid-1980s he took over the primary responsibility for the son who was a product of his broken first marriage, but he publicly and unfairly humiliated his sister ("She gets mad when the mailman is late with her welfare check; that's how dependent she is") to make a political point; furthermore, it is reported that he never offered her any help when she was going through difficult times (White, 1991).

Is he the judge who, on looking out the window of his office at busloads of Black prisoners, said to himself, "There but for the grace of God go I"? Or is he an "ambitious political climber" (Strasser & Coyle, 1991) who, while Chairman of the Equal Employment Opportunity Commission, attended a reception honoring the ambassador from South Africa, a country then advocating apartheid?

The Complexity of Individual Lives

Some might say that Clarence Thomas's personality—because of his upbringing and the changes in his life—is more multifaceted and complicated than the personality of the typical person. I doubt it. Each of us reflects the accumulation and assimilation of thousands of daily decisions and experiences. To describe only one day in the life of one individual, ecological psychologists Roger Barker and Herbert Wright (1951) required more than 400 pages of print. And their task was simply to record the *behaviors,* not the thoughts, feelings, and attitudes, of one boy. Multiply these by the experiences of 365 days a year, for however many years, and contemplate the mass of environmental stimulation that each of us receives every 24 hours. The sheer immensity of information demands processing, even if it is incorporated into an existing personality structure, or even if it is later ignored. And much is not ignored.

This perspective causes some observers of the human condition to conclude that each of us is unique, and hence efforts to seek common explanations are fruitless. But others emphasize the consistencies between individuals and, more importantly, that a scientific approach emphasizes communalities. Box 1.2 discusses this distinction as a basic issue in the study of personality development

---

BOX 1.2

What Units Shall We Employ?

In studying personality, should we focus on characteristics that—in some degree—are common to all persons, or should we focus on each unique individual? Identifying the appropriate unit for the analysis of personality has been an issue for than 50 years (see, e.g., Carlson, 1971b). This distinction is sometimes characterized as the choice between the nomothetic and idiographic approaches (Cohler, 1993).

The nomothetic approach seeks to uncover scientific laws that describe relationships between characteristics present in most or all people. Thus an emphasis is describing a taxonomy of qualities central to all individuals. The Big Five traits of personality (Goldberg, 1990) have been proposed by personality trait theorists as such basic building blocks; technically, such traits are *descriptions* of personality, but the emergent five-factor model has also been advanced as a theory of personality (John & Robins, 1993).

In contrast, the idiographic approach emphasizes individual uniqueness. But two types of uniqueness can be theoretically distinguished. The more extreme view would propose that the elements by which personality is organized or structured are different in each individual; hence, the individual has to be the unit of analysis. Gordon Allport (1961)—often offered as an example of idiographic advocacy—instead insisted on what he called a "morphogenic" perspective that presumed a unique *organization* of elements within each person, but a common set of traits from which the individual's unique combination was formed (Cohler, 1993).

The latter conception of the idiographic approach is compatible with the role construct theory of George Kelly (1955), described in Volume 1, Chapter 1, in the sense that each person chooses from common constructs but uniquely selects which to emphasize. This makes sense; one of the strongest arguments for the Big Five as basic units of personality is that these are the terms that people commonly use to describe other people. It is natural that each of us—even in our uniqueness—relies on these as tools.

---

in adulthood. Other overarching issues are described in subsequent sections of this chapter.

.

Recurring Issues

Volume 1 described and evaluated contrasting conceptions of how personality develops during adulthood. As each is applied to different aspects of adulthood in forthcoming chapters, its contribution to an overriding conception of personality will be reexamined. But in regard to a number of issues these conceptions differ; the next sections provide, first, brief illustrations of some specific issues and, then, focus on examples of basic controversies: the role of values in determining the "good life," and the effect of heredity versus environment.

Is the System an Open One or a Closed One?

How do people regulate the input of new experience described earlier? Some people can be so open to new experience that they are constantly overwhelmed. Others can be so shut off to all outside stimulation that they live in worlds of autism or schizophrenia. For example, some people refuse to recognize changes in their wives or husbands and continue to interact with their spouses as they did when they first got married.

The goal, perhaps, is to regulate the flow of new experience in a way that enables people to remain essentially stable over most of the rest of their lives, while being open to new experiences (Troll, 1982). But just when are these regulating structures developed, and how much do these structures actually accommodate? And, do these structures themselves change over adulthood? The developmental psychologist John Anderson (quoted by Troll, 1982, p. 5) proposed that the aging person possesses a progressively more closed system. This issue will be examined in more detail in Chapter 7.

Continuity Versus Abrupt Change

A theme of Volume 1 was the issue of whether personality in adulthood was best characterized as reflecting stability or change. One conception of change in adulthood emphasizes that it is a gradual response to accumulating bits of information and experience (Troll, 1982). Interestingly, this is the way most people see their own lives. Often, when change seems to outsiders to be abrupt or dramatic—the shift to an entirely different line of work (Chapter 2), or a seemingly sudden breakup of a long marriage (Chapter 5)—the person will say, "Oh no, I've been leading up to this for a long time."

Some developmental psychologists agree; they conceptualize life as an unfolding process; Jaffe and Allman (1982) say, "The life process consists of a somewhat orderly sequence of developmental stages and tasks, which are punctuated at each point by individual crises and difficulties" (p. 3). But others give the crises more prominence; Levinson's (1980) theory, described in Volume 1, Chapter 7, views adulthood as alternating between periods of major upheaval and periods of quietude.

What Is "The Good Life"?

Each of the perspectives introduced in Volume 1 perpetuates implicit value judgments about what is the best adaptation to changing tasks and ages in adulthood. But there certainly are problems in determining what is "good." Smelser (1980) notes:

Growth . . . is a relative concept. Like pattern, its presence or absence is dictated in part by questions posed and by the scope of the life span considered. Whether or not a given process is regarded as growth depends also on the criteria by which the term is defined. Two investigators may agree on the empirical fact that in the later years of adulthood men and women become more resigned and conservative in a variety of ways. But whether this is to be interpreted as growth to some plateau of vision and wisdom or whether it is to be seen as defeat and retreat is unclear, and neither interpretation depends on the facts but on a framework for evaluation that the individual investigator uses. (p. 22)

To the mathematician, engineer, or physical scientist for whom "the facts speak for themselves," the value-colored nature of conclusions by adult personality theorists must be frustrating and elusive. Can there be any firm, objective, agreed-on conclusions about the nature of development? I believe there are, but still we will see this issue recurring through virtually every chapter of this book.

Values should be made explicit, of course, and sometimes they are not. When values are clearly articulated, people can choose between them. And sources of ideas should be identified. To some degree, theoretical concepts on this topic stem from the personal experience of the theoretician (see Volume 1, Chapter 2). But many of the ideas in this book, regardless of the individualistic nature of their origins, have stood the test of time and have been accepted by others.

Is Biology Destiny?

Among the theories in Volume 1, the psychoanalytic viewpoint heavily relies on biological origins for personality development in childhood. As a spin-off of the psychoanalytic view, the life script approach has little to say about constitutional factors. As stage theories extended the wellsprings of development beyond the first 5 years of childhood, emphasis shifted from biological to cultural determinants. The dialectical approach rejects the assumption from biology that homeostasis is desirable (or even attainable) with respect to personality development.

Though linked together, and though both have had a recent resurgence as explanations, we need to distinguish between biological determinants and hereditary ones. Recent reactions of depressed persons to the drug Prozac (Kramer, 1993) have led observers—noting massive changes in these persons' personalities—to question the basics of personality. Now taken by some 8 million persons, Prozac has typical effects—assertiveness, vivacity, mental acuity—far different from the responses of these persons previously (Gates, 1993). Prozac maintains high levels of the neurotransmitter serotonin, a mood regulator. But do its effects mean personality is simply a function of brain chemistry? Psychiatrist Peter Kramer (quoted by Gates, 1993, p. 71) concludes, "It's difficult to resist the . . . visceral certainty that who people are is largely biologically determined."

The Resurgence of Heredity as an Explanation

Sixty years ago, heated controversy existed between adherents of heredity and environment as explanations especially of a person's

IQ level, but of one's personality as well. But support for heredity declined in the 1960s, as the mood of the country encouraged a belief that environmental interventions (such as Project Head Start) could abolish limitations in educational performance and instill improved academic motivations. Since then, support for heredity as a determinant of personality has had a resurgence, even what Plomin (1990, p. 3) calls a "remarkable turnaround."

For example, recent work by Kagan and Snidman (1991) concludes that a small number of children are born with a biological disposition to be shy. This section will focus on the issue of the *heritability* of personality. Heritability refers to the relative contribution of the genes to individual differences in a particular trait (Loehlin, 1992).

Research methods that for decades had been applied to the question of the determinants of intelligence level have begun to be used to study personality determinants; these include a comparison of similarities in identical twins with similarities in fraternal twins and in siblings. Although identical twins have the same genes, fraternal twins—on the average—share only about half their genes (Loehlin, 1992). The use of foster children as subjects provides a fruitful method when the environment in the foster home differs dramatically from that of the natural parents' home. But perhaps the most useful procedure capitalizes on occasions in which pairs of identical twins had to be removed from the environment of their biological parent or parents and separated by placing one child in a different home from the other.

As an example of such a study, Pedersen, Plomin, McClearn, and Friberg (1988) compared the similarity in personality in both identical twins and fraternal twins, some pairs of whom were reared together and some of whom were reared apart. The study capitalized on data from Sweden, which has a population-based twin registry that includes 25,000 pairs of twins. When tested, most of the subjects were over 50 years of age; the mean age was 58.6 years. But for those who had been brought up in separate homes, all pairs were separated by age 10, and almost half had been separated by their first birthday. The total numbers of pairs in the study were: 99 pairs of identical twins reared apart, 160 pairs of identical twins reared together, 229 pairs of fraternal twins reared apart, and 212 pairs of fraternal twins reared together. All the subjects were mailed personality inventories and asked to complete them; these included Eysenck's measures of neuroticism and extroversion, as well as other scales measuring impulsivity and sensation seeking.

The percentage of the variance attributable to genetic sources was 41% for extroversion, 31% for neuroticism, 45% for impulsivity, and 23% for sensation-seeking. These are, indeed, impressive figures, indicating that heredity plays a significant role in influencing responses to personality inventories, even when the subjects are middle-aged adults or older. (The figure for extroversion, 41% of the variance, is very similar to the 35% to 39% found in Loehlin's 1992 review.) Environmental similarity had nonsignificant effects on most measures; less than 10% of the variance was accounted for by the environment, as found in some similar studies (Plomin, 1990), but not all. For example, using 7,144 adult twin pairs in Finland, Rose and his colleagues (Rose, Koskenvuo, Kaprio, Sarna, & Langinvainio, 1988) conclude that the greater similarity within a pair of identical twins than fraternal twins is a result of both genetic dispositions and the pattern of their social interactions.

Some other studies have found even higher percentages of variance attributed to heredity; from 41% to 74%. For example, Tellegen et al. (1988) compared 44 pairs of identical twins raised apart (with an average age of 36), along with a large samples of identical twins reared together and fraternal twins reared together. Correlation coefficients for identical twins reared apart included .61 for absorption (imagination), .53 for traditionalism, .48 for alienation, and correlations of .29 to .61 for other personality measures. As Plomin (1990) notes, these correlations, for identical twins brought up in separate families, are as high as those found for identical twins reared together. That is, the inevitable differences in environment produced by the adoptive families apparently had little effect.

Sometimes the similarities in personality and values extend to surprising details. Begley (1987) describes one case:

Take the renowned case of Jim Springer and Jim Lewis, identical twins separated just four weeks after they were born in Ohio 48 years ago. Reunited 39 years later in a study on twins at the University of Minnesota, they discovered that they had married and divorced women named Linda, married second wives named Betty and named their first sons James Allan and James Alan, respectively. That's not all: They both drive the same model of blue Chevrolets and they both enjoyed woodworking (and had built identical benches around trees in their backyards). They often vacationed on the same small beach in St. Petersburg, Fla., and owned dogs named Toy. (p. 59; from NEWS-WEEK, November 23, 1987. © 1987, Newsweek, Inc. All rights reserved. Reprinted by permission.)

A coincidence, or a genetic determination?

Interactionist Views and Reconciliations

The research results summarized in the previous section have caused psychologists to seek newer and more sophisticated conceptions of the causes of personality. As Troll (1982) observes, among developmental psychologists who are interested in the early years of life, many have resolved the conflict between heredity and development by adopting an interactionist view. That is, "Neither heredity (biology) nor environment (experience) can be thought of apart from the other; both are intertwined from the first moment of conception" (Troll, 1982, p. 3). Furthermore, as Loehlin observes, "particular combinations of genes and environments may lead to consequences not predictable from the two considered separately" (1992, p. 7).

Advocacy of an interactionist position reminds us that three different views can be distinguished; in a provocative presentation, Dean Keith Simonton (1993) has applied these to the development of genius—which reflects intelligence plus personality. Simonton builds on the quotation from Shakespeare's *Twelfth Night:* "Some men are born great, some achieve greatness, and some have greatness thrust on them."

Advocates of hereditary influences—"Some men are born great"—rely on Sir Francis Galton's classic study of English families, *Hereditary Genius* (1869), which argued that natural ability and zeal were inherited and if you had these, you were bound to achieve.

Galton's work was a major influence on psychologist Lewis Terman (who developed the Stanford-Binet intelligence test) and his *Genetic Studies of Genius* (Terman, 1925). He also influenced modern behavioral genetics, by initiating both the previously described twin studies (Galton, 1875) and the *pedigree method,* or the tracing of ability through several generations of the same families.

Simonton (1993) describes research on pathological pedigrees and concludes that geniuses and creative people score higher on the clinical subscales of the Minnesota Multiphasic Personality Inventory (MMPI) and other measures of pathology. The incidence rates of mental illness in creative people are higher than the average, but, more interestingly, there is a curvilinear relationship between level of pathology and eminence. If you have too much or too little pathology, you are not creative (Simonton, 1993), as too little pathology leaves you with too conventional an orientation, and too much prevents focus on the task at hand.

Simonton concludes that there is sufficient evidence that mental pathology is partly inherited. Genius also runs in families, so that some siblings get just the right amount, while other siblings become too mundane or too bizarre. Simonton (1993), referring to it as the "missing siblings" problem, asks why we do not see more successful brothers and sisters of geniuses? Why were all the siblings of Shakespeare, for example, or Benjamin Franklin, so ordinary? Only a small number of siblings get just the right combination, a point to be developed more when we deal with *emergenesis* in the next section.

In contrast to the hereditarians, cultural determinists would subscribe to Shakespeare's statement that "some men have greatness thrust on them." They note that many contributions by seemingly creative people reflect the phenomenon of multiple discovery; Newton and Liebnitz discovered the calculus at the same time; Alfred Wallace and Charles Darwin developed their theories of evolution at the same time. Creativity is partly determined by developments from the culture and society.

The third perspective, claiming that "some do achieve greatness," reflects the psychological approach. Heredity is not enough; some kind of stimulation—even if it takes the form of a traumatic event—is necessary for greatness to occur. Opportunity to work with a mentor is very helpful. Extending this further, the field of developmental behavior genetics accepts the proposition that the impact of genetic and environmental influences cannot be completely disentangled (Goldsmith, 1990).

By now it should be clear that the question "is biology destiny?" is not answered straightforwardly.

The field of behavior genetics is one of the most rapidly developing fields of specialization relevant to the topic of this book. One of the most recent and sophisticated conceptions in behavior genetics seeks to explain the remarkable similarities in identical twins reared apart, consistencies that cannot be explained by a shared environment. Developed by researchers from the Minnesota Study of Twins Reared Apart (Bouchard, Lykken, McGue, Segal, & Tellegen, 1990), the concept of *emergenesis* refers to a trait that is the result of a *configuration* of genes "or perhaps a configuration of mere basic traits that are themselves partly genetic in origin" (Lykken, McGue, Tellegen, & Bouchard, 1992). Lykken (1982) proposed that the marked similarity in identical twins—even when reared separately—in contrast to the lack of similarity in fraternal twins is strongly suggestive of an emergenic trait. Especially this emphasis on a unique cluster of determinants seems applicable when applied to some of the very specific traits or behaviors shown in the more than 100 pairs of subjects studied by the Minnesota Study of Twins Reared Apart. Consider the following (in this excerpt "MZA" refers to monozygote, or identical, twins reared apart):

A pair of British MZAs, who had met for the first time as adults just a month previously, both firmly refused in their separate interviews to express opinions on controversial topics. . . . Another pair were both habitual gigglers, although each had been raised by adoptive parents whom they described as undemonstrative and dour, and neither had known anyone who laughed as freely as she did until she finally met her twin. . . . A pair of male MZAs, at their first adult reunion, discovered that they both used Vademecum toothpaste, Canoe shaving lotion, Vitalis hair tonic, and Lucky Strike cigarettes. . . . Only two of these more than 200 individual twins reared apart were afraid to enter the acoustically shielded chamber used in our psychophysiology laboratory; both separately agreed to continue if the door was wired open—they were a pair of MZA twins. When at the beach, both women had always insisted on entering the water backwards and then only up to their knees; they were thus concordant, not only in their phobic tendencies but also in the specific manifestations of that timidity. There were two gunsmith hobbyists among the group of twins; two women who habitually wore seven rings; . . . two who obsessively counted things; two who had been married five times . . . in each case, an MZA pair. (Lykken et al., 1992, pp. 1565-1566)

And recall, these pairs were in all cases twins who had been separated in childhood! The average age of separation for subjects in this study was 5 months, and the longest that any pair was together was the first 4 years of life (Bouchard et al., 1990).

Referring back to Simonton's distinction among origins of greatness, it may be that some geniuses possess such a configuration of specific inherited traits that they possess no family pedigree to predict this, nor do their siblings or offspring show such signs of genius. Simonton (1993) puts Michelangelo, Shakespeare, Beethoven, and Sir Isaac Newton in this category of "Galtonian isolates."

The evidence presented to support the conclusion of a strong genetic influence on personality is impressive but its impact can be exaggerated. In an important way, an appropriate response is the same as the one to the conclusions of the personality trait theorists reviewed in Volume 1; yes, personality is consistent from childhood to adulthood if it is defined through the use of traits and applied to specific behaviors. Among the various levels of conceptualizing personality (see Volume 1, Box 10.1), the basic trait level shows highest heritability. But so far, no strong evidence has been provided to indicate that goals and "projects" of Level 2, or the narrative view of identity at Level 3, are inherited. As Chaplin (1990) observes, "Our understanding of human personality will improve when we consider personality at different levels of abstraction" (p. 941).

Furthermore, the results presented here fail to specify the role of the environment as it either passively or actively influences individual differences in personality traits. Contemporary theorizing sees the environment as multifaceted (Wachs, 1992). An impressive book by Arnold Buss (1988) takes the types of traits studied by the hereditarians and speculates about how parent-child matches and mismatches on each trait might modify those traits in the individual. How does one's genetic makeup affect reactions to certain experiences and choices? How does environmental stimulation work? The resurgence in the recognition of the role of heredity is a healthy move toward balance, but the important questions remain to be answered.

Less emphasized than the question of what determines personality in identical twins is the question: Do the personalities of two twins become more similar or more different with age? A useful review (McCartney, Harris, & Bernieri, 1990) examined the correlations for a number of intelligence and personality variables for sets of identical and fraternal twins in 103 studies. The reviewers' general conclusion: Among the older pairs, the two twins were less similar to each other than among the younger. Some strong qualifications exist for this conclusion; in effect, the meta-analysis was a cross-sectional study, no longitudinal follow-up existed of the same pairs, and the numbers of cases for some measures was quite small. The authors title their review "Growing Up and Growing Apart" and, as Loehlin (1992, p. 83) notes, the most straightforward interpretation is that the growing apart is mostly environmental in origin. Each twin has a more individually distinctive environment as he or she gets older; this was true even for the identical twins.

S U M M A R Y

The distinguished psychologist Jerome Bruner has said that "the major activity of all human beings is to extract meaning from their encounters with the world" (quoted by Fisher, 1989, p. 11). Theorists of adult development face a number of issues when they seek to give meaning to personality in adulthood. For example, value judgments are inevitable when describing "healthy" personality development. But perhaps most important is the emphasis placed on heredity; some theories overlook it. The conclusion of this chapter is that recent research leads us to argue it cannot be ignored as a contributor to personality. However, environment interacts with heredity at the very beginning of development and continues to do so throughout adulthood.

2

Occupational Changes in Adulthood

There is no substitute for hard work.

Thomas Alva Edison

Volume 1 of this book portrayed various conceptions of personality development and psychosocial development during adulthood. Subsequent chapters in Volume 2 apply these concepts to important aspects of adult life: careers, intimate relations and marriage, sexual attitudes and behavior, sex roles, political and religious values, mental abilities, and adaptation to aging. For each of these topics, my emphasis is on developmental concerns, or the changing nature of the phenomenon across the 50 or more years of adulthood. The chapter-length coverage of each of these aspects also permits further investigation of the validity and applicability of the theories presented in the first volume.

In the case of occupational choice, one of the most respected theories of career development—that by Donald Super (1971, 1986, 1990)—follows the individual's career through the entire era of adolescence and adulthood. Super emphasizes changes in self-concept and their inevitable impacts on choice and change of career. Conveniently for the structure of this book, Super employs a stage theory of occupational development (although he has been faulted by some for failing to incorporate emerging concepts and methods from life-span developmental psychology; see, e.g., Vondracek, Lerner, & Schulenberg, 1986). The first stage, occurring between the ages of 15 and 25, is characterized by exploration and trial, with consideration of several avenues, either systematically or in a trial-and-error fashion. The second stage, called the establishment phase, occurs between the ages of 25 and 45, and involves the implementation of a career choice and stabilization within an occupation. In keeping with Gould's concepts described in Volume 1, Chapter 6, the individual expects that hard work—even, for some, the extreme of "apple polishing"—will provide recognition and advancement, and the young worker may seek additional technical training to facilitate progress up the occupational ladder. Emphasis here is on conformity to the lifestyle of "superiors" in the organization, and a rather stable career pattern. The maintenance stage, applicable according to Super at ages 45 to 55, involves continuity of vocational behavior along established lines, although a reevaluation phase may occur here, too. An outcome is a sense of becoming resigned to one's failure to reach the anticipated level of achievement.

By use of *maintenance* to label this stage Super does not necessarily mean that development is constant (Whitbourne & Weinstock, 1979). There is even a dialectical flavor to Super's (1957) treatment of this stage; he writes that:

> Perfect equilibrium is never reached, that vocational adjustment is a continuous process throughout the whole of life and that even the maintenance stage is not, as the name may be thought to imply, a period of undiluted enjoyment of the fruits of labor. Instead, the labor continues, although perhaps somewhat less arduously because its pattern is by now well established. (p. 149)

At age 55 begins a deceleration stage or "disengagement" that prepares the worker for retirement. The last stage is the retirement period around age 65; the worker may experience a severe discontinuity in both work role and self-concept (see Chapter 7 for elaboration).

An application of a stage theory of development to one type of occupation—college professor—is illustrated in Box 2.1.

BOX 2.1

A Stage Theory of Faculty Career Development

Nevitt Sanford (1971) and his colleagues (Brown & Shukraft, 1971; Ralph, 1973) interviewed college and university faculty about their professional development for several years; these interviews, with about 300 professors in eight different institutions, went into considerable depth. They were guided by a comprehensive interview schedule; the average length of each interview was about 3 hours.

Sanford (1971) concludes that "college professors develop as individuals in much the same way that other people do" (p. 360). Their development is believed to be progressive and marked by distinguishable stages; however, in contrast to Super, Sanford and his colleagues do not try to assign specific chronological ages to these stages.

The thinking of David Hunt (1966) is reflected in this work. Five stages have been conceptualized. The first, a *formative period,* really is a prologue, a preadult development of identity. The last stage, *generativity,* is not dealt with as extensively as the three intermediate stages. Sanford describes three stages in detail:

1. Achievement of *sense of competence* (also called *competence formation*) in one's discipline or specialty. It represents "the act of focusing one's identity, of setting on a specific career direction as a durable and sustaining life stance" (Brown & Shukraft, 1971, p. 52). The way this developmental task is approached and achieved depends to a great degree on what has happened to the faculty member in his or her past (during the formative period). It depends, for example, on whether the person's childhood was relatively "isolated" or "social." Sanford reports that "the overwhelming majority" of the professors in his samples were isolated children. In one liberal arts college, half were only children. Most learned early in life "to enjoy being rewarded by adults for academic achievement and they learn late, if at all, to participate in the rough and tumble of campus politics" (p. 361). Sanford hypothesizes that those college professors who were "social" children—and were mischievous and sometimes disobedient—came rather late upon the discovery of their academic potentialities and that these professors "have a hard time getting over the feeling that they may not be doing the right thing in the classroom" (p. 361) even though they may be successful in campus politics.

(Continued)

BOX 2.1 (Continued)

---

2. The next stage is one of *self-discovery* or *alternation* in which the professor "gives attention to other abilities, interests, and aspirations and so expands his [or her] personality" (p. 361). This would appear to be similar to Levinson's Period 6, "the midlife transition," as Brown and Shukraft note that what occurs here is "the encounter between the visions, ideals, and expectations of the initial career decision and events and experiences in the actual situation" (p. 52). Sanford notes that at this stage the professor is ready to change, but change is difficult, because he "has made commitments and must defend what he has done, while also dealing with expectations of families and colleagues who, often at some pain, have grown used to him as he is" (p. 361).
3. A third stage is *integration* or *discovery of others*: "Now the professor is prepared to use all of his skills in genuine relationships with other people; he may find it comfortable and enjoyable to take a parental role with some students—those who can stand it or will accept it" (Sanford, 1971, p. 361). This stage resembles Levinson's period of restabilization; here Sanford and his colleagues build on Erik Erikson's formation described in Volume 1, Chapter 1.

It should be apparent to you that Super's vocational-development theory contains many of the same qualities of the general stage theories of Volume 1, even to its specifying of precise (and too confining) age limits for each stage. And the theory also suffers the limitation of previous ones in its implicit male bias; theories built on the experience of men assume a career pattern that is linear and uninterrupted (Perun & Bielby, 1981). For women, it is common for the combination of work and family responsibilities to produce an interrupted career pattern.

As is detailed in a later section of this chapter, psychologists who conceptualize the career development of women have responded to the challenge in several ways (Brooks, 1990). One approach is to apply a theory from one realm to another. For example, Hackett and Betz (1981) use the concept of self-efficacy, one's beliefs about one's own capabilities to perform a task; they propose that the different sex-role socialization experienced by women prevents them from gaining the same access to relevant information as men have. So, women's expectations are lower, contributing to the restricted range of options and the underutilization of their abilities, characteristic in recent times in the workforce of this country. A review of the empirical literature on these ideas, by Linda Brooks (1990), finds considerable support for the expectation that one's self-efficacy level is related to vocational behavior. Some results lend support to the conclusion that "women may be more heterogenous than men with regard to efficacy beliefs about traditional and nontraditional occupations" (Brooks, 1990, p. 372).

Similarly, Gottfredson (1981) has proposed that gender-typing of certain occupations leads women to develop compromises in the choice of careers.

A second approach to the challenge of explaining women's career pathways is to suggest ways that additional concepts can be incorporated into existing theory (Brooks, 1990). Consider, for example, work identity. Most theories have reflected a masculine bias—a concept of a separate and objective self. Theories of the development of women (Chodorow, 1978; Gilligan, 1982) note that many women describe their identity on the basis of their relationships to others; connectedness rather than separateness is central to their self-concept. It would follow that women would prefer "work environments where this component of their identity could be expressed and valued" (Forrest & Mikolaitis, 1986, p. 83).

A third theoretical approach is to create a new comprehensive theory specifically to describe the career-choice process of women. Helen Astin's (1984) sociopsychological model includes constructs of motivation, expectations, sex-role socialization, and structure of opportunity. These are not static, especially the latter construct, accounting for changes in women's aspirations and choices in recent years. Astin's theory is intuitively appealing, but as Brooks notes, it has been criticized on philosophy-of-science grounds (Fitzgerald & Betz, 1984), and it lacks published evaluative research to date.

The Place of Work in One's Adult Identity

For young people who have completed their schooling and are now ready to enter the world of work on a full-time and "permanent" basis, change has characterized their lives up to this point. Although they realize that their jobs may be one of the most lasting features of their adult life, they may not be prepared for such an enduring commitment. Undergraduate students have, on occasion, confided to me that the idea of working in the same job for 40 years is utterly incomprehensible to them. And well it might; even the professional literature in occupational psychology has virtually a gap (Hall, 1986) with regard to research on maintenance of one's career during midlife.

Yet we all realize that one's identity as a worker is central. Soon after we meet someone, we are likely to ask, "What kind of work do you do?" We ask this not only because we assume that we will know more about the person from the answer, but because we, too, value our work identity. When given a "Twenty Statements" test that asks the person to provide responses to the question "Who Am I?", most adults mention their occupation among the initial five self-labels.

Furthermore, Americans by and large are working as many hours as they are allowed; employees typically state they would prefer longer hours and higher incomes to more leisure and smaller pay-checks (Church, 1987). Absenteeism in the United States is lower than that in England, Canada, Denmark, France, or the Netherlands (Church, 1987).

The place of work in the identity of Americans is indirectly emphasized by figures that conclude that length of paid vacations in the United States compares unfavorably with those of most other advanced countries (Kinsley, 1990). Compared to the average American's 12 paid vacation days, the British get 25, the French a little more, and the Germans 30 a year. Even the Japanese average 16 days of paid vacation per year.

Yet our feelings toward our own work identity may reflect a love-hate relationship. Sarason (1977, pp. 13-14) notes that the question, "How do you like your job?" triggers different and sometimes ambivalent feelings about our work. At a superficial level, our initial response is usually "Well, of course, I like it." But at a deeper level we may question what we are doing. Our work identity, like our self-identity, may go through periods of relative turmoil and then relative stability. And with younger adults of the "baby-boomer" generation, Hall and Richter's (1985) study indicates that a new set of values affects the attitudes toward work held by this cohort. Baby boomers place high priority on the balance between work life and family life, partly because the preponderance of two-career families has forced them to. Based on a long-term longitudinal study of two cohorts (Howard & Bray, 1988), AT&T manager baby boomers are less dominant, more energetic, and more nurturant than the earlier generation of managers.

Society places expectations on us to enjoy our work, especially if our occupation is a prestigious, well-paying one. As more and more people move into high-level professions, they are all expected to experience satisfaction and fulfillment in their work. But what if they do not? What if they burn out or lose interest? Sarason (1977) observes:

> To express dissatisfaction or boredom with or a waning interest in one's work—particularly if one's work is judged by society as fascinating and important, as in the case of many professions—is no easy matter. To face up to such dissatisfaction is literally to question what one is and to have to justify continuing as one has. It is no less difficult, upsetting, and propelling than to come to the realization that one no longer wishes to live with one's spouse. Our experience suggests that to talk candidly about one's relationship to one's work is as difficult as talking about one's sex life. We define ourselves, and are defined by others, by what we do: our work. To question this definition produces internal conflict, in part precisely because we know that we have come to see ourselves quite differently from others. (p. 57)

This is a provocative statement from one of the most experienced observers of career change in adulthood. Perhaps you think it is too extreme in its statement of the difficulty we have in expressing dissatisfaction with our jobs. Many of us recall the Johnny Paycheck song, "Take This Job and Shove It." But note that Sarason is especially referring to jobs that outsiders see as "fascinating and important." Society may tolerate—or even expect—ditch diggers or garbage collectors to grouse about their working conditions. But for heart surgeons or architects to vacillate about their career identity creates questions and chagrin, partly because we reason, "If they are not satisfied in their high-paying, important positions, how can we be satisfied with our mediocre jobs?"

Sarason's claim that it is just as hard to talk frankly about one's job dissatisfaction as it is to reveal one's sex life may also strike the reader as too extreme. But Sarason (1977) observes that "our society has made it easier to change marriage partners than to change careers (partially or drastically), but the dynamics behind both types of changes are similar if not identical" (p. 71).

Ideally, one's personality and one's choice of an occupation should be congruent. John Holland's (1963, 1966, 1985, 1987) widely cited theory of career development sees choice of a career as a three-stage process in which self-knowledge and knowledge of the world of work have matured to a point that an intelligent and congruent career choice could be made. In Holland's view, our vocational interests are an extension of our personalities. The more a person resembles one of Holland's personality types or subtypes, the more likely the person is to seek environments (including work environments) that reflect those personality types (Weinrach & Srebalus, 1990). As noted earlier, women, in general, might seek different types of work environments than men seek, because of distinctions between connectedness and separateness in their identities. One cause of job dissatisfaction is a lack of a good match between the person's work orientation and the rewards generated by his or her occupation. Work orientations have been classified into intrinsic and extrinsic orientations. Intrinsic aspects of a job include the nature of the job task, the degree to which it is challenging and fulfilling, its opportunity for personal growth, and its proper level of difficulty. In contrast, an extrinsic orientation reflects the wage level, the working conditions (how clean, how comfortable), and the job security. For some workers, intrinsic factors are more important, whereas for others, extrinsic aspects take precedence. And even for the same worker, there may be a shift from intrinsic to extrinsic motivations over the span of adulthood.

Occupations differ in the kinds of rewards they provide. Sometimes it is not feasible to establish a match between the person's needs and what the occupation offers, but the worker may continue in the job for many years despite this lack of congruence. The position may have initially offered challenge or excitement, but then inertia sets in, as the work becomes routine.

A dialectical analysis is helpful in understanding persons who, in midlife, shift positions. Why would a person give up a well-paying, prestigious position? A personality trait theorist might stereotype such people as perpetually dissatisfied and emotionally unstable.

But research evidence (Krantz, 1977) suggests that people who change jobs in the middle of adulthood are no more maladjusted than the rest of us. Changes are often a response to dialectical tugs—toward intrinsic rewards rather than earlier extrinsic rewards, for example. They often reflect rational attempts to move from what have become unsatisfactory occupational situations. Krantz (1977) concludes, "The fundamental difference between those of us 'normals' who stay in the trajectory of our lives and careers and those who choose to change that direction is the solution chosen, not in the problems themselves" (p. 167).

Special Problems of the Professional Person

Before further analysis of career change during midlife, we need to devote extended attention to the special problems of those persons in professional or executive positions who lose their interest in their work. In one sense, society's assumption is correct; people in those positions that pay more and carry more perquisites are more satisfied with their jobs. Few, if any, physicians want to change jobs with coal miners or bricklayers. But the exceptional case illustrates the dialectical thrust of the phenomenon. John Coleman (1974), while an economist and college president, decided to break the lockstep and vary the rhythm of his life by spending his sabbatical leave working anonymously in menial jobs. For 2 months, at the age of 54, he dug trenches and laid pipe in Georgia, and then worked for $2.50 an hour as a garbage collector in College Park, Maryland. (Some years later, in 1986, Coleman resigned his position as president of a charitable foundation and took over the ownership and hands-on management of a country inn in Chester, Vermont.)

Not many people at Coleman's level of eminence would emulate his actions. But some, at least, would acknowledge that, for them, professional work generates its own types of discontent. Why? Sarason (1977) offers three reasons:

Lack of Control Over One's Work Schedule

For most people in the professions, the work has intrinsic rewards (as well as extrinsic ones). A surfeit of riches abounds in that there is always too much work to do. As the person becomes more proficient and more recognized, more opportunities beckon. Accomplished family physicians soon have so many patients that they are working exhausting hours. The entrepreneur sees more and more markets develop, but each requires a finite portion of his or her time and energy. The renowned scholar gets so many invitations to write chapters and give speeches that each loses its appeal and becomes an ordeal. Outsiders may suggest the solution is "Just say no" to requests that cause an expansion of services or an exhaustion of energies. But many professional persons credit their success to their willingness to work harder than their colleagues or to their unique collection of skills and abilities, and it is hard for them to decline opportunities that provide recognition or offer challenges. The proficient physician may feel an obligation to his or her community; the scholar may fear that saying "no" is the first indication of a dying interest in his or her search for truth. Although they long for a manageable work schedule, their very nature makes this unattainable.

The reaction of famed cellist Yo-Yo Ma to this conflict is described in Box 2.2.

Conflict Between One's Self-Concept and One's Reputation in the Community

A second source of dissatisfaction for professional persons is the discrepancy they feel between the level of esteem accorded them by their clients, or society in general, and their own self-concepts. A heart surgeon may be idolized by patients who see the cardiologist as a miracle worker who has saved them from death, but the physician's own reaction may be, "I didn't do a very good job with that patient; I was too slow, I made mistakes." One physician has confided, "The more my patients treat me as a god, the more I feel like a hypocrite." Similarly, students may respect and commend a professor for the sophistication and erudition of her lectures, even as the professor castigates herself for failing to review the most recent sources. Although the discrepancy between client's views of us and our own self-concepts may be a source of discomfort at any job level, Sarason seems accurate in identifying it as a particular problem in occupations that (a) run the risk of public adulation and (b) include an expertise beyond the common knowledge of the layperson.

BOX 2.2

Controlling One's Work Schedule

Yo-Yo Ma describes the challenges of his highly successful career as follows:

During my first years of performing, all the travelling and concertizing seemed terribly exciting. My management would call and ask if I'd like to give a certain series of concerts two years later. I'd be in the middle of dinner, and I'd say, "Fine, sure"—but eventually I'd be faced with actually having to play those concerts. I'd end up with as many as a hundred and fifty concerts a season. I was always flirting with getting burned out from exhaustion.

So, I finally sat down and wrote out a list of all the things I care most about. First of all, I promised myself that if I ever felt really burned out and lost enthusiasm for giving concerts I'd be responsible enough to quit. . . . Second, I decided that every concert I played—no matter where, no matter if the city was big or small—was going to be special. Third, I accepted the fact that only one person is responsible for what's going on, and that person is me. Fame and success are always being dangled before you. But you have to choose your drugs carefully. I have yet to find something that beats the power of being in love, or the power of music at its most magical. So if someone suggests adding just one more concert at the end of a tour—it's always just one more—you just have to say no. . . . Finally, I decided that it's not enough just to make time to be at home, I have to preserve the quality of that time. So, aside from practicing, I don't let professional obligations encroach upon my family life.

An extreme example of this type of conflict is reflected in the *impostor phenomenon,* in which professional persons fear that they have been overestimated, and that at any moment the truth about them will come out. Being successful can be stressful, and psychologist Pauline Rose Clance (1985), author of a book on this topic, estimates that such private feelings of being a fraud are shared by as many as 70% of all successful individuals and that many such self-labeled "impostors" are perfectionists who can never achieve their own standards.

Lack of Challenge

A third source of dissatisfaction stems from our professional activities that were previously challenging but are so no longer. It is difficult for professional people to talk about declining motivation, because their work is often seen by clients, family, and friends as an endlessly fascinating and rewarding line of endeavor (Sarason, 1977). To reflect such concerns is to raise questions in the minds of others about one's competence or emotional stability. Sarason (1977) concludes:

> If an individual is by conventional criteria doing well (e.g., he is gaining recognition, his income is increasing, he is respected for his knowledge and expertise, he has a comfortable home, travels, etc.), we unreflectively assume that his feelings about his work are isomorphic, so to speak, with these "objective" indices. (p. 114)

As in "Richard Cory," the poem in which the highly successful, well-respected millionaire commits suicide, we ask why? See Box 2.3 for one example of society's reaction.

For many a professional person, dissatisfactions like those in the above paragraphs accrue over the years, so that by the late 30s or early 40s they have forced the person into a painful reexamination of his or her work identity. "For the professional person mid-life is, like the beginning of adolescence, experienced as an eruption of internal stirrings which had best not be articulated" (Sarason, 1977, p. 105).

Yet sometimes it *is* articulated. In 1976 Josiah Thompson was a professor of philosophy with tenure at Haverford College in Pennsylvania. But while on sabbatical leave in the San Francisco Bay area—with no progress on the scholarly book he was to write and his marriage deteriorating—he decided, "almost capriciously," to apply for a job at a detective agency. With this sudden shift, from a job with security and prestige to one with less salary and more

---

BOX 2.3

Reactions to Professional Job Burnout

What happens when job dissatisfaction in a professional person disconfirms society's evaluation of the person? Robert F. was 42 and superintendent of schools in a Midwestern suburban community that contained a university. A Ph.D. from a leading university, he had been a classroom teacher and a principal. His salary as a school superintendent in the mid-1970s was $42,000. He resigned in the middle of the school year; his work had lost its satisfaction.

When friends heard that he had resigned, they first assumed that he had accepted a "better" superintendency. When he told them that he had no other job, they thought he was being coy or secretive. On further thought, many speculated that he was in trouble, or ill, or in an unhappy marriage. After a couple of weeks, a number of his friends finally accepted his affirmation of job dissatisfaction, and some expressed their admiration and envy for his action.

SOURCE: Sarason, 1977, p. 112.

---

peril, he became a $10-an-hour private investigator (Lehman, 1988; Thompson, 1988).

But is not some amount of dissatisfaction true of everyone? The stage theorists described in Volume 1 would certainly propose so. Sarason (1977) argues that it is more so for the professional person who

> came to his career with greater expectations that he was embarking on a quest in which all his capacities and curiosities would be exploited, the vibrant sense of challenge, growth, and achievement sustained, and his sense of personal growth and importance strengthened; the material rewards he would obtain would be as icing on a delicious cake. (p. 106)

The "One Life, One Career" Imperative

Dissatisfactions like those above can lead to a change in careers, sometimes a seemingly drastic shift. One cause for the consternation when a person changes vocations in midlife is the implicit assumption in our society of "one life, one career," or as Sarason (1977) colorfully expresses it, society views the developmental task of the young individual as deciding "from a smorgasbord of possibilities the one vocational dish he will feed on over the course of his life" (p. 123). The early choice of a career is expected in our society. Children early on are quizzed, "What do you want to be when you grow up?" Not usually tolerated are answers such as, "Well, I'd like to be a marine biologist for 10 years, then I'd like to design houses, and then be a farmer." Colleges require their undergraduates to declare a major field, leading them toward seemingly irrevocable career commitments. Sometimes, the decision to go to graduate school or law school is primarily motivated by a desire to delay deciding on a career.

Frequency and Causes of Occupational Change

Despite these pressures toward continuity, many people do change jobs during adulthood. Sommers and Eck (1977) report that 30% of the workforce and 10% of technicians and professional people experienced a career change in a 5-year period. Osherson (1980) estimates that 5 million citizens of the United States change their occupation in a given year.

Mary Gratch spent a decade after her college graduation trying to become an actress. Once she achieved that goal—a full-time position in a classical repertory company—she decided it was not sufficient. "It wasn't challenging enough mentally or emotionally," she said (quoted by Belkin, 1992, p. C19). Mary Gratch has completed her 4th year of medical school at the age of 37, seeking a career in medical education.

Why does this happen? Three different explanations have been suggested. The "counterculture hypothesis" concludes that dissatisfaction with the present social system has led individuals to leave the mainstream of society. The rapid growth of communes in the early 1970s supported this claim; many members of communes were former professional persons, executives, and managers who "dropped out of the rat race" that they felt corporate life was (Roberts, 1971).

They sought participation in a different type of social system, one that did not possess the values of competitiveness, materialism, regimentation, depersonalization, and status distinctions they found present in the white-collar world. Krantz (1977), in his observation of the "Santa Fe experience" (to be described in the next section), also concludes that the predominant motive was the rejection of a previous lifestyle. As one midlife career changer told Moffitt (1986), "Yes, maybe there's a little drop in the standard of living, but there's a big jump in the quality of life" (p. 47).

A second explanation—sometimes labeled the "developmental hypothesis"—pictures the career shift as a manifestation of a personal crisis. A man may experience such a crisis at midlife when he realizes that he is not accomplishing his lifelong goals, or, in Levinson's terms, not attaining his "dream." Osherson (1980) has portrayed the crisis as one of *loss,* of coming to terms with the lost self, or the discrepancy between who you are and who you expected to be. Sarason (1977) has used the example of the Frenchman Paul Gauguin, who chucked his banking career and his family responsibilities to go to the South Seas to paint. For such persons, the urgency of acting—the "now or never" aspect—is a driving force to radical change. A 45-year-old man who abandoned his high-paying job without any definite plans for another told an interviewer that he had liked his work: "I was actually enjoying myself more than I had in years. It was just that if I was ever going to try something different, I had to do it now" (Moffitt, 1986, p. 47).

The remaining explanation places focus on sociological rather than intrapersonal causes for occupational change. In periods of rapid social, economic, and technological change, such as we currently are experiencing, careers become obsolete, or at least need upgrading. Typists become word processors; bookkeepers become computer operators; librarians become learning-resources specialists. Shifts in the skills needed by society lead to shifts in jobs. The escalating cost of living has demanded that more wives and mothers work outside the home; by the same token, a second salary in the family may make more feasible a career change that requires a period of retraining or further education, and hence temporarily no income.

Empirical Studies of Men Who Change Careers

Two empirical studies of men who changed careers in midlife have been completed by psychologists (Krantz, 1977; Osherson, 1980). Although neither has a large number of subjects—one interviewed 30 men, the other 20—their conclusions are similar, and each provides detailed examples of the reasons for the changes.

David Krantz interviewed 30 men, all of whom moved to Santa Fe, New Mexico, and changed jobs. All were well educated, with at least a bachelor's degree; many had postgraduate education. Aged 32 to 56 at the time of Krantz's interview, each man had a least 5 years' experience before his change. And many of the shifts were quite radical; a New York City banker became a waiter in a ski resort, a Broadway set designer became a bartender, an advertising agency head switched to directing a small art gallery, a social worker became a construction worker, an eminent TV producer became a bus driver, and a stockbroker shifted to an ice cream store owner.

Despite the diverse occupations chosen, Krantz found many common themes in the reasons for the changes. For these men, the change extended beyond just that of their occupation. "For all the people interviewed, the decision to change careers involved far more than simply giving up the immediate activities involved in the work setting" (Krantz, 1977, p. 172). For some, the choice involved rejecting an unacceptable future reality, such as living in an urban environment, where they felt alienated and unsafe, or in an eroding family structure because of work demands or a long commute. The shift also symbolized a freedom from the restraints of their previous jobs. These men were searching for control over their own lives. Furthermore, they had reevaluated and redefined the significance of work as a definition of their lives. For some, work has remained central; for others, less so. For the latter, their identities are now less defined by their jobs, material possessions, or family background. An editor and publisher, Phillip Moffitt (1986), after interviewing people who had shifted careers, concluded, "What I think is starting to occur is not a phenomenon of failure, but of success. . . . These are people with the strong self-image necessary to maintain an identity without the prop of a career or professional label: Doctor, Lawyer, Businessman" (p. 47). One of these men told

Krantz (1977), "People in Santa Fe do not stand on formality or judge you by what you've accomplished" (p. 183). Moving to Santa Fe—a city that has come to symbolize this transformation—was also symbolic to these men; the change in physical location was an important step in removing constraints. Traveling in a sense causes us to be different people, or at least it varies what have become habitual ways of acting.

In the second empirical study, Osherson (1980) analyzed the life histories of 20 men, each of whom, as a result of a midlife crisis, left an established professional career to become a creative artist or craftsman. Initially they were research scientists, executives, business managers, lawyers, and professors; of the 20, 18 had gone to graduate school. All had spent at least 3 years, after their training, in a professional career; they were between the ages of 35 and 50 when interviewed. All were now—and had been for from 3 to 10 years—either an actor, a potter, or a visual artist.

Like Krantz's subjects, the men in Osherson's sample reflected changes beyond simply their occupational identities. Nine of the 13 marriages dissolved during this period.

On the basis of his interviews, Osherson concludes that these men were seeking to recapture a part of their selfhood that had been lost. He uses Levinson's analysis of shifts toward feminine (i.e., artistic) values during midlife. The focus on a values substitution also explains a recently increasing trend for men in their middle years to enter seminaries to study for the ministry. In the 13 years from 1975 and 1988, the average age of seminarians increased from 25 to 33 (Sullivan, 1988), and older persons (i.e., over age 30) now comprise 44% of the 52,000 seminary students in the United States (Associated Press, 1987a). Interviews with these people reflect a generalized feeling that their previous life had its good points but "it didn't deal with values and the solid issues of people's lives" (Associated Press, 1987a, p. 8A).

One example is William McElraney, a member of a long-time Dallas family who worked in banking and oil businesses for several years after obtaining his M.B.A. degree. But he then decided to become a minister, because "It clarified what I'm doing here—who I'm called to be during my lifetime. It has to do with responding to life in as faithful a way as one knows how" (quoted by Watts, 1989, p. 23).

Is a Crisis Necessary to Bring About Change?

To what extent do the changes described in the previous section result from a crisis? Does the second of the three explanations reflect a general trend? Lawrence (1980) selected 10 persons who had changed jobs between the ages of 35 and 55, in an effort to determine if a drastic upheaval in their lives had been associated with their occupational change. Five of these subjects were men; 5 were women. Among their job shifts were: librarian to writer, small business owner to career counselor, professor of physics to musician, and clerical worker to custodian. Lawrence had hypothesized that a midlife career change is the outcome of the resolution of a midlife crisis, but she observed a crisis pattern in only 3 of her 10 subjects. In one of these the crisis was externally generated; the owner of a family business suffered unanticipated difficulties with the Internal Revenue Service, forcing him to sell his business and look for new work. A second was both internal and external; a clerical worker, without any family ties, faced the loss of a person she had been in love with for 18 years. She became a custodian, but still remained single. The third example, the most internally caused crisis, was a Jesuit priest who, affected by the death of his brother, was forced to examine his inability to express his feelings. He resigned from the priesthood, married, and became a college administrator. So, for each of these three, a personal change preceded the career change.

But for the other seven it was hard to detect any precipitating crisis; the personal change associated with the career change took place throughout the career-change process. Some of them planned a change for a long time. Even though outsiders may have characterized their job shifts as sudden or dramatic, the career changers perceived a continuity in their lives. Lawrence (1980) notes, "Although these subjects made externally identifiable career changes, it is clear that in all ten cases, a direct relationship existed internally between the kind of work they did and enjoyed in their first career and what they chose to do in the second" (p. 44). From the inside the shift was not spontaneous; rather, they saw it as evolutionary over a period of time.

The study of middle-aged men who shifted careers for the ministry also concludes that the change did not usually stem from an identifiable crisis. Ellis Larsen, who has completed a survey of these men, is quoted as stating, "Most of the men had sensed a calling to the ministry early in life, but for some reason, weren't able to follow it then" (Associated Press, 1987a, p. 8A).

Occupational Development in Women

Previous sections of this chapter noted that the frequently cited theories of occupational choice systematically fail to account for women's development. Leona Tyler (1977) has pungently expressed the state of theorizing: "Much of what we know about the stages through which an individual passes as he [sic] prepares to find his [sic] place in the world of work might appropriately be labeled 'The Vocational Development of Middle Class Males' " (p. 40). It has only been the past decade and a half that has seen efforts at remedying this deficit; Nieva and Gutek's Women and Work: A Psychological Perspective, published in 1981, provided an organizational psychology perspective, and more recently, Astin (1984) developed a theory of career development to reflect the unique challenges to women, while also applicable to men. Betz and Fitzgerald (1987) systematically assessed women's work from a careers perspective. But even the much-more-desired recent developments, such as the latter book, mostly focus on educated women, thus excluding the jobs held by the majority of working women (Gutek, 1989).

Reviews of the literature (Betz & Fitzgerald, 1987; Fitzgerald & Crites, 1980; Perun & Bielby, 1981) note several distinctions between women's occupational development and men's: (a) The determinants are different; (b) the trajectory of the work cycle or career pattern is less predictable and more complex in women; (c) the process of synchronizing work and family responsibilities throughout adulthood may be more difficult for women than for men. As a result, women may be in more conflict at some occupational stages about priorities in their life structure. For example, the late 20s are considered a primary time for career building in men; for women these are also primary childbearing years. For men, midlife is a time of reevaluation and possible change; women at midlife may be returning to a career or even initially establishing one. Therefore reassessment for them may be entirely different.

As we saw in Volume 1, Chapter 7, women may be classified into several types of groupings, based on their emphasis on one role or another. Rossi (1965), for example, classified women into *pioneer* or *traditional* categories based on the types of careers they pursued. Traditional women chose those occupational fields consistent with generalized conceptions of women's roles; they were more traditional in their own orientations, but not necessarily less likely to be employed. Pioneer women entered fields that were predominantly male. They tended to have more commitment to a career than did traditional women, and their career patterns tended to be stable and uninterrupted.

Super (1957, 1971, 1990), in a laudable attempt to adapt his career-development theory for the situation faced by women, identified seven career patterns or routes taken by women through their working lives. These were:

1. stable homemaking and marriage shortly after completion of schooling, with no work experience outside the home;
2. conventional career pattern; that is, women who worked briefly after graduation until marriage and did not return to work outside the home;
3. stable working outside the home, with consistent continuous work;
4. double-track or consistent work and homemaking responsibilities;
5. interrupted career pattern with working, nonworking, then working with return to the same or different job;
6. unstable career pattern with several working, nonworking alternations with no particular recurrent pattern and little consistency; and
7. a multiple trial pattern of successive unrelated jobs.

Whenever the empirical evaluation of women's occupational development is contemplated, the use of a longitudinal methodology is especially necessary, because of the career interruption that many women experience. For example, Mulvey (1963) followed up a high school graduating class 20 to 27 years later. She concluded that a major determinant of the subjects' life satisfaction was the degree to which the woman chose her career pattern. The women who were most dissatisfied were those whose career patterns were controlled by either financial or other factors and not by their personal choices.

More recent empirical study of women on the job reflects this conclusion. Larwood and Gattiker (1987) examined the career development of successful employees in several corporations and concluded that "movement of women up the career ladder was irregular and seemed affected more by external forces outside the women's control than was the men's occupational success" (Hansen, 1989, p. 760).

SUMMARY

For men in our society, a stage theory generally has sufficed as a theory-based explanation for the pattern of career development. But a dialectical analysis needs to be superimposed on these stages, in order to deal with (a) the disruptions in career choice that occur for some men and (b) the dissatisfactions expressed by some men in professional positions. For women in our society, career trajectory is less clear-cut because of the multiple roles assigned to women in our society.

3

Cognitive Abilities During Adulthood

Aging need not silence outstanding creativity in the last years.

Dean Keith Simonton

Daniel Levinson, Roger Gould, and other personality theorists who have concentrated on adulthood concluded that changes take place in the mid-lives of some of us, leading to less commitment to a vocation or even to a shift to another type of career. According to these theorists, the driving force to succeed—characteristic of the 20s and early 30s—diminishes, or is replaced by other motives.

Do changes in mental abilities interact with or even cause these hypothesized changes in vocational orientation? Stereotypes abound about the loss of memory and other cognitive skills in the elderly; for some, creativity is the prerogative solely of youth (Simonton, 1990). Such reactions are much too simplified, however; the effects of aging are as multiple as are the abilities that potentially are affected.

The purpose of this chapter is to examine research findings and conclusions about age changes in a variety of cognitive abilities—creativity, learning and memory, intelligence, and language ability—in an effort to determine whether or where decline occurs.

This is a matter of practical as well as theoretical concern. Stereo-types of cognitive decline with advancing age can be self-fulfilling. Assumptions that a diminishing in scientific or creative productiv-ity occurs after age 40, along with the shifting age structure of the American scientific population, have led to a conclusion that a decline in science in the United States is inevitable (Oromaner, 1981; Yuasa, 1974; cited by Simonton, 1988).

Changes in Creativity During Adulthood

How does creativity proceed across the life span? Do achieve-ments in a career peak at a particular age? Do people get more creative as they get older? If not, what inhibits creativity with increasing age? And if it is the case that mental productivity declines with increasing age, is the explanation decreasing intelligence, lessened creativity, motivational changes, or something else? We will find various answers in the following section, although a pro-vocative statement by an eminent psychologist can serve as a stimu-lus. Donald Hebb (1978), in an account of his own intellectual abilities written when he was 74, reported, "Today, I have none of that drive, that engrossing, dominating need to fiddle with and manipulate ideas and data in psychology. . . . The real change, I conclude, is a lowered ability to think; the loss of interest in psy-chological projects is secondary to that" (p. 23). Hebb's view should not be taken, however, as a statement applicable to all. One of the fascinating issues is the question why creativity remains alive and well in the later years of some people but not others.

Defining Creativity

A general definition of creativity emphasizes that it is the ability to make or produce something new or unique (Cohen, 1977). A psychiatrist has defined it as "the healthy search for novelty" (Gedo, 1990, p. 35). But like other abstract concepts, we are challenged to specify it more precisely even though we claim to know when we see it.

Psychologists, even though sometimes recognizing creativity as an important characteristic, have had difficulty in isolating it

(Torrance, 1988). A number of operational definitions have been advanced, and many tests to measure creativity are available. Although psychologists generally agree that creative acts generate products that are original, unusual, appropriate, and yet simple and straightforward, these tests differ greatly in the way they conceptualize and measure creativity (Milgram, 1990).

One type of approach seeks to distinguish between individuals with respect to the fertility of their cognitive associative skills. J. P. Guilford's (1950, 1967) early measure, the Unusual Uses Test, asked subjects to "think of as many unusual uses of a brick as you can" (Cohen, 1977, p. 66). The Torrance Tests of Creative Thinking developed by E. Paul Torrance (1963, 1974, 1987) include many based on the Guilford model, finding similarities between unlike things and differences between things that seem alike.

Another example in this genre, the Remote Associates Test, developed by Sarnoff Mednick (1962, 1963), presents the subject with sets of three words, with instructions to generate a fourth word that is associated with each of the three. For example, if one were presented with *cookies, sixteen,* and *heart,* a word that might be associated with each is *sweet.* As Dacey (1982, 1989) notes, this procedure reflects Mednick's belief that creativity is a process by which ideas already in the mind are associated in unusual, original, or useful combinations. What makes creative people distinctive, in this view, is that they persist in exploring more and more associations in their minds.

For example, a creative inventor might be challenged by a blind friend to come up with some way for a television set to tell a blind person, audibly, what channel is on. The blind person uses the television to listen to talk shows, news reports, and other programs, but is handicapped by not being able to see the readings from a channel selector. The inventor develops a remote control mechanism with larger buttons, with Braille markings on the top of each button.

Mednick goes on to propose that "familiarity breeds rigidity," or the more we know about a subject, the less likely we are to be creative about it. Certain procedures or principles become so entrenched that we no longer question or seek new associations. If this is the case, it may explain why theoretical physicists and master chess players are said to have reached the period of their peak performance by the age of 36. For example, Elo's (1965) longitudinal study of master chess players concluded that at age 63, almost 30 years beyond their peak, they were performing at a level like that back when they were only 20—but not as well as they did in their late 30s. Mednick's proposition also gives a hint as to a way to revitalize creativity in midlife or later life, an issue deferred for later in this section.

A different conception of creativity sees it as a task of restructuring. Rather than methodically exploring one association after another, creative people, in this view, deal with whole problems and restructure them in their entirety. Michael Wertheimer (cited by Dacey, 1982), for example, proposes that in creative activity one develops an overview of the entire structure and only then is there a manipulation of parts. A creative musician gets a half-formed idea of a finished piece of music and then works backward to complete the idea. This analysis conforms with the comments of Ludwig van Beethoven about his ability to hold the theme for a symphony in his mind for years, as he worked out the parts and the notes for particular instruments.

This conception of creativity is quite tolerant of opportunities for creative work with increasing age. The person in his or her 50s, 60s, or 70s, with greater knowledge and possibly a greater number of perspectives, might better be able to produce creative solutions. The composer Franz Joseph Haydn illustrated this view, in that some of his most brilliant compositions were done toward the end of his long career. Haydn lived for 77 years; at age 63, in the year 1795, he composed his trumpet concerto, still considered the premier trumpet concerto in the world, and in his late 60s and early 70s he composed his famous oratorios, *The Creation* and *The Four Seasons*. Likewise, Graham Greene and James Michener were still writing novels at the age of 84, and Alexander von Humboldt was working on the fifth volume of his masterpiece, *Kosmos*, when he died in his 90th year (Simonton, 1990).

It is quite conceivable that each of these contrasting conceptions of creativity is correct; for certain tasks, in certain settings, a different approach may be appropriate. "Creativity" in scientific research, or crime detection, may involve constant manipulation of jigsawlike pieces of information, until the right combination emerges. Intuition and the sudden awareness of relationships are central (Cohen, 1977).

But creativity in painting or musical composition may require developing a "big picture" and *then* relating aspects within it to each other. We need to keep these distinctions in mind as we review the empirical findings on creativity and age (Kausler, 1982).

Surveys of Creativity in Adulthood

Albert Einstein once said that "a person who has not made his [*sic*] great contribution to science before the age of 30 will never do so" (quoted by Gladwell, 1990, p. 38), but many of the major creative contributions have emerged when their progenitors were approaching 40. When he wrote *Hamlet, King Lear,* and *Macbeth,* Shakespeare was in his late 30s and early 40s; Tolstoy was 38 when he published *War and Peace;* Beethoven composed his magnificent Fifth Symphony when he was 37; Michelangelo completed the Sistine Chapel also at the age of 37 (Simonton, 1984). Does the fortieth year signify the culmination of a creative career?

Not necessarily. The seemingly straightforward question "At what ages do people make their most creative contributions?" is not easily answered. Lehman (1953), in an early review, used biographical information about several thousand highly productive individuals born after the year 1774. He concluded that creative output increases fairly rapidly up to one's late 30s or early 40s; then there is a gradual decline that leads to a considerable decrease in middle age. He found that 80% of the high-quality productions were made by people younger than age 50. Scientists were their most productive between the ages of 30 and 39, but writers and historians—in contrast to the general trend—were most productive between their mid-40s and mid-50s. But note the emphasis here is on the quantity of work and fails to take into account the *quality* of creative work. Jaques (1965) points to many artists and musicians whose work in their 40s became more careful and painstaking, more "sculpted," hence their rate of productivity decreased as the quality improves. Yet Manniche and Falk (1957), determining the age at which Nobel Prize winners did the work for which they received the prize, found that mostly the late 20s or 30s were the determinants.

Conclusions about the early peak for creative or groundbreaking works touched sensitive areas (especially among older psychologists!) and hence were not without criticism (Botwinick, 1967).

Dennis (1958, 1966) faulted Lehman's study because it included so many individuals who died before they reached old age. To avoid including subjects with differing longevities, Dennis analyzed the biographies of 738 creative persons, all of whom lived to age 79 or beyond. His conclusions were different from Lehman's; for example, the peak period for scholars and scientists (except mathematicians) was the 40s to the 60s, with some still producing in their 70s. (These groups had little creative output in their 20s.) Artists had a somewhat different pattern, with a peak period in their 40s, but they were almost as productive in their 60s and 70s as they were in their 20s.

Dennis interpreted the difference in the patterns as a result of scientists needing a longer period of training and greater experience accumulating and interpreting data. Also, artists operated as individuals, whereas scientists often worked in groups. If, as in Beard's (1874) view, creativity is composed of two essential elements—enthusiasm and experience—the greater experience needed by the scientists would account for the "delay" in the scientists reaching their creative peak. But, in careful studies of productivity and creativity in 10 classical composers and 10 eminent psychologists, Dean Simonton (1977, 1985) found that the ratio of their creative works to all their products did not systematically change with age. That is, the quality of their work in later years was just as highly regarded as that of their early or middle years. Simonton (1984) has advanced this "constant probability of success" model as a general conclusion; that is, that "the proportion of top-quality products stays relatively constant throughout a creator's career" (p. 97). As such, it refutes a conclusion that a peak period exists, at least for quality works.

Previous studies focused on persons with demonstrable creativity or giftedness. Jaquish and Ripple (1980), at Cornell University, took a different approach. Drawing samples of children, adolescents, young adults, middle-aged adults, and elderly, they administered to the subjects a measure of creativity that assessed three aspects of divergent thinking (fluency, frequency, and originality). After comparing average scores for the different age groups, they concluded that persons ages 40 to 60 did significantly better than did those persons in the 18-25 and 26-39 age groups. For those people in the oldest age group (ages 61 to 84), creativity scores were significantly lower than those of any of the younger age groups, but the difference was greater with respect to quantity of creative products than for quality. For the middle-aged and elderly groups, those participants with more favorable self-concepts were more creative (rs of .41 and .43).

This relationship with self-esteem is especially important because of the vast individual differences with respect to creativity in old age. Verdi composed *Falstaff* at the age of 80. Pablo Casals played the cello brilliantly at the age of 90. At the age of 84, the philosopher Mortimer Adler published his 15th book in the past 10 years. When abilities continue to be used, they do not decline as quickly or at all. The motto "Use it or lose it" seems to apply to creativity, too.

But it would simplify matters too much if we left the topic of creativity with the possible implication that ability differences are the only important determinants. As these examples of creativity in older ages reflect, creative productions are the result of heightened motivation, also. The apparent decline in creativity may reflect in the aspiration levels of older adults; there may be less urge to accomplish new things or to make one's mark anew (Pruyser, 1987). Similarly, as Renner, Alpaugh, and Birren (1978) argue, an environmental-press explanation may fit. That is, the environment of many older people may discourage creative or divergent thinking; creativity may not diminish with age as much as the demand for it does (Kausler, 1982).

Creative scientists may get seduced into administrative positions that distract them with new responsibilities (Gladwell, 1990). As Simonton notes (1990, p. 628), one reason why Lehman's conclusions about a peak in creative output around age 40 drew such hostile critiques is the assumption that the later "loss" reflected a decline in intellectual capacities. The age curve is best interpreted as a career curve (Simonton, 1990), the way a creative career evolves over time.

How does one reverse the general trend of a decline in creativity with increasing age past 40? Simonton (1990), whose research on age differences in creativity is the most thorough and extensive, concludes that developing new ideas is not a function of biological age per se, but rather the result of confronting a new intellectual environment. Thus one secret to continued creative success is to enter a new field after one's productivity has peaked in a previous field (Gladwell, 1990).

Simonton is optimistic about the maintenance of creativity for other reasons:

1. The decrement of creativity is rarely so great that the individual is devoid of creativity at life's end (Simonton, 1990). In fact, on the average the rate of creative output in the 70s is about half of that at the optimum age (Simonton, 1988). "As long as a person's health holds out, no theoretical or empirical reason exists to expect the absence of creativity in senior citizens" (Simonton, 1990, p. 627).

2. Even some of the more debilitating infirmities of old age can be surmounted by the self-actualization process that motivates creativity (Simonton, 1990, p. 627). Among numerous examples, Bach and Handel both continued to compose despite blindness in later life; Matisse, despite being in a wheelchair, continued to paint with a crayon attached to a long bamboo pole. Among contemporary creative individuals, the theoretical physicist Stephen Hawking generates new ideas despite almost total paralysis.

3. The level of creative productivity in elderly years depends on the individual's creative potential at the outset of his or her career. Gladwell (1990) notes that the influential 19th-century mathematician K. F. Gauss is said to have started his career with so many ideas that a lifetime of activity was not enough to evaluate all of them. Told that his wife was dying, the intensity of his quest led him reportedly to mutter, "Tell her to wait a moment till I'm through" (p. 38).

4. Creativity can undergo a resurgence in the later years of life, and especially in life's last years (Simonton, 1990, p. 630). Sometimes during the late 60s and 70s an increase in output appears (Simonton, 1988). This secondary peak in output may be a manifestation of an Eriksonian final-stage contemplation of death and review of one's life accomplishments.

Does any empirical evidence exist for the existence of such a "swan-song" phenomenon? Simonton (1989) examined 1,919 compositions by 172 classical music composers, assessed each of numerous aesthetic qualities, and determined how many years before

the composers' death the piece was composed. A clear pattern
emerged:

> As the composers approached their final years, when death was raising
> a fist to knock on the door, they began to produce compositions that
> are more brief, that have simpler and more restrained melodic lines,
> and yet that score high in aesthetic significance according to musi-
> cologists and that eventually become popular mainstays of the classical
> repertoire. It is as if when the composers see the end approaching
> fast on the horizon, warning that their last artistic temperaments dwell
> among their current works in progress, they put their utmost into
> every creation, yielding truly noteworthy products. (Simonton, 1990,
> p. 630)

Age Differences
in Learning and Memory

Do people in middle adulthood begin to display memory changes
that are pervasive? Is memory loss a part of normal aging? If so, is
there one *type* of memory to lose? Or more?

No simple answer exists, partly because of the complexity of
memory. But psychology also offers several perspectives on the
nature of memory impairment during the aging process; Light
(1991) notes that these "range from the optimistic view that poorer
memory in old age arises from inefficient use of encoding and
retrieval strategies (a problem subject to remedial intervention), to
less optimistic views that declining memory ability is the conse-
quence of irreversible age-related changes in basic mechanisms
underlying cognition" (p. 334). Space limitations permit a review
of only some of these.

Craik (1992) notes that one of the most striking features that
emerges from studies of age differences in memory is that the
decline is very significant under some conditions but almost non-
existent in others. For example, the type of memory task referred
to as "priming" or "implicit memory" shows little change with age
(Light, Singh, & Capps, 1986). An example is the task in which a
subject studies a list of words and is later given words with letters
missing to complete (Craik, 1992). Naturally, it is easier to complete

words that were on the previous list than words that were not. The ability to complete these words for which one has been primed remains intact for older people (Richardson-Klavehn & Bjork, 1988). Similarly, the research done by Kellas, Simpson, and Ferraro (1988) concludes that the recognition of isolated words does not show a universal decline with age.

But other types of tasks show very consistent and significant decrements with age; examples include the free recall of a list of unrelated words, the ability to recall names of people and unusual objects, and dichotic listening (the ability to reproduce two short sequences of numbers presented simultaneously, one sequence to each ear).

How do we explain these differences? One possibility is that the long-term memory abilities of older adults differ little from those of young adults. From middle age on, the content of long-term memory may become selective, with focus more on reminiscences from their youth and early adulthood than from more recent times (Goleman, 1987; Rubin, 1986). Psychologist David C. Rubin concludes, "It seems to be that reminiscence flows more freely about the period in life that comes to define you: the time of your first date, marriage, job, child" (quoted by Goleman, 1987, p. 17).

But Craik's (1992) review concludes that some tasks that reflect the operation of each memory store (long-term vs. short-term) decline with age and some do not. Rather, he emphasizes different types of *processing operations* as the explanation; that older people have particular difficulties with types of processing that require self-initiation. But when the process is driven by the stimulus and the context, such as in recognition memory, older people perform comparably to their younger counterparts (Craik, 1992; Hoffman & Nelson, 1990).

Another approach capitalized and elaborates on Endel Tulving's (1972, 1985) classification of types of memory:

1. Episodic memory, the conscious recollection of personal experiences tied to specific times and places. This is seen as most affected by aging, especially after age 70 (Goleman, 1990; Mitchell, 1989).
2. Semantic memory, or memory for words, language, specific facts: "basic" memory.

3. Procedural or implicit memory, or remembering "how-to" or "auto-matic" operations, from how to answer a telephone to how to operate a personal computer.

The most serious deficiency of the elderly is in regard to self-generated ways to *organize* material to be learned or remembered. When the elderly are provided an organizational structure to use for memorizing information, they perform just about as well as young adults (Hultsch, 1969, 1971, 1974). Similarly, older adults show "little disadvantage compared to the young in remembering sentences and discourse materials" (Walsh, 1983, p. 174).

If we extrapolate these results to persons at middle adulthood, we may conclude with some confidence that memory deficits do not usually account for any differences in career commitment that may surface during the ages of 40 to the late 50s. A greater effect may come from self-fulfilling prophecies stemming from messages that tell middle-aged people that once we are past our 30s, life is a continuous decline. Several recent studies conclude that compared to young adults, older adults are more likely to blame themselves for their memory failure (Erber, Szuchman, & Rothberg, 1990; Rebok & Balcerak, 1989; Weaver & Lachman, 1990). When young adults make internal attributions for poor memory, they see the causes for their performance to be less stable and more subject to change. They tend to attribute their performance to factors such as effort, tiredness, or mood—all causes that may not be present in the future (Weaver & Lachman, 1990). Older adults are more likely to see their memory loss as uncontrollable and irreversible (Lachman, 1991).

Age Differences in Intelligence

Might changes in level of mental ability during adulthood account for the changes discussed earlier in this chapter? Does intelligence decline as one gets older? Certainly opinions abound about such declines. Dacey (1982, p. 125) quotes Mark Twain in his 1884 book *Puddin'head Wilson*: "It was a very curious thing. When I was about 13, my father's intelligence started to drop. His mental ability continued to decline until I reached 21, when these abilities miraculously began to improve." But "young people project more negatives on later years than reality suggests is correct" states James Birren, former director of the Andrus Gerontology Center at the University of Southern California (quoted in Gunderson, 1987, p. 6D).

Dacey's (1982) approach to answering the questions in the above paragraph is, I believe, a very helpful one. He contrasts three different responses: Yes, intelligence does decline with age; No, it does not; and Yes, it declines in some ways but no, in other ways it does not. Each viewpoint is reviewed below.

David Wechsler (1958), author of one of the most widely used intelligence tests, believed that most cognitive abilities peak between the ages of 18 and 25, and then decline. Wechsler proposed that this "occurs in all mental measures of ability including those employed in tests of intelligence" (p. 135). Wechsler's conclusions were based on extensive research data, but they were all cross-sectional data, in which older people (often with less education and fewer cultural opportunities) were compared to younger adults (Schaie, 1983, p. 138). Longitudinal studies of changes in IQ scores tend to lead to the opposite conclusion, that intelligence does not decline with age. For example, Terman's study of gifted children, which began in 1931, retested its subjects in 1941, in 1956, and in 1969. In the last testing, when the subjects were around 40 years old, their IQ scores had increased an average of 10 points from what they had been at age 30 (Kangas & Bradway, 1971).

Also, in a fortuitous happenstance, psychologist William Owens (1953, 1959) found test scores 30 years later for 363 people who had enrolled in Ohio State University in 1919. He was able to locate and retest 127 of them; at the time of retesting they were around the age of 47. All but one of 127 showed an increase in IQ over this 30-year interval. In 1966, when these people were 61 years old, 97 of them were retested again and none of their scores had changed significantly. These are impressive results, not only because they reflect stability during adulthood, but also because they further support a conclusion that Wechsler's results were affected by the educational differences in his subjects of differing ages; that is, that age and cohort were confounded and that "education may be one of the prime causes of such cohort effects" (Denney, 1982, p. 812). In fact, Botwinick (1978) offers a general conclusion that "longitudinal studies tend to reflect less decline than cross-sectional studies and they often show decline starting later in life" (p. 224).

Fluid Versus Crystallized Intelligence

But one's IQ score is a reflection of many different mental abilities; intelligence is no longer viewed as a unitary concept. A potentially fruitful analysis of changes with age makes a distinction between two types, fluid and crystallized intelligence. Horn and Cattell (1967) use the term *crystallized intelligence* to refer to those skills that we acquire through education and exposure to our culture. As Schaie (1983) notes, "Crystallized abilities depend upon the acquisition of certain kinds of information and skills transmitted by the culture that are not available to the individual simply by virtue of his characteristics as human being" (p. 139). One's vocabulary level, level of information, and mechanical knowledge are examples of crystallized intelligence. Horn and Cattell conclude that level of crystallized intelligence does not normally decline over the period of adulthood; in fact, it increases, at least from the ages of 20 to 60.

The other type of mental ability, labeled *fluid intelligence,* does decline with age. Fluid intelligence covers those abilities that are related to the physiological characteristics of the organism and hence are culture-free, including reaction time, spatial visualization, memory span, and verbal reasoning. For example, what letter comes next in the series SUXBGM? There is a sort of paradox here; our knowledge of words maintains itself or even improves, but our ability to use words in reasoning diminishes. Horn (1970, 1982) claims that the decline in such reasoning is equal to about 5 IQ points from the ages 25 to 40, and about 5 points for every 10 years of living beyond the age of 40. He speculates that perhaps it accelerates with advanced age.

Of relevance to the distinction between fluid and crystallized intelligence is Kemper's (1987) research on the age differences in the ability to process information expressed in complex sentences. Kemper finds the most common difficulty occurs when a long subordinate clause precedes a main clause. Normally, when you hear such a clause, you must wait until hearing the main clause before processing it; the main clause gives the context. Consider the sentence: "Because Bill left the party without his coat, John was upset." The wait for the main clause appears to require a processing step that deteriorates with increasing age (Howell, 1987). Kemper believes that this decline does not usually emerge until the late 60s

---

BOX 3.1

Changes in Diaries Over Age

In a fascinating use of archival materials, Susan Kemper (1987, 1990) located and content-analyzed sets of diaries kept by the same eight adults (6 men and 2 women) over a period of 70 or more years. The authors were all born between 1856 and 1876 in the United States; they died between 1943 and 1967. All diary entries were made when the writers were adults; that is, in their 20s or older.

Several characteristics were assessed to see if they changed over time. For example, the diarists' narratives became structurally more complex as they grew older. (Structural complexity can range from a listing of successive events that are not linked in any meaningful way to complex stories with causally connected multiple episodes, along with a coda that usually draws a lesson from the complexity of events.) In actuality, stories at the more structurally complex level (Level 8) were produced only by diarists in their 70s and 80s.

But at the same time, with increasing age of diarists, the entries became less cohesive, with an increased number of anaphoric and exophoric errors. An example of an anaphoric error is the following: the diary entry has mentioned two male characters but later refers to "he" without clarifying which character is meant. Exophoric errors refer to situations in which the referent of a definite description cannot be established.

Kemper sees the increase in errors with age as a reflection of age-related declines in working memory, possibly in limitations in its absolute capacity, or decreases in the speed of operations, or strategic differences in the allocation of attention. The demands placed on working memory by the use of complex syntactic structures can affect older adults' performance of a variety of tasks involving written or oral language. But despite these limitations, these diarists became skilled storytellers.

---

and early 70s (if at all) and then becomes stronger in the late 70s and early 80s. Further manifestations of age differences in language skill are found in Box 3.1.

Among the components of fluid intelligence, the ability measured by the Digit Symbol Subtest on the Wechsler Adult Intelligence Scale-Revised (WAIS-R) is the one most affected by aging. In a cross-sectional study of 177 healthy older persons, Joy, Fein, and Kaplan (1992) found a progressive decline with age; in fact, the subjects' age accounted for 40% of the variance in performance. But the prime components of the Digit Symbol substitution task appear to be motor speed and coordination.

Wisdom

One of the problems in evaluating the question of changes in intelligence during adulthood comes from the operational definition of intelligence based on performance on standardized IQ tests. Often such tests contain speeded components as in the Digit Symbol Test; that is, one's scores are determined by how quickly one answers. It is on these speeded types of measures that the greatest decline occurs with age; in contrast, "on abilities where speed is not of primary importance, there is very little change in intellectual function for an individual throughout adulthood" (Schaie, 1983, pp. 144-145).

The definition of *intelligence* given by the typical man or woman on the street is usually broader than that used by psychologists; the broader definition may include such varied aspects as "street smarts" and "wisdom." The latter quality, especially, may grow throughout adulthood, although its magnitude is not directly assessed by intelligence tests. Its growth refutes claims that adults do not develop past midlife (Gallagher, 1993) or that they suffer a cognitive deficit. An example is provided by Gallagher:

> Any adult who has debated with a bright adolescent about, say, the likelihood that the world's nations will erase their boundaries and create a passportless global citizenry knows that there are two types of intelligence: the abstract, objective, Platonic-dualism sort that peaks early, and the practical, subjective type, born of shirtsleeves experience, which comes later. When asked the way to Rome, the young trace the most direct route very quickly, while their elders ponder: "Why Rome? Is this trip really a good idea? At what time of year? For business or for pleasure? Alone or with others?" (p. 68)

Wisdom appears to blend qualities of cognition, emotion, and intuition (Clayton & Birren, 1980). It has been defined as expert knowledge involving good judgment and advice with respect to the fundamental pragmatics of life (Baltes & Smith, 1990). It has been proposed to be composed of social competence (Maciel, Sowarka, Smith, & Baltes, 1992), mature personality functioning (Orwoll & Perlmutter, 1990), and exceptional social intelligence (Cantor & Kihlstrom, 1985). More specifically, openness to experience and introversion are seen by respondents to contribute to wisdom, if not necessarily determining it (Maciel, Staudinger, Smith, & Baltes, 1991).

For some, wisdom includes an understanding that fundamental similarities exist that are evident in the dimensions of human experience (Kekes, 1983). People may be considered wise if they apply their knowledge and experience to difficult life decisions (Szuchman, 1991).

Underlying the conception of the wise decision may be greater utilization by the person of a dialectical analysis (see Volume 1, Chapter 8). That is, the person may look at each side of a problem and seek an integration or synthesis. Sinnott and Guttman (1978), studying the resolution of personal problems in adults approximately 70 years of age, found that about 25% resolved their conflicts via the implementation of a dialectic synthesis of conflicting aspects. Basseches (1980) reported increasing preference for a dialectical perspective in older subjects.

Wisdom is associated with maturity and age, although it is not seen as acquired by chronological age alone. Recall that wisdom is the ideal accomplishment of Erikson's last stage of psychosocial development.

Furthermore, older persons show more cautiousness than do younger adults (Botwinick, 1978). Schaie (1983) observes, "Young people in most test situations tend to make many more errors of commission than omission, but the reverse is true for the elderly. . . . Cautiousness may often be adaptive, but in this instance it may make the elderly appear less able than they actually are" (p. 147).

"Less able" especially if speed of reaction is the measure. Paul Baltes (1987), in cross-sectional research on problem solving, finds that on some measures young adults can do in 2 seconds what it takes older persons 8 seconds to complete. But the results are quite different on tasks Baltes designed to measure "wisdom," for example, how to respond to a friend who has decided to commit suicide.

"The highest grades we record occur somewhere around sixty," Baltes is quoted as saying (Gallagher, 1993, p. 68); "Wisdom peaks in midlife or later."

4

Sex Roles

Man may work from sun to sun,
But woman's work is never done.

Old saying

Perhaps the most significant development in psychological thinking over the past two decades is the emergence of gender to accompany race and social class as "the primordial axes around which social life is organized" (Michael Kimmel, quoted by Brooks, 1991, p. 19). First came a realization of the male bias in psychological theory and research, along with recognition of the detrimental nature of gender stereotypes. The emergence of feminism as a force in society and as a perspective in psychology contributed to a critical examination of the supposed benefits and significant constraints of traditional gender roles, and later, led to development of the "men's movement." (See also Box 4.1.)

The Power of Sex-Role Stereotypes

Late in 1987, Secretary of Transportation Elizabeth Dole resigned her powerful cabinet position in order to assist her husband, Senator Robert Dole, in his campaign for nomination by the Republican party as its presidential candidate. Critics asked why she was pres-

---

BOX 4.1

Why Gender Differences?

Beyond biological differences in the two sexes, differential socialization of sons and daughters contributes greatly. A review by Jeanne H. Block (1984) provides the following conclusions:

1. Mothers and fathers appear to encourage achievement and competition more in their sons than in their daughters.
2. Independence or the assumption of responsibility is emphasized more for boys than for girls (especially by fathers).
3. Punishment is more salient in treatment of boys than of girls.
4. Relationships between parents and daughters are characterized by greater warmth and physical closeness and greater assumption of trustworthiness.

---

sured to resign to avoid a conflict of interest when male candidates who themselves held public offices were not (Cohen, 1987).

Half a decade later, the nation saw the wife of a president, Hillary Rodham Clinton, assume an influential—albeit unpaid—role in her husband's administration. Yet, despite the difference with Mrs. Dole's action, critical reactions still resulted; some welcomed the opportunity for a bright woman to implement health policy, while others felt she was too influential. As Deborah Tannen (1992) has written, there exists "a double bind that affects all successful or accomplished women—indeed, all women who do not fit stereotypical images of femininity: women who are not clearly submissive are seen as dominating and are reviled for it" (p. A-17; copyright © 1992 by Deborah Tannen. Permission granted by International Creative Management, Inc.).

Each in its different way, these examples reflect the power of sex-role stereotypes (or gender-role stereotypes) in our society. Each sex is evaluated differently, based on the pervasiveness of sex-role norms, or beliefs about appropriate behavior for women and men. These perceptions and evaluations affect the opportunities for development for persons of each gender throughout adulthood.

Masculinity, Femininity, and Androgyny

Society often has avoided a basic clarification. We are aware of the distinction between male and female, and generally we can agree about the differences between the concepts of masculinity and femininity (see below). But society has assumed that being male means possessing masculinity and being female means possessing femininity, and many people in contemporary life have conformed to these expectations; in fact, they have been trained to do so. (Gender schema theory, one attempt to explain how this happens, is described in Box 4.2.)

But for several decades psychologists have been dissatisfied with the lumping together of maleness and masculinity, or with the inexorable yoking of femaleness and femininity. Psychologists have thus undertaken the construction of personality scales to assess the qualities of masculinity and femininity that presumably could be found among males *and* females. That is, they have assumed that, psychologically, some men and some women may be more similar to each other than different from each other. They believe that an emphasis on these psychological qualities can contribute something extra to our effort to understand behavior.

Constantinople (1973) reviewed the early research on this issue. She noted that although the early investigators differed in some of the details of their measurement procedures, they consistently made two assumptions: (a) that masculinity and femininity represent two opposite poles on a scale and (b) that the dimension of masculinity/femininity is unidimensional, rather than being a complex conglomerate of characteristics. But a change in perspective has taken place more recently, as investigators examining male/female differences began to argue that masculinity and femininity are quite separable sets of characteristics and that both men and women can possess varying degrees of each set (Bakan, 1966; Block, 1973; Carlson, 1971a).

These theory-derived conclusions generated a number of important measurement developments, in which researchers devised scales to measure femininity and masculinity separately (Bem, 1974; Berzins, Welling, & Wetter, 1975; Heilbrun, 1976; Spence, Helmreich, & Stapp, 1974). The assumption underlying each of these investigations is that one set of characteristics can be consid-

---

BOX 4.2

Gender Schema Theory

How do we develop stereotypes about sex roles or gender roles? Sandra Bem (1981, 1982, 1983, 1984, 1985, 1987) has proposed gender schema theory, which reflects partially a cognitive developmental framework, along with social learning theory and cultural factors (Basow, 1992). Gender-schema processing is considered a readiness on the part of children to encode and organize information according to how the culture defines sex roles. For example, a child may observe that boys usually are described as "strong" or "brave," whereas girls are more often described as "nice" or "sweet."

As Basow (1992) notes, cultural stereotypes become self-fulfilling prophecies because the child learns not only that the sexes differ but, more importantly, that certain attributes are associated more with one sex than the other. The extreme degree to which our society classifies behaviors and objects into "masculine" versus "feminine" only intensifies the development of a gender schema in children.

Gender schema theory has received its share of criticisms (e.g., Deaux, Kite, & Lewis, 1985; Devine, 1989; Freedman & Frantzve, 1992; Kite & Deaux, 1986) but, as Basow (1992) concludes, they do not necessarily disprove the major premise of the theory, that "people do process the world in terms of schemata and that sex-typed individuals are particularly likely to use a gender schema as their primary way of organizing their world and self-concept" (p. 126).

---

ered masculine (or *agentic* in Bakan's terms) and another set can be considered feminine (or *communal*). Usually the masculine scales contain terms such as *independent, competitive,* and *self-confident,* whereas the femininity scales contain words such as *kind, gentle, warm.* Although males as a group score higher on the masculinity scale and females as a group score higher on the femininity scale, the two scales are unrelated (Bem, 1974; Spence & Helmreich, 1978). In other words, a particular individual might score high on both scales, low on both, or high on one and low on the other. Statistically, this means that the correlation between the two scales approaches zero. In more descriptive terms, it means that both females and males can be either high or low in either femininity or masculinity; in contrast to the assumption of earlier investigators, the presence of one set of characteristics does not imply the absence of the other.

Psychological Androgyny

To categorize people who possess these varying combinations of characteristics, investigators have borrowed the term *androgyny* (originally used by the ancient Greeks to refer to individuals who combined the physical characteristics of both sexes). In its use here, the term refers to a combination of *psychological* characteristics (see Box 4.3 for elaboration). A person who scored above the median on both the femininity scale *and* the masculinity scale would be classified as androgynous. If the person scored above the median on only one of the scales, he or she would be labeled as masculine sex-typed or feminine sex-typed, depending on which scale was high. Those persons scoring below the median on both scales have been labeled *undifferentiated.*

Using this method of categorization, Spence and Helmreich (1978) examined the masculinity and femininity scores of different groups of people. Among a typical college-student sample, approximately one third of the males were masculine sex-typed and one third of the females were feminine sex-typed. One fourth to one third of the students scored as androgynous; the remaining students were either undifferentiated or were sex-typed in atypical ways (masculine-sex-typed females and feminine-sex-typed males).

Although it is relatively easy to place people in one of these four categories, considerable disagreement exists over what these categories mean (Locksley & Colten, 1979; Morawski, 1987; Pedhazur & Tetenbaum, 1979). For Sandra Bem (1974, 1977, 1979), whose work on this topic was the first to be widely recognized, the androgynous person was originally an ideal toward which we should strive. By combining positive masculine and feminine characteristics, the androgynous person functions effectively in a wide variety of situations that call for either masculine or feminine behavior. She proposed that sex-typed persons, in contrast, are more limited, because they are able to operate effectively in some situations but not in others. Other investigators take a more cautious approach, arguing that the personality characteristics of masculinity or femi-

BOX 4.3

The Concept of Androgyny

Morawski (1987) has listed the following as the core assumptions shared by operational conceptualizations of androgyny:

1. Categories of masculinity and femininity are assumed to be independent dimensions, hence not necessarily mutually exclusive.
2. Masculinity and femininity, as psychological categories, are unrelated to biological sex and to sexuality.
3. The categories are derived by aggregating responses to stereotypic descriptions that distinguish gender roles and expectations.
4. These sex-typed characteristics are assumed to be a function of individual traits as well as popular conceptions about masculinity and femininity.
5. The categories retain the same content as the previous M-F scales; masculine is direct, instrumental, and independent, whereas feminine is indirect, expressive, and dependent.
6. Androgyny is identified as a high level of both femininity and masculinity within an individual.
7. The categories of feminine, masculine, and androgynous are held to be predictive of certain social behaviors, although the models differ in specifying which behaviors are related to the measures.
8. Androgyny, or high levels of both masculinity and femininity, is believed to be desirable. Although there are differences between the models, they generally posit that the androgynous person has a greater range of options for behaving and, therefore, is more flexible and adjusted.
9. The androgyny construct is situated in conventional frameworks of psychology. Whether explained through self- and cognitive-schemata or through trait theory, androgyny adheres to current canons in psychology.

SOURCE: Morawski, 1987, p. 50. Used with permission.

ninity may or may not relate to what we typically consider sex-role behaviors. For example, the personality characteristics of femininity may not be entirely related to homemaking skills; rather, running a home may be related to both masculine and feminine (or agentic and communal) characteristics (Spence & Helmreich, 1978). Still other critics have argued that the notion of androgyny is a phenomenon that is peculiar to the United States, where individuality is valued and interdependency is scorned (Sampson, 1977). According to this view, traditional sex roles and characteristics may be functional in most societies and at most times—or, at a minimum, the advantages of the androgynous personality remain to be demonstrated.

Sandra Bem herself has renounced her commitment to androgyny as a goal, concluding that androgyny theory is "insufficiently radical" because it implies that masculinity and femininity have a reality of their own, beyond serving as internalized constructs (Bem, 1981, p. 363).

Even more idealistic a view is one by Rebecca and Hefner (1982), claiming that androgyny does not go far enough. In an article titled "The Future of Sex Roles," they write:

> Although the work on androgyny is a major advance in our view of sex roles, we still do not know if this abstract concept captures all the different ways that people behave in real life. We do not know how a person becomes androgynous, if androgyny has a distinct place in the development of sex roles, or if, indeed, androgyny is itself an end point. The sweeping societal changes in roles for women and men that are already occurring remind us that we must not be content with any one concept of the nature of people. This is why we have thought out a developmental model of sex-role transcendence which tries to capture the emerging possibilities—possibilities that might be quite different from the way of life that we now know. Transcendence means to go beyond what we know. In the area of sex roles it means to go beyond the rigid definitions of masculinity and femininity so that these terms lose their meaning. (p. 161)

Rebecca and Hefner (1982) in their article mean by transcendence an atmosphere in which choices are no longer traced even to the concepts of masculinity and femininity. Apparently their criticism of androgyny is that it is defined as a combination of sex-related traits. They state:

> Transcendence, then, involves several levels of change. It has to do with going completely beyond (transcending) present gender specific behavior, personality, and expectations. This is something quite different from a mere time-sharing of masculine and feminine characteristics in the same person, nor is it a mere freeing of both females and males to be both masculine and feminine. It requires the invention of new ways of being that are not merely fusions of what we already know. . . . A woman will be nurturant not because it is feminine but because she needs or wants to be nurturant. (p. 162)

As we can see, the notion of androgyny has accumulated its share of controversy since it was introduced into the psychological literature. Theoretical controversy has been accompanied by abundant research, and we are continually learning more about what it means to be androgynous. It is important to remember, however, that in regard to an operational definition, androgyny is just a convenient label for a combination of high scores on both masculinity (instrumental) and femininity (expressive) scales. Looking at the scales separately, we find that they are related to different kinds of behavior. People who score high on the masculinity scale generally have higher self-esteem. They are also more likely to have high achievement needs, to be dominant, and to be aggressive, compared with people who score low on masculinity (Taylor & Hall, 1982). High scores on the femininity scale are related to different kinds of behavior. For example, high femininity is related to the ability to show empathy, sociability, and skill in decoding nonverbal communications (Spence & Helmreich, 1978; Taylor & Hall, 1982).

The androgynous person, by definition, has both these kinds of skills, and in many situations this combination may be advantageous. In conversations, for example, both instrumental and expressive skills may be useful. Being instrumental may allow you to initiate discussion and introduce new topics; being expressive may allow you to relate to the other person and interpret his or her mood. Research has shown that androgynous people are more comfortable in conversational settings (Ickes, 1981). In one set of studies, male and female subjects representing various combinations of masculinity and femininity scores met each other in a waiting room (Ickes & Barnes, 1977, 1978). Their conversations were recorded on videotape and analyzed, and each member was also asked how much he or she had enjoyed the conversation. The results may contradict some common assumptions. The lowest levels of interaction and lowest levels of reported enjoyment were found among pairs in which the male was traditionally masculine sex-typed (high in masculinity and low in femininity) and the female was feminine sex-typed (high in femininity and low in masculinity). In contrast, when both persons were androgynous, levels of interaction and mutual enjoyment were high. These results support the hypothesis that the possession of both instrumental and expressive skills leads to more rewarding encounters.

Sex Roles in Young Adulthood

The extended analysis of masculinity, femininity, and their relationships in the previous section provides a foundation for a developmental analysis of the impact of sex roles during adulthood. At different periods during the adult years, these sex roles carry different manifestations.

As Dacey (1982) observes, young adult men and women share many goals in common. Erikson's task of establishing intimacy was described in Volume 1, as well as Gould's claim that the 20s were the ages when young people had to relinquish their connection with their parents. At the same time, young adulthood is often considered to be the period in which male/female differences are their greatest (Dacey, 1982). This section concentrates on different issues for women (role conflict) and for men (fear of femininity) during the young adult period.

Role Conflict

In this book, roles have been defined as expectations for behavior; thus *role conflict* is defined as any situation in which incompatible expectations are placed on a person because of his or her membership in a position. Role conflict creates tension because it almost inevitably forces the person to violate someone's expectations. In a useful review, Sales (1978) proposes that, compared to men, women are more likely to experience role conflict, especially in the workplace. They have special limitations placed on them because of the pervasiveness of the feminine sex role in our society. That is, a woman can either ignore the role demands coming from an expectation of being feminine and choose to behave "just like a man" on the job, or she can moderate her assertiveness and display the aspects of her personality that she values (or knows are effective in winning over her co-workers).

More specifically, in order to succeed in roles previously dominated by males, a woman must be confident, ambitious, and enterprising, or in general, demonstrate *instrumental* behaviors (Davis, Sommers-Flanagan, & Kessi, 1990). In contrast, those qualities generally considered feminine are *expressive* traits: gentleness, sensitivity, and supportiveness. A manifestation of the suggested conflict for some women in our society is the proliferation of books on subjects such as "smart women who make foolish choices" or "women who love too much." Weisbard (1988) observes that the successful marketing of these books reflects an assumption that the modern woman who is independent and fulfilled in her career remains unhappy and unfulfilled in her personal life.

Similarly, Sales (1978) writes:

> When competing roles are added to a woman's role repertoire, the potential for role conflict mounts. A husband socialized in traditional ways expects his wife to be supportive, respectful of his work obligations, and admiring of his competence. . . . A woman who is herself a job-holder may not nurture her husband's ego as well as a wife whose only contact with the work world is through her husband. . . . It is hard for a woman who is independent and assertive at work to become the compliant wife on her return home. (p. 159)

Role Overload

Somewhat different, but overlapping with role conflict, is the problem of role overload; the latter places a burden on individuals through the expectations of fulfilling too many roles, or of spending more time than available in fulfilling each of the roles. The emphasis here is on time demands, and as a result, role overload is a common

---

BOX 4.4

An Example of Role Overload

Sandra Bernstein, like millions of others in dual-career marriages, engages in the daily high-wire act of balancing work and family responsibilities. But unlike most of them, she is able to pinpoint the moment when she nearly slipped off the wire.

Ms. Bernstein, a family therapist in the Philadelphia suburb of Hatfield, Pennsylvania, was on the phone counseling a suicidal patient. Suddenly, from her office window she saw lightning from a distant thunderstorm. It was heading in the direction of the soccer field in another town where she knew her son Josh was playing with his friends.

"I realized my husband and I hadn't arranged to have him picked up for another hour, and he had no one to take him home in the storm," she said. "At that moment, I felt I had to make the impossible choice between my patient and my son."

In the end she stayed on the phone until her patient was in stable emotional condition, then drove through the storm to pick up her son. Although the tale has a happy ending—both patient and son are fine—Ms. Bernstein said she believes that she may never live through another moment that so clearly illustrates the contradictory pressures on those who cope with the two-career life.

SOURCE: Collins, 1987, p. 19. Copyright © 1987 by The New York Times Company. Reprinted by permission.

---

plight of young women who attempt to be "superwomen" by combining work, marriage, and family roles.

Close to 70% of American mothers with children at home are in the out-of-home workforce (Richardson, 1992). Their multitude of duties demands extensive time; Box 4.4 presents a typical dilemma.

What to do? Sales (1978) writes:

Role overload can be resolved by withdrawing from some roles or by renegotiating expectations with role partners. Husbands may be asked to share in household tasks, children may if old enough be asked to assume more responsibilities, alternative child care or housekeeping services may be devised, or bosses may be told that their demands are excessive. Although these solutions are often difficult to implement, they are the only ways of effectively eliminating role overload. (p. 160)

Dual-Career Couples. Dual-career couples report many advantages from their relationship: realization of personal fulfillment, financial rewards, and enhancement of family; but some couples were unable to alter expectations brought to the marriage. These couples reported disadvantages: not enough time to fulfill all roles in marriage and conflicts about specific roles (Stanton & Berger, 1987).

During the past 10 years, psychology has begun to recognize and study the dual-career couple as a special phenomenon in adult development (O'Neil, Fishman, & Kinsella-Shaw, 1987), and to identify the difficulties and conflicts that dual-career families encounter (Crosby, 1987; Gilbert, 1984, 1985; Gilbert, Hanson, & Davis, 1982; Walker & Wallston, 1985). How each spouse's career develops, for example, affects the other spouse's career development. The differentiation in gender roles tends to get obscured in dual-career families (O'Neil et al., 1987).

In a prescient article, Rapoport and Rapoport (1969) described the typical dilemmas of dual-career couples as arising from a clash between their own personal norms and society's views about appropriate behavior. These included career transitions, transitions in the family life cycle, and events in the life space of the children. Some specific factors are listed in Box 4.5. Even though the increased number of women in the outside-the-home workforce has eased some of the rigid community norms about a mother's role in child care, dual-career couples can still experience conflicts both at home and on the job, and vast differences occur with respect to marital satisfaction in dual-career couples (Gilbert & Davidson, 1989). For instance, Houseknecht and Macke (1981) found that a supportive husband, congruent role expectations, shared life expectations, and freedom from childbearing were among the factors contributing to marital adjustment in wives. But—as you would expect—role conflict increases in a dual-earner couple when there are greater differences between spouses in time spent on domestic responsibilities (Wiersma & van den Berg, 1991), and two-career marriages in which the partners share household tasks are the happiest.

BOX 4.5

Factors That Influence How
Couples Combine Work and Family Roles

Personal Factors

Personality (e.g., how important is it for a person to have an intimate relationship, to be emotionally close with children, to be number one in her or his field?)

Attitudes and values (e.g., what are a person's beliefs about who should rear a child, who should be breadwinners?)

Interests and abilities (e.g., how committed is a person to his or her work, how satisfying is it to them, how successful are they at what they do?)

Stages in the career and life cycles (e.g., is one spouse peaking career-wise and the other opting for early retirement?)

Concept of self as a man/woman (e.g., does being feminine mean being the primary nurturer and taking the back seat career-wise?)

Relationship Factors

Sources of power in the relationship (e.g., who decides on major purchases? Who has the final say?)

Tasks that need to be done to maintain the family (e.g., who does the grocery shopping? Who pays the bills?)

Concepts of equity (e.g., what seems fair and do the spouses agree on this?)

Spouse support (e.g., to what degree can one spouse, particularly the husband, put his or her needs aside and support the other spouse?)

Shared values/expectations (e.g., to what degree do spouses share life goals, views of men and women?)

Environmental Factors

The work situation (e.g., how flexible are work hours? Can one work at home if a child is sick?)

Employer's views (e.g., if a parent leaves at 5:00 to watch a child perform, will she or he be viewed as not ambitious enough?)

Societal norms and attitudes (e.g., is quality child care readily available? Do employers offer paid paternity leave?)

Support systems (e.g., are there friends or relatives to help out with parenting? Are colleagues supportive?)

SOURCE: Gilbert & Davidson, 1989, Table 9.1, p. 201. Used with permission.

An increasing number of women with children do not have a husband at home who can share household tasks. During the decade of the 1980s the number of single mothers increased by 35%. And when there is a husband present, typically he spends only about a quarter of the time on household tasks that his wife does, and he carries out many fewer of those tasks than she does (Burros, 1988; Gunter & Gunter, 1991).

Role Discontinuity

A third difficulty facing young women is role discontinuity, or the stressful response to the sharp shifts in the pattern of sex roles over time. Sales (1978) suggests that women are much more likely to experience role discontinuity than are men. The pattern is most diverse for women with children: They typically work until the first child is born; then they reduce or abandon work in preschool years. Perhaps they work part time while their children are in school, and they may work full time in their forties. These shifting role demands require continued adjustments for many women. Other women may experience problems because they are unable to acknowledge a status change; for example, when a new parent still feels constrained to fulfill all of her social obligations.

Sales (1978) and Dacey (1982) suggest the following as ways that role transitions may be eased for the person:

1. the person may develop the ability to adopt to changing social expectations;
2. the person may use available social supports to ease role entrance;
3. people may informally seek information about the new role from others; and
4. the stress is lessened if other valued roles are part of the person's repertoire.

Gender-Role Conflict in Young Men

Young men in our society face another type of conflict. The heavy-handed nature of being socialized to become a man can create oppressive effects. We are aware of the deleterious effects of sexism on women's opportunities, but men are also oppressed by rigid socialization processes that limit their potential to be fully functional human beings (Pleck, 1981, 1982). The *masculine mystique* reflects a set of values and beliefs that define optimal masculinity in our society. Part of the masculine mystique implies that femininity is inferior to masculinity as a gender orientation (O'Neil, 1981a).

O'Neil and Egan (1992) have specified five stages or phases in a gender-role journey if men are to move away from the masculine mystique to new roles. These are:

Phase 1: a restrictive view of gender roles, with traditional distinctions in the sexes; lack of awareness of the deleterious effects of sexism.

Phase 2: an ambivalence about gender roles and a confusion about masculine and feminine identities; experiences sporadic irritation about sexism; begins to contemplate making gender-role changes.

Phase 3: an emerging expression of anger about sexism and a recognition that sexism is a form of interpersonal violence; begins to use anger to make personal changes.

Phase 4: an activism stage, in which the person pursues an exploration of how gender roles and sexism have affected his or her life and makes gender-role changes that make behavior less restrictive and conflictual.

Phase 5: a celebration and integration of gender roles; experiences a "gender-role freedom" in personal and professional relationships; continues active efforts to educate the public about gender roles and the violence of sexism.

As noted above, many men have been socialized to behave in sexist ways; they have difficulty in developing and integrating new male roles that are compatible with nonsexist behavior. Yet sex-role strain occurs; it is, in fact, the result when rigid gender roles restrict people's abilities to actualize their human potential. Garnets and Pleck (1979) operationally define sex-role strain "as a discrepancy between the real self and that part of the ideal self-concept that is culturally associated with gender" (p. 278).

Rigid gender roles lead, in some men, to what has been labeled *fear of femininity* by James M. O'Neil (O'Neil, 1981b; O'Neil, Helms, Gable, David, & Wrightsman, 1986). Fear of femininity is defined as a strong concern that oneself possesses (or is seen as possessing) feminine values, attitudes, and behaviors, and that these will reflect negatively on oneself (O'Neil et al., 1986). That is, a man may fear that people will see him as stereotypically, negatively feminine—weak, submissive, and dependent. O'Neil has proposed that six components of fear of femininity are functional:

1. Restricted emotionality, or difficulty in expressing one's own feelings, or denying others their rights to emotional expressiveness, especially with regard to such feelings as tenderness and vulnerability.
2. Homophobia or having fears of homosexuals or fears of being homosexual, including possessing unfounded beliefs, myths, and stereotypes about gay people.
3. Socialized control, power, and competition, or the desire to regulate, to restrain, or to have others or situations under one's command, striving against others with the purpose of winning or gaining something.
4. Restricted sexual and affectionate behavior, or having limited ways of expressing one's sexual needs and affections to others.
5. Obsession with achievement and success, or having a persistent preoccupation with work, accomplishment, and eminence as means of substantiating and demonstrating one's value.
6. Health care problems, or having difficulties maintaining positive health care in respect to diet, exercise, relaxation, and stress, and a healthy lifestyle.

Scores on the Gender-Role Conflict Scale (GRCS), a measure of the above qualities, have shown several relationships indicating the power of the phenomenon. For example, these qualities were positively related to anxiety and depression and negatively related to degree of social intimacy and level of self-esteem in college men (Good & Mintz, 1990; Sharpe & Heppner, 1991). In keeping with the focus on health-care problems, Stillson, O'Neil, and Owen (1991) reported that male gender-role conflict predicted extent of physical symptoms. As Harrison (1978) warned many years ago, exaggerated masculinity can be hazardous to one's health.

O'Neil proposed that fear of femininity is strongest in young adulthood, and then begins to diminish. O'Neil and Fishman (1986) propose that men redefine their career and gender-role identities over the life cycle, and especially experience gender-role conflict during periods of career transition.

Sex Roles in Middle Adulthood

Something different happens during middle adulthood. Now that the children are gone, the man can let the anima aspect of his personality emerge, as well as the animus (see Volume 1, Chapter 3). Meanwhile, the woman may be preparing to reenter the job world, or increase her commitment to it. A role reversal begins to occur in each sex.

The Empty Nest Syndrome

As the preceding paragraph states, many women face an almost complete loss of one role while in the forties, as children reach adulthood and leave home to establish independent lives. Role discontinuity can be severe for the woman whose prime focus has been on nurturance and provision of child care for 20 years.

But more women react positively to the empty nest. Women whose children have left are more satisfied, less self-pitying, and less easily hurt than women whose children are still at home (Lowenthal et al., 1975). They generally show fewer depressive symptoms when their children are on their own (Radloff, 1975). Also, women's feelings about marriage show marked improvement once children have left home.

Menopause

Role discontinuity may be increased in traditionally oriented women at about the same time; menopause, by marking the end of fertility, may make these women now feel useless and barren. Such feelings are strikingly similar to those experienced by some men at retirement. (For contemporary women, in contrast, the subjective end of their fertility probably occurred about the time of their final pregnancy and birth.)

But the negative impact of menopause is often exaggerated (Sheehy, 1992). Germaine Greer (1992) characterizes the new period of her life as the "post-menopausal zest." Only about 4% of women thought menopause was the worst thing about middle age. *Severe* hot flashes are reported by only 10% of women experiencing menopause, vaginal dryness by only 5% (Voda, 1982). Karen

Matthews and her colleagues (Matthews et al., 1990) review studies and conclude that natural (i.e., nonsurgical) menopause is a benign event for most healthy women; in fact, women who have experienced menopause evaluate it much more positively than either premenopausal women or men (Dan & Bernhard, 1989).

Sex Roles in Later Adulthood

In later adulthood two developments are important. One, called the cross-over phenomenon, is an accentuation of the role reversal begun by some couples in middle adulthood. Neugarten (1968) describes it as follows: "Women as they age seem to become more tolerant of their own aggressive, egocentric impulses, whereas men, as they age, [become more tolerant] of their own nurturative and affiliative impulses" (p. 71).

Sales (1978) adds the following:

> Women play a more dominant role in marital decision making than they did in earlier periods. Referred to as *peak wife-dominance*, both husbands and wives often consider the wife the dominant partner. . . . This pattern, which is a dramatic reversal of the earlier marital power structure, is further evidence of the increased assertiveness that women show in middle age. . . . For many traditional women, the mid-life crisis seems to culminate in their final unleashing from earlier sex-role personality constraints. They may be aided in their transition by the corresponding decline in their husband's need to play his marital role according to social prescriptions. Both partners, newly comfortable with expressing their personal rather than their sexual imperatives, may reshape their marriage into a more rewarding form. (pp. 183-184)

This leads to the second phenomenon, a movement toward "normal unisexuality" (Dacey, 1982). That is, the differences between men and women, so many of which seemed to be based on sexuality, are no longer as important. Older men and women seem to have more in common with each other.

In later adulthood, other issues may develop that lead once again to different reactions by the two sexes. For example, Chapter 7 describes the reaction of men and women to the loss of their spouses.

5

Sexual Relationships and Marriage

*Marriage is, remember, a male institution. Men created it,
and men like it. Men need marriage more than women do
and suffer more profoundly outside it.*

Dalma Heyn

Is there life after marriage? Chapter 2 described the effort to escape
the pervasiveness of the "one-career imperative" in contemporary
society. An equivalent issue is the commitment to a lifetime marriage. Newspapers and magazines tell us of the increasing percentage of marriages that end in divorce. A dialectical analysis is useful
here: At times, commitment to a marriage may be comfortable and
reassuring; at other times, this commitment may be threatening.
Perhaps this is one of the explanations for the fact that despite the
centrality of "long-term marriage" as a value in our society, the
median length of a first marriage in the United States, as of 1992,
was only slightly more than 6 years (Usdansky, 1992).

How do married couples respond? What changes take place during a long-term marriage? How does the sexual aspect of a relationship change over the course of 20, 30, or 50 years? These are some

71

of the questions faced in a chapter that attempts to provide a developmental analysis of sexual behavior and marriage.

Establishing a Sexual Relationship

Some 50 years ago, most American couples had their first sexual intimacy on their wedding night; today fewer than one of every five couples postpone sexual intercourse until their marriage. Hence, as a background for analyzing the sexual aspect of a marriage relationship, it is necessary to review the findings on the extent of premarital sexual behavior.

Obtaining accurate data on sexual activity outside of marriage is, of course, difficult to do, because of reluctance on the part of some respondents to reveal personal information. Furthermore, many of the studies on this topic used as their subjects "captive samples" of high school or college students, who may not accurately represent the entire population of young unmarried people. We face a dilemma; we need to report these findings, because they are better than no information; still, we need to be careful not to generalize specific incidence rates too widely.

According to a survey conducted by the Alan Guttmacher Institute (Lawson, 1991), 60% of teenaged boys and 50% of teenaged girls have had sexual intercourse; for 19-year-olds, the percentages are 86% and 75%. Indications are that teenagers are becoming sexually active at younger ages than before. Pregnancy rates for teenaged girls remained constant over the 1980s—at 127 per 1,000 girls, the rate in the United States is far higher than in other industrialized countries (Painter, 1991). One of every 25 high school students reported having a sexually transmitted disease (Associated Press, 1992).

Standing back from the figures for specific studies of sexual experience of college students—studies done at different times over the past 30 years—we detect several trends. The percentage of ummarried young people who report sexual experience has increased dramatically. The major change came in the 1960s and early 1970s, along with a spirit of questioning everything and a value on adventurousness. In general, percentage of respondents reporting being sexually active increased in those studies that were done up to around 1983; since then, there has been little or no increase. Increased concern over the effects of sexual promiscuity, including the incidence of AIDS, has contributed to the stabilizing of the premarital sexual incidence rate.

Perhaps of equal importance is the increasingly casual attitude toward nonmarital sexual intercourse. A survey of 999 students on 104 college campuses found only 9% saying it would be "very shameful" if an unmarried friend became pregnant; 53% say it is "not shameful at all" (Stewart, 1986). Furthermore, when University of Michigan undergraduates were asked which event would trouble them more—if their partner had intercourse with someone else or if their partner had formed a deep emotional attachment with someone else—60% of the men chose the first option. Of the women, 85% chose the second option.

The values that are salient in our society shift from decade to decade and year to year; Chapter 6 describes the impact of these shifting values on a number of topics. These shifts, some of which are predictable, some of which result from unanticipated conditions, reinforce the utility of a dialectical approach to the analysis of sexual relationships. One way of conceptualizing these values is provided by the sociologist Isador Rubin (1965); Box 5.1 describes these six differing value positions regarding the purpose of sexual activity. A quick examination of this list will lead to an awareness that each value is advocated by certain segments of our society, and from time to time, different values are the norm in our society.

Given the shift in percentage of young people who have engaged in sexual intercourse prior to marriage, it may be concluded that movement has been away from the traditional asceticism described in Box 5.1 toward the next couple of values. This change in the norm has implications for sexual morale during marriage, and it is that topic to which we next turn.

Sexual Morale in Marriage

Several years ago the columnist Ann Landers (1989a, 1989b) asked her female readers to respond to the question: "Would you be content to be held close and treated tenderly, and forget about 'the act'?" More than 90,000 women responded, and 72% of these said

---

BOX 5.1

Rubin's List of Six Value
Positions Regarding Sexual Behavior

---

1. Traditional Asceticism: The sole purpose of sexual behavior is procreation and it should strictly be limited to marriage. Thus sexual activity is a necessary evil, and young people who are instilled with this traditional value often have difficulty expressing their sexual nature.

2. Enlightened Asceticism: Sexual activity needs to be carefully monitored and controlled. Although it is not considered evil as such, and people are encouraged to express their needs and feelings, sexual activity should be exercised only under carefully delimited conditions.

3. Humanistic Liberalism: This "relativistic" position proposes that an evaluation of sexual activity should be based on the relationship of the people who are engaging in it. One viewpoint that fits this category is that of "situation ethics"; this liberal position endorses any type of sexual activity as long as it is justified by the consequences.

4. Humanistic Radicalism: After careful education, any type of sexual activity is accepted. There is no blanket rejection of any type of behavior as long as no physical or emotional harm results.

5. Fun Morality: The view here is that the main reason for sex is to have fun. There should be no limits on frequency or type, as long as no one is physically abused.

6. Sexual Anarchy: An extreme position that advocates no restrictions on any type of sexual behavior.

---

yes. Of those, 40% were under the age of 40. Publication of these results led to a variety of responses in the mass media, mostly with reactions of consternation and surprise. Sex therapist Ruth Westheimer even called it "dangerous" because it was misleading. Although 90,000 respondents is an impressive number, we cannot conclude that 72% of women in general are satisfied only with close feelings of genuine intimacy without sexual intercourse.

Unfortunately, a tendency exists to equate sexual morale with frequency of intercourse. The latter is a contributor to morale, but not a complete determinant.

There is evidence that sexual morale is high early in a marriage despite whatever difficulties are encountered. Intercourse occurs frequently in the early months of marriage and decreases in frequency over the length of the marriage. It has been estimated (Broderick, 1982) that the average frequency of sexual intercourse per month is as follows:

- during the first 6 months of a marriage: 12 per month
- marriage of 2 years: 8 per month
- marriage of 5 years: 7 per month
- marriage of 10 years: 6 per month
- marriage of 25 years: 4 per month
- marriage of 30 years: 3 per month

A more recent survey found that sexual frequency dropped from about 6 or 7 times per month for couples under age 40 to slightly less than one time a month for those over age 70 (Haney, 1990).

The inexorable linear quality of the above figures, and especially the "decline" in frequency, should not be overinterpreted and most certainly should not be used as a norm table by someone who wants to "keep score." These figures are based on large numbers of couples, but there are problems in concluding from them that with decreasing frequency, a particular couple shows a decline in the morale of its marriage. For example, divorce rates peak after the third or fourth years of marriage; also it is during this general period that pregnancy is more likely to occur. The decrease in frequency of intercourse during pregnancy (especially in the third trimester) is found in many cultures, not only in the United States, but in Thailand, Czechoslovakia, and other countries.

The occurrence of pregnancy is one example of the conclusion that frequency of intercourse is not the only indication of sexual satisfaction (Broderick, 1982). Women who have a positive attitude toward their pregnancy tend to improve or at least maintain the quality of their sexual relationships with their husbands, whereas those with negative attitudes experience a decrease in sexual satisfaction. Several explanations may be proposed for this:

1. *Stimulus generalization:* This term refers to the reaction of the woman who loses enthusiasm for everything associated with an unwanted or unpleasant pregnancy, including the activity that brought it about.
2. Negative manifestations of the pregnancy (fatigue, nausea, sleeplessness) seem to be more frequent when the woman's attitude toward the pregnancy is unfavorable.
3. The quality of the couple's affection for each other prior to pregnancy predicts the pregnant woman's degree of satisfaction (Broderick, 1982).

But most pregnant women apparently succeed in maintaining a level of sexual activity that closely reflects their desires. And even though their interest in sexual intercourse declines in the third trimester of pregnancy, their interest in being held does not diminish.

Sexual-intercourse incidence rates based on length of the marriage neglect the awareness of sexual needs in older women. The groundbreaking surveys of sexual behavior by Alfred Kinsey and his colleagues in the late 1940s and early 1950s concluded that women reached their peak of sexual functioning in their middle years. But Kinsey's survey almost overlooked the study of older persons. In his study of women (Kinsey, Pomeroy, Martin, & Gebhard, 1953), only 56 women over the age of 60 were included in his sample respondents. One of the problems is a sexual double standard: older men are considered "more sexual" whereas older women are not. This is ironic, given that most older men do experience some decline in the physiological aspects of sexual intercourse, whereas women are more able to maintain sexual responsiveness at older ages.

More recent scholarly work (e.g., Weg, 1989) emphasizes the continued sexual desire, capacity, and pleasure in midlife. Weg (1989) uses the concept of *sensuality/sexuality* to broaden the concept of sexuality by including intimacy and communication as well as genital contact.

Although there is a gradual diminishment of sexual response in males over the adult life cycle, a substantial percentage of men continue to function even into advanced old age. Masters and Johnson's (1966) study of sexual physiological responses found that men in their 60s took two or three times longer to respond to direct sexual stimulation, and other studies have found that younger males (ages 19-30) responded six times quicker than older groups (ages 48-65).

Five studies of sexual potency in aging males (summarized by Broderick, 1982) found that for men in their early 60s, from 60% to 82% (in different studies) maintained their sexual potency; in men in their late 60s, these percentages were from 50% to 75%. Somewhere between 25% and 45% of men in their late 70s were still sexually potent.

As noted before, women's orgasmic capacity seems unaffected by aging. Older women may need extra lubrication but their orgasmic capacity remains the same or better. Masters and Johnson (1966) reported that women often experienced increased erotic feelings after menopause, perhaps because they were relieved of fear of pregnancy and its responsibilities. However, this distinction may be a function of the "pre-pill" generation—women who were of childbearing age before this type of birth control was available (Broderick, 1982).

All reports agree that the frequency of sexual intercourse drops off strongly in old age. Pearlman (1972) reports that only 20% of elderly men have sexual intercourse two or more times a month. But it is hard to know how much the diminished rate is a function of biology, of health, of relationships, or of expectations. It may not be an exaggeration to claim that society disapproves of sex among the elderly. We stereotype sex as an activity of youth; the message our culture often transmits is that love is only for the young and beautiful (Bulcroft & O'Conner-Roden, 1986). Attitude surveys show that people assume the elderly are uninterested in sex. This is an extension of college students' mistaken beliefs about the frequency of their parents' sexual activity. Pocs and Godow (1977) asked college students to estimate their parents' frequency of sexual activity. On the average, students estimated their parents had sexual intercourse less than half as often as that indicated by surveys of sexual incidence rates in couples of their parents' age. Some 6% of the students refused even to answer questions about their parents' behavior. Responded one: "Whoever thinks about their parents' sexual relations, except perverts?" One fourth of the students estimated that their parents never had sex or had it less than once a year.

Sexual Relationships
in "Successful" Marriages

A substantial correlation exists between satisfaction with frequency of intercourse and overall marital satisfaction; that is, couples who are happy in the relationship engage in about as much sexual behavior as they like. But again, such a correlation reflects a general trend, and there remain vast differences and discrepancies. One of the most revealing of the studies that illustrate this diversity is that by Cuber and Harroff (1965), who interviewed 100 married couples (ages 35 to 55) who were "successful" in the ways that most people measure success. Every couple had been married for at least 10 years and was still married at the time of the interview; in fact, none of these couples claimed that they ever seriously had considered divorce or separation. They were "socially conspicuous" because of the nature of their work in business, government, the military, medicine, education, or the arts. The husband was at the top of his profession or business organization. But despite these similarities the sociologists found vast differences in the sexual relationships among these "successful" couples, leading them to classify the couples in five types.

About one sixth of the couples had a "vital" relationship; sexual intercourse was frequent and mutually rewarding. Communication between the two people flourished; they shared life experiences and each considered the other indispensable; an activity was uninteresting if the spouse was not a part of it. Romance lived in a continuing vibrant relationship.

Cuber and Harroff (1965) classified a few of the couples into a "total relationship" category, really an extension of the vital relationship. The difference is that in the "total relationship" the points of "vital meshing" between partners are more numerous; "in some cases all of the important life foci are vitally shared" (p. 58). The authors, however, report that this kind of relationship is rare.

In contrast, another one sixth of the couples the authors called "the conflict-habituated." They constantly quarreled; they deliberately hurt each other emotionally. Sexual behavior between them was only one of several battlefields. Sometimes they were involved with lovers outside the marriage. Cuber and Harroff (1965) note that the intermittent conflict was rarely concealed from their children, even though the parents claimed otherwise. They observe, "There is a subtle valence in these conflict-habituated relationships. It is easily missed in casual observation. So central is the necessity from channeling conflict and bridling hostility that these considerations come to preoccupy much of the interaction" (p. 46).

In between these two groups, the sociologists distinguished two other types. About one third of the marriage relationships they labeled "devitalized." These couples had previously had a vital relationship but had lost that quality. The zest was gone; one called her marriage "dull." They both missed and resented the former vitality, and thus had become quite apathetic about marriage itself. These couples did not share many interests and activities, and did not spend much time with each other. Sex was quite often perfunctory or absent; occasional discreet affairs were tolerated. In many of these couples there were certain aspects of their relationship—their children, their house—that they shared and found satisfying; hence the social scientists did not classify them as extreme as the "conflict-habituated."

The fourth group, comprising about one third of the couples, was labeled the "passive-congenial" type. These couples had settled into a comfortable, loyal relationship; as a matter of fact, they were happy with their less intense relationship. Many of these couples had put more of their energy into other activities than their marriages. They took each other for granted but saw this as a virtue rather than a vice; they had not expected the intensity of the courtship phase to continue and so were not embittered when it did not. They express little conflict with each other, although "some admit that they tiptoe rather gingerly over and around a residue of subtle resentments and frustrations" (Cuber & Harroff, 1965, p. 51).

It should be emphasized that all of the couples in the above study were in long-term marriages, despite the differing ways they have adapted. A recent study indicates that how couples fight may have little to do with keeping a marriage together (Morin, 1993); how *often* arguments take place was a stronger predictor of marriage survival in a study of couples married longer than 8 years.

Divorce, Remarriage, and Sexual Relationships

Of those who become divorced, approximately 80% remarry. A half century ago, only one of every three divorced persons remarried, partly because of the stigma of divorce (Dacey, 1982). In 1952, the fact that U.S. presidential candidate Adlai Stevenson was divorced was a significant factor in many voters' reactions to him; in 1980, there was hardly any public notice over the fact that presidential candidate Ronald Reagan was divorced and remarried.

Among women born between 1945 and 1949, 17% of their first marriages had ended in divorce by age 30, and one third of all marriages today involve at least one party who has been married before. For divorced people who remarry, women wait an average of 3.4 years, whereas men wait a little less, 3.1 years (Schmid, 1987).

No substantial research exists comparing the sexual adjustment of remarried persons with that of once-married couples of the same ages. But Pietropinto and Simenauer (1979) reported that more than half of the remarried respondents to their survey said that their sex life was now excellent and 21% reported having sex at least five times a week, as opposed to 15% of first-married people.

Sexual Behavior Outside of Marriage

We are all aware of the vast variety of sexual relationships outside of marriage; differences exist with regard to the sex of the partner, the permanence of the relationship, the commitment to it, and many other aspects. Three major types exist: homosexual relationships, heterosexual relationships between two people unmarried but living together, and extramarital relationships. Each will be briefly described below, with emphasis on whatever knowledge is available on the developmental nature of the relationship.

Homosexual Relationships

The decade of the 1990s has seen a massive increase in society's awareness of homosexuality. The whole topic remains quite controversial, but two aspects generated special degrees of disagreement in the mid-90s: the incidence rate of homosexuality and its causes.

Incidence of Homosexuality

A national survey of male sexual behavior, carried out by the Alan Guttmacher Institute and published in 1993, found that 2.3% of the 3,300 men surveyed (ages 20-39) had engaged in homosexual sexual behavior and that 1.1% considered themselves exclusively homosexual (Barringer, 1993). (The study used face-to-face interviews in which all subjects were guaranteed anonymity.) Its findings were in marked contrast to those of Kinsey's study, done in 1948, which concluded that from 6% to 10% of men and 5% of women were primarily homosexual, as well as a 1989 anonymous survey that had concluded that one out of every five American men had had a homosexual experience (Knight-Ridder News Service, 1989). In fact, the conventional wisdom in American society had assimilated the belief that one tenth of the American male population was gay, and a quarterly magazine for gays and lesbians, first published in 1992, is even titled "Ten Percent" (Painton, 1993). And even after this survey, many experts estimate that the percentage of men who are homosexual is somewhere between this 1% figure and Kinsey's 6% to 10%—from 2% to 4% (Schmalz, 1993).

Homosexuality: Genetic or Learned?

Chapter 1 dealt with the question of hereditary influences on personality, and reported recent data indicating a significant influence, based on studies of identical twins who were brought up in separate families. Does such a methodology lead to similar conclusions with regard to homosexuality? The author of one of the largest such studies, psychologist J. Michael Bailey, concludes that genetic background accounts for 50% to 70% of the variance in sexual orientation; "the reason why male sexual orientation runs in families appears to be genetic and not environmental," he is quoted as saying (Adler, 1992, p. 12).

The study (Bailey & Pillard, 1991) utilized more than 100 fraternal or identical male twins, plus 46 adopted men and their brothers. The subjects ranged in age from 9 to 65 (mean = 33 years); at least one in each pair was homosexual or bisexual in orientation, having responded to the researchers' advertisement. The more genetically similar the brothers were, the more likely both were to be homosexual. Of the 56 sets of identical twins, 52% were both gay, but only 22% of the 54 sets of fraternal twins were both homosexual in orientation. Only 11% of adopted brothers were both gay.

Do these findings apply to women also? Bailey and Pillard (1991) repeated their procedures with a sample of women who responded to advertisements in gay media. Of those lesbians who had an identical twin, 48% of the time the other twin was also gay. For fraternal twins, the rate was 16%, and for genetically unrelated adoptive sisters, 6%. The similarity to the men's data is striking, and clearly supports the thesis that the "predisposition to homosexuality is largely an inborn trait" (Daly, 1993, p. 38).

Like the studies on heritability coefficients in Chapter 1, the significance of these results can be exaggerated. Definitions of homosexuality in these studies were based on self-reports. Using as subjects those who respond to advertisements is not sufficient for an epidemiologically acceptable procedure. Accounting for 50% to 70% of the variance still leaves room for other factors. And hormonal factors during utero may be confounded with genetic similarity. Even a recent study (Hamer, Hu, Magnuson, Hu, & Pattanucci, 1993), linking some instances of male homosexuality to a small stretch of DNA on the X chromosome, needs to find out whether heterosexual brothers have such markers.

Bell and Weinberg's (1978) study, conducted by the Kinsey Institute at Indiana University, is perhaps the most useful in providing a classification of the lifestyles of homosexual men and women. They generated five categories that described 70% of the persons in their San Francisco sample:

1. The "close-couple" relationship: These couples reflected intimacy, exclusivity, and continuity. About 15% of the male pairs and a higher percentage of the women were in this type of sexual relationship.
2. "Open-couple" relationship: These pairs lived together but their relationship did not preclude other sexual partners even though jealousy was a pervasive problem when such liaisons existed. This type of relationship reflected characteristic behavior of 25% of the men.
3. "Functional" relationship: This type of homosexual person had many sexual partners and few commitments or regrets.
4. "Dysfunctional" homosexual lifestyle: This type of person had few partners or sexual activity, but was tortured by self-doubt and guilt.

5. The asexual lifestyle: The person who is less active than those in previous categories.

Reports of the sexual behavior of homosexual men published as recently as 15 years ago (see, e.g., Lief, 1978) emphasized a characteristic promiscuity, with frequent encounters with strangers. With the rise in the incidence of AIDS, such patterns are changing, and doubtless such typologies as even the carefully done one by Bell and Weinberg are no longer correct with regard to percentages of people in particular categories.

Prior to the advent of fears about AIDS, female homosexual lifestyles, more often than the men's, emphasized a long-term, committed relationship with a single partner. Lesbians reported less sexual activity than either heterosexual couples or male couples (Blumstein & Schwartz, 1983).

Unmarried, Heterosexual Relationships

The decade of the 1970s saw an eightfold increase in the number of cohabiting couples in the United States under age 25; among those ages 25-44, it increased sixfold (Cherlin, 1979). For the first half of the decade of the 1980s this trend continued; 1985 was the first year in more than a decade that the number of unmarried couples living together was less than the year before (Schmid, 1985). Even with the slight decrease, there were still 1,983,000 cohabiting couples in the United States (Kelley, 1985). Even surveys now more than a decade old (Pietropinto & Simenauer, 1979) reported that 14% of married couples had lived together prior to marriage, and of those married for a second time (or more), 35% had cohabited. More recent figures increase these percentages to 30% and 60% (Barringer, 1989).

As Dacey (1982) notes, cohabitation is not usually a permanent substitute for marriage. Either the living-together relationship ends after a while—Dacey estimates a year or less—or the couple decides to get married. Cherlin (1979), after observing the progress of cohabitation in Sweden, France, and the United States, views it as an emerging first stage of marriage. Surveys of premarriage records in one county in Oregon concluded that 53% of the couples who took out marriage licenses were living together prior to marriage (Jacob, 1986).

Despite the "trial marriage" connotation of cohabitation, recent studies indicate that couples in the United States who lived together prior to marriage were more likely to separate and divorce after marriage than were couples who did not live together prior to marriage. Within the first decade of marriage, 38% of those couples who had lived together had split up, compared to 27% of those who did not cohabit (Barringer, 1989).

Extramarital Relationships

Extramarital relationships are a staple of television soap operas, trashy and not-so-trashy fiction, and the lifestyles of some of "the rich and famous." Kinsey's studies, published in 1948 and 1953, reported that 50% of the males and 25% of the females in these samples had had at least one such experience. (But Kinsey's samples were not representative samples; they were composed entirely of volunteers.) Other estimates of incidence of extramarital relationships are sometimes lower, but the sex difference remained distinct, until more recent reports.

It should be noted, however, that the earlier problems with inconsistency of results between surveys continue. Two different surveys of infidelity among women (the Janus survey and the Cosmopolitan readers survey)—both published in 1993—reported rates of 26% and 39%, respectively (Adler, 1993). The Janus survey (Janus & Janus, 1993), which reported 26% of women having had an affair, claimed 35% of married men had.

The most up-to-date estimates show a smaller discrepancy between the sexes, with the women's rate of extramarital relationships having increased, whereas the reported rate for men has stayed about the same. In fact, a Yale University survey of 25,000 respondents (Stewart, 1985) found that women in their 30s are just as likely as men of that age range to participate in a sexual affair.

Other sex differences exist. Men are more likely to engage in an initial sexual affair during the first 5 years of marriage, whereas for women this decision is more common after 15 or 20 years of marriage.

Despite the strong disapproval voiced about infidelity, many married people feel that they can be tempted into it. Only 39% of the population view themselves as totally beyond temptation (28% of husbands and 49% of wives).

Why, then, does infidelity exist? Dissatisfaction with the marriage itself is given as the most frequent reason. But we need to recognize that an extramarital affair can be generated by a variety of causes. Cuber and Harroff's (1965) typology of five types of marriage described earlier in the chapter, is helpful here. They concluded that:

> Infidelity . . . occurs in most of the five types, the total relationship being the exception. But it occurs for quite different reasons. In the conflict-habituated it seems frequently to be only another outlet for hostility. The call girl and the woman picked up in a bar are more than just available women; they are symbols of resentment of the wife. This is not always so, but reported to us often enough to be worth noting. Infidelity among the passive-congenial, on the other hand, is typically in line with the stereotype of the middle-aged man who "strays out of sheer boredom with the uneventful, deadly prose" of his private life. And the devitalized man or woman frequently is trying for an hour or a year to recapture the lost mood. But the vital are sometimes adulterous, too; some are simply emancipated—almost bohemian. To some of them sexual aggrandizement is an accepted fact of life. Frequently the infidelity is condoned by the partner and in some instances even provides an indirect (through empathy) kind of gratification. The act of infidelity in such cases is not construed as disloyalty or as a threat to continuity, but rather as a kind of basic human right which the loved one ought to be permitted to have—and which the other perhaps wants for himself (or herself). (p. 62)

This last reason is magnified in the recent *The Erotic Silence of the American Wife* (Heyn, 1992), which argues that adultery for women is a revolutionary way for a woman to abandon the sexless, stifling, self-sacrificing style characteristic of "The Perfect Wife." Although Dalma Heyn interviewed a small number of unfaithful wives, she makes "sweeping generalizations about the malleability and self-deception of American wives and their inability to assert their own needs within the marital relationship" (Smolowe, 1992, p. 74).

A second important reason is the premarital sexual frequency of the person. The greater number of sexual partners the person had before marriage, the more likely he or she is to be extramaritally active sexually.

Evolutionary reasons for infidelity (and divorce) are also offered; anthropologist Helen E. Fisher (1992) concludes that most couples, in their fertile years, remain together long enough to establish the safety and security of their children and then seek new partners. The evolutionary explanation is that we seek the greatest possible diversity for our offspring.

Marriage—A Lasting Institution?

Despite the pattern of other types of sexual relationships described in the last few sections, and despite the numerous criticisms of marriage, it is still considered a significant event that changes the lives of both its participants. Even in the late 1960s and early 1970s, when young Americans were scrutinizing every conventional value, about 80% of the weddings in the United States included a religious ceremony.

Is marriage an institution that is universally valued? In one sense, not as much as it used to be, but in another sense, it remains as strong as before. Some indications that it has weakened: The proportion of women ages 30-34 who have never married has nearly tripled, from 6% in 1970 to 16% in 1990 (Manning, 1991). In 1957 a survey of representative U.S. adults (Veroff & Feld, 1971) found that 80% of them believed that only sick or immoral people would not want to marry, but in 1976 a repetition of this study (Douvan, 1979) reported that only 25% felt that not marrying was wrong. Similarly, the percentage of women who hope to get married has decreased, and the median age at marriage increased more than 2 years (to 26.1 for men and 23.9 for women) from 1970 to 1990 (Manning, 1991; Schmid, 1987).

Some observers (e.g., McFarlane, 1987) are concerned about implications of this delay to marry, one being that it reflects a fear of making a binding pledge to someone else. Jonda McFarlane (1987) writes:

> Those who fear the commitment of marriage, who avoid the trouble and the responsibility in the name of more time, more money or more pleasure, cheat only themselves. Those who wait until they reach all their other goals before presenting themselves to a deserving mate often find their success empty. (p. 8)

This is one viewpoint, but society's values, manifested in the choices of young and marriageable people, reflect a dialectical shift from one tug to another. I expect that at some point in the future the average age at marriage will shift downward again.

But as we saw earlier in this chapter, the vast majority of those who end a first marriage in divorce remarry—five sixths of the men and three fourths of the women. As noted earlier, in recent years, more than 30% of people who marry have been married at least once before. From one half to two thirds of these remarriages last until one of the married partners dies. And remarried people are substantially happier than separated or divorced people. Each year in the United States the number of new marriages increases (Schmid, 1987) and marriage is an institution that will doubtless continue as the foundation for intimate relationships, despite the trend toward increased cohabitation and significant divorce rates (see Box 5.2 for clarification). Especially, then, it is appropriate to examine how a marital relationship develops, the topic of the next section.

The Development
of the Marital Relationship

Social scientists have sought to specify a sequence of developments that lead to marriage.

Social psychologist George Levinger (1979) has presented a descriptive analysis of marital relationships based on the combination of attractions and barriers that are present. Some of the attractions that he identifies are material rewards, such as family income; others are either symbolic, such as status, or affectional, such as companionship and sexual enjoyment. Barriers are conceived of as the potential costs of divorcing, such as financial expenses, feelings toward children, and religious constraints. Finally, Levinger suggests that people also weigh the alternative attractions, such as the value of independence or a preferred companion or sexual partner. This framework is helpful in a general way in identifying some of the factors that may come into play when individuals decide whether to maintain or discontinue a relationship. We can predict that when the attractions of the present relationship decrease, the barriers to escape from the relationship diminish, and the strength

---

BOX 5.2

What Is the Divorce Rate, Anyway?

Often the mass media tell us that 50% of marriages in the United States end in divorce. This is a misleading statement. It appears to be based inappropriately—on a document back in 1984 from the U.S. National Center on Health Statistics, which reported that there were 2,400,000 new marriages and 1,200,000 divorces during that year. Yes, if we divide 1,200,000 by 2,400,000 we get 50%, but it is misleading to conclude from that that half of marriages terminate through divorce or dissolution. Those 1,200,000 divorces are composed of marriages that began perhaps years or decades before. Louis Harris of the Harris Poll estimates that the divorce rate is much lower, that about 13% of marriages end in divorce. In any single year, he concluded, only about 2% of existing marriages break up (Associated Press, 1987b).

---

of the alternative attractions increases, then, at that point, an individual would choose to get out of the relationship.

A comprehensive list, developed by Adams (1979), is reprinted in Box 5.3; no list can deal with every consideration and eventuality, however. Just as "the progress of true love is never smooth," so too must every conceptualization fall short by the nature of its purported simplicity and rationality.

Attraction Versus Attachment

The development of a close relationship takes time. Those qualities that contribute to the early stages, such as physical attraction, may not be related to important factors at the later stages, such as attachment. Research findings conclude that what brings a couple together "almost inevitably" recedes into the background as the relationship matures (Goleman, 1985, p. B-5). Lillian Troll (1982) has sagely written:

An examination of long-term relationships—parent/child, sibling, old friend, and long-married couple relationships—suggests that there may

BOX 5.3

The Sequence of
Developments Leading to Marriage

1. attraction to marriage itself—a conscious, expressed desire to marry
2. propinquity—geographical closeness, availability
3. early attraction, based on such surface behaviors of the partners as:
   a. gregariousness
   b. poise
   c. similar interests and abilities
   d. physical appearance and attractiveness
   e. similarity to one's ideal image
4. perpetuation of attraction, aided by:
   a. reactions by others, including being labeled as a couple
   b. disclosure: opening oneself up to each other
   c. pair rapport, being comfortable in each other's presence
5. commitment and intimacy; establishing a bond
6. deeper attraction, enhanced by:
   a. value consensus or coorientation, providing validation of each other's viewpoints
   b. feelings of competence reinforced
   c. perception of other similarities in the partner, such as:
      1. attractiveness
      2. levels of emotional maturity
      3. affective expressiveness
      4. self-esteem
      5. race, ethnic group, or religion, if important
      6. birth-order matching
      7. deciding that this is "right for me" or "the best I can get"
      8. marriage

SOURCE: Adapted from Adams, 1979.

be an inverse relationship between attraction and attachment. In the beginning of a relationship, attraction is high, because part of the impetus is novelty and discovery. But attachment is low, because bonds are not yet cemented. . . . In the course of repeated interaction, however, novelty is gone and attraction reduced—but attachment may have become very strong. The two members of the dyad have become part of each other; they have achieved a joint identity. A breakup at this time may never be completely overcome. (p. 294)

As marriage continues, intense communication and self-disclosure may decrease, whereas loyalty, investment, and commitment to the relationship may increase.

Recent thinking about love and the developmental nature of an intimate relationship reflects these trends.

For example, in the early stage of a relationship, spouses are particularly likely to make attributions about the causes for the partner's behavior (Holtzworth-Munroe & Jacobson, 1985). As the marriage progresses, these attributions decline in frequency and importance unless conflict predominates in the interactions between the partners (Baucom, 1987). Robert Sternberg (1986) has proposed that love has three major elements—intimacy, passion, and commitment—and that these three elements develop at different rates in the course of a relationship. *Intimacy* represents the warmth and closeness in a relationship. It develops gradually over the course of a relationship, continuing to grow (although at a progressively slower rate) as the partners share experiences and feelings. *Passion* represents the more intense aspect of the relationship; passion typically develops very quickly but then drops off as the partners become accustomed to each other. Los Angeles psychologist Berta Davis (quoted by Gindick, 1985) calls this phase "a wondrous sense of specialness" that a couple experiences at the beginning of the relationship but that is doomed to be short lived. *Commitment* can be of two types. A short-term commitment involves the decision that one loves another person; a long-term commitment involves willingness to maintain that love and to make the relationship succeed. This aspect of love typically develops slowly at first, and then speeds up as the rewards and costs of the relationship become clear.

Psychologist Ellen McGrath (quoted by Gindick, 1985) sees commitment as a more genuine aspect than passion:

It's based on knowing who you are. You're appreciative of them [the partner] because they care for you even knowing who you are. And they are that way about you. It's a more real stage. It's more comfort-able. If people base a relationship on [commitment], a relationship has a better chance of succeeding. (p. B-5)

Communication in Marriage

The importance of communication in marriage is reflected in the typology of marriages developed by Mary Anne Fitzpatrick (1988). She distinguishes among three types:

Traditional Marriages

Traditional marriages place more emphasis on stability in the relationship than spontaneity in communication. In this conven-tional orientation, there is a high degree of sharing and companion-ship. The woman takes the husband's name; she is not particularly assertive, but tends not to avoid conflict with her spouse. Infidelity is always inexcusable.

Independent Marriages

Couples in independent marriages hold fairly unconventional views about marriage; they believe relationships should not con-strain an individual's freedom in any way. These couples may main-tain a high level of companionship and sharing, but also may have separate physical spaces. They report some assertiveness in their relationships with their spouses; they tend not to avoid conflicts.

Separates

Separates couples seem to hold to opposing ideological views on relationships at the same time. Whereas a "separate" is as conven-tional with respect to marital and family issues as a "traditional," he or she simultaneously supports the values advocated by "in-dependents." Individual freedom is emphasized over relationship maintenance.

This suggests that "separates" are ambivalent about the value they put on a relationship, and it is true that they have significantly less companionship and sharing in their marriage. They attempt to keep some psychological distance in their relationship to their spouse; they avoid open marital conflicts but report some attempts at persuasion and assertiveness toward their spouse.

Communication styles play a central role in recent efforts to forecast which marriages will end up in divorce. Psychologist John Gottman (1993), based on interviews with couples in their homes, was able to predict with impressive accuracy which pairs would separate within 3 years. Four communication aspects—criticism, contempt, defensiveness, and withdrawal—played central roles.

Satisfaction With One's Marriage

Ann Landers, in 1989, asked her readers, "Has your sex life gone downhill since marriage? If so, why?" A total of 141,210 persons responded (52% of whom were male), and 82% said that sex after marriage "was much less pleasurable" (Landers, 1989a). Perhaps the dissatisfied were more likely to respond; certainly the respondents are not representative. But we can learn from the types of responses; these include how the sameness becomes monotonous and boring, or how the lack of communication, or the deterioration in the partner's physique, health, or hygiene, can increase dissatisfaction.

Surveys of couples report some increased dissatisfaction over time but not to the magnitude elicited by Ann Landers's question. Pauker and Arond (1989) interviewed 346 persons married between 1 and 18 months and found that 37% admitted to being more critical of their mates since marriage and 29% reported an increase in arguments. Similarly, in a survey of dating couples or newly weds, Buss (1989) found that women complained most about men who were sexually aggressive, unfaithful, abusive, condescending, and emotionally constricted. Men were most troubled by women who were unfaithful, abusive, self-centered, condescending, sexually withholding, neglectful, or moody.

The previous section emphasizes that a long-term marriage is a frequently changing phenomenon, with different needs and costs surfacing at different times in the relationship. "Satisfaction" with one's marriage thus needs to be viewed in dialectical terms, with shifts in its degrees and emphases. Box 5.4 illustrates the dialectical conception in detail.

BOX 5.4

The Dialectic of Marriage

Irving Sarnoff and Suzanne Sarnoff (1989), a psychologist couple, emphasize the dialectical nature of marriage; powerful impulses can bring a couple together or pull them apart. Even though we seek to enjoy fully the love we have sought, we "fear the merger it inevitably requires" (p. 55). To resolve the dialectical dilemmas, a successful marriage, according to the Sarnoffs, moves through six stages:

Stage 1: Coupling and Concealing

Newlyweds make love frequently, thus attaining "an incomparable union of body and mind" (p. 56), but such intense intimacy is physically and emotionally threatening, perhaps leading the couple to hide some of their innermost thoughts from each other.

Stage 2: Reproducing and Retreating

Deciding to have a child is a way of expanding opportunities for love and intimacy. But pregnancy can lead the man to envy his wife's power as a birth-giver, and it can lead the woman to covet her husband's freedom from discomforts and danger. "In a sense, he resents his wife because she's pregnant; she resents him because he is not" (Sarnoff & Sarnoff, 1989, p. 56).

Stage 3: Nurturing and Negating

Presence of a child or children leads each spouse to revert to his or her traditional roles, because they are threatened with the loss of their individuality. He may become absorbed in his career; she may end up doing most of the housekeeping and child-rearing, even though she holds a job.

Stage 4: Focusing and Fragmenting

At this stage the issue of centrality is the number of desired children. The couple risks fragmenting their relationship just when they could benefit themselves. Some couples may pursue separate, sex-segregated hobbies.

Stage 5: Renewing and Regressing

Middle-aged couples get a second chance to establish a vitality in their marriage after their children leave the home. But this may mean

(Continued)

BOX 5.4 (Continued)

---

the loss of the daily satisfactions and challenges of parenting. "Couples may feel at a loss, at least temporarily, about how to relate exclusively as husband and wife" (p. 57).

Stage 6: Keeping and Drifting

Sarnoff and Sarnoff note that spouses ages 65 to 70 have a magnificent chance to deepen the satisfaction of their relationship, by maximizing their interdependence. But "too often, this enriching objective is threatened by their joint fear of death and the ambiguity of not knowing who will go first. Afraid of depending too much on someone who may soon be gone, they find ways to drift apart well before death separates them" (p. 57).

The overall concept of "marriage satisfaction" has been an elusive one for other reasons, too. Generally, two criteria have been applied to define a satisfactory marriage: Stability and happiness. In fact, these two have been associated; in our society, many people assume that a long-term marriage must be a happy one. But happiness and stability are not the same thing; as we saw earlier in the chapter, many marriages may reflect "success" in lasting more than 15 years and leading to economic wealth and social prominence, and yet be devoid of sexual compatibility.

Happiness in one's marriage is also related to one's expectations. Highly educated persons have higher expectations, including the expectations of self-actualization and romantic love through marriage. The less educated may have fewer options and hence lower expectations.

Sex Differences

In general, husbands tend to find their marriages more satisfactory than do wives.

A survey of 2,330 men found that most of them (actually 77%) who were in their first marriages would marry their wives again, if given a chance (Cruver, 1986). (Slightly more than 80% of the remarried men would again marry their current wives.) In contrast, a survey in *Women's Day* magazine reported that only half of 3,009 women surveyed would remarry their husbands. (For women in second marriages, the figure increased to 63%.) Even more extreme in its expression of wives' dissatisfaction is the survey by Shere Hite (1987), who concluded that 98% of the women in her sample want to make "basic changes" in their love relationships. But Hite's analysis is based on the 4,500 women out of 100,000 who responded to a mail questionnaire. This 4.5% return rate is much too low to conclude that the sample is representative.

When asked to list "what you *do not* like about your marriage," 45% of the men listed nothing, whereas only 25% of the women responded that way (Cruver, 1986). A husband's dissatisfaction does not seem to increase over the length of the marriage as much as a wife's does. Women's affiliative needs are often satisfied just by getting married and being married. But their reactions change. Of women married less than 2 years, 52% were very satisfied and none were dissatisfied. But of women married 20 years or more, only 6% were very satisfied and 21% were very dissatisfied.

In fact, men generally say they are satisfied with their marriages if their overall lives are going well, but women who are unhappy with their marriages are unhappy in other aspects of their lives. A "figure-versus-ground" contrast seems to exist here; marriage is more often secondary to a man's self-esteem, compared to its primary role for the woman.

There is an irony here. Jessie Bernard (1973) observes that even though marriage is a condition desired more by women than by men, it is much more beneficial to men. For example, married women have worse mental health than either single women or married men. Single women have many fewer psychological-distress symptoms than do married women.

Age Differences

Stage theories and dialectical approaches to adult development receive support from an analysis of age differences in marital satisfaction. As you would expect, honeymooning couples are the groups most satisfied with their marriages. But the next most satisfied is the elderly, followed by those in the "launching phase" (when children are leaving home). Least satisfied with their marriages are parents whose youngest children have just entered school, and parents of teenagers. Satisfaction figures for men were: married 10 years or less, 74%; married 10-20 years, 70%; married more than 20 years, 81% (Cruver, 1986). Sexual aspects of the marriage become less important determinants of satisfaction later in life (Pineo, 1961).

Friends and Spouses

A significant example of the evolving nature of the marital relationship is the couple's choice of and definition of "friends." Each partner in a new marriage has her or his own friends, but there is a gradual shift toward "couple friends" (Troll, 1982). Traditionally, such new pairs of friends have been more often recruited by the man, through his work (Babchuk & Bates, 1963); despite the fact that most newly married women also have jobs outside the home, male dominance still prevails here.

Probably one of the reasons for this is the sex difference in choice of friends. Men focus on similarity; "he's like me," or "we like the same things so we get along." Men choose friends who fulfill certain functions; "my poker-playing buddies," "my tennis partner," "my friend who advises me on taxes." Women more often choose friends with whom they can develop a relationship in which reciprocity and mutuality are salient; their friends are more likely to be "all-purpose" friends who provide support and sharing rather than fulfilling a specific need or function (Candy, 1977, cited by Troll, 1982).

In younger couples, each partner tends to name friends of his or her own sex and age (Hess, 1972). But in couples married 50 years, both of the factors were less important (Parron, 1979, cited by Troll, 1982). In these couples, there was considerable overlap in the friends of the husband and the wife.

The Longitudinal Study of Married Couples

Previous sections of this chapter have implied the presence of a pattern of changes in the marital relationship over time. The most effective methodology for determining what changes have taken place is a longitudinal one. This section describes two studies of married couples, using a longitudinal method.

The project directed by Ted L. Huston (Huston, Robins, Atkinson, & McHale, 1987) concentrated on the early part of a marriage. A total of 168 couples were interviewed a series of times at three periods during their first two and a half years of marriage. Husbands and wives were interviewed separately.

The focus of the interviews by Huston and his colleagues was on the tasks and activities recently carried out by each member of the married couple; in essence, it was a behavioral self-report. Although the goal of the researchers was a comprehensive description of activities and relationships shared by the couple, our focus here is on the changes in the affective quality of the interaction during this period. Huston et al. (1987) report, "Both the parent and nonparent groups declined considerably in the frequency with which they expressed affection or otherwise behaved in ways that brought pleasure to the partner. . . . We found that couples declined substantially on each of the positive behaviors . . . except 'talking together about the day's events' " (p. 64). However, there was no significant increase in negative behaviors over this time period.

The second longitudinal study was a much more extended one. Maas and Kuypers (1974) followed the development of some of the couples who were parents of the children in the Berkeley (California) Growth Study. (Other results of this important project were described in Volume 1, Chapter 9, on the issue of consistency of personality.) A total of 142 parents were reinterviewed when they were between the ages of 60 and 82; 95 of these were women and 47 were men. All 47 of the fathers had remained married for more than 40 years to the mother of the child who was the subject in the original longitudinal study. Their wives were included in the sample of 95 women (most of the other women in the sample were widowed). Maas and Kuypers decided to classify the men and women separately, based on their present lifestyles. Four types of lifestyle emerged from the men, two thirds of whom were retired. (However, whether the man worked or did not still work was not a salient determinant of his classification into a particular lifestyle category.) A description of each type follows.

Family-Centered Fathers (N = 19)

Central to these men's lives were matters of marriage, parenting, and grandparenting. Most of their satisfactions came from the marital relationships and their grandchildren. In contrast to the other three types of men, they see their children and grandchildren frequently. They are also active in clubs and other formal groups, but are little involved in church. They are moderately satisfied with life and report that they rarely or never think of death.

In viewing their past lives, they report that stability is the key. Overall, 90% of them followed a single career line, and have kept the same friends over the years.

Hobbyist Fathers (N = 11)

Leisure-time activities and interests are at the core of the lives of these men. They engage in more recreational activities than do the men in the other groupings; interestingly, most of these activities are done alone. They report more interests than they had in their 40s, but we get the sense that these activities are "out there" and serve a function for these persons, rather than being an integral part of their lives. This instrumental orientation can be detected with regard to these men's relationships with their wives, too; many of them report being able to count on their wives "to do things" for them.

A withdrawn lifestyle characterizes these men. They are loners; they do not see their grandchildren very often. Yet they frequently attend church; 45% do weekly, compared to only 5% to 12% of the men in the other types. And they are the group who report the greatest satisfaction with their lifestyle and their home life.

Remotely Sociable Fathers (N = 9)

These men have a low level of involvement as marriage partners. They do not communicate with their wives very much and report being dissatisfied with their marriages. They stay busy and report having lots of "friends"—in fact they visit with other men more frequently than any other group. But their gregariousness appears to be superficial; they are not very involved in these relationships.

With respect to their relationships with their children and grandchildren, they are the opposite of the family-centered fathers described in the first category; they see the relationships with their own children as not close at present, as becoming increasingly remote with age, and as lacking in affection or function. But they are optimistic about "how the world is going today" and few have made plans for death, such as preparing a will or purchasing a burial plot.

The men in this group tended to come from upper class backgrounds; they were satisfied with their early life and experienced occupational and social success back then.

Unwell-Disengaged Fathers (N = 8)

These men have a compliant-submissive relationship with their wives; in these marriages one or the other spouse makes all the important life decisions. But as a group, they feel they cannot count on their wives to "do for" them.

Basically, these men have withdrawn from the world. Theirs are the highest ratings on "life dissatisfaction" and their marriages seem to be changing for the worse. They engage in few recreational activities; do not interact much with their grandchildren; and have little energy. Throughout their lives they reported poor health and less stamina; in fact, they have been preoccupied with health concerns their whole lives. Their lifestyle seems to be a consistent one rather than a result of some recent experiences or changes; they report that even when their children were young, they were distant from them.

For the 95 women in Maas and Kuypers's (1974) study, six discriminable patterns emerged; several of these were quite different from the men's. They were the following:

Husband-Centered Wives (N = 23)

For these women, the center of their daily living was their husbands; they do most activities with them, and they have little involvement in other activities. They do not see their siblings, children, or grandchildren very much; in this respect they differ from the family-centered fathers in the first category. They are very satisfied with their home life and lifestyle; they are in relatively good health.

Visiting Mothers (N = 16)

These women are characterized by high energy and social activity. They are highly involved as hostesses or guests, as parents, or as group members. Social life is the core of their lifestyle, especially informal social interaction. They possess a large social network of relatives and friends; also the church is important to them (80%—by far the highest percentage of any type—belong to a church).

These women have a relatively large number of children and grandchildren, they appear to have a good relationship with them, and they do not obtrusively try to control their children.

Even though the husbands of 14 of these 16 women are still alive, the marital arena is not the central focus of their lifestyle. Perhaps one reason—but it could be an effect rather than a cause—is that more than half of the husbands still work (a relatively high percentage, compared to the other types).

Uncentered Mothers (N = 21)

The central nature of the daily lifestyle of these women is hard to characterize but it is essentially negative. They have few recreational interests, few club memberships, few close friends or confidants, and few activities of any type done with other persons. They do see their children and grandchildren often but report they are not as involved with them as the women in other groups are. They are dissatisfied with their present financial situations and with their health.

Overall, 17 of the 21 women in this group (81%) no longer have a marital partner. Apparently the death of their husbands was a shattering event for many of these women, as they had had a family-centered life. They had more children than the women in the other groups.

Furthermore, they live under the most disadvantageous conditions; they are the oldest group (almost three-fourths are in their 70s or older); they are in poor health; and the majority live alone.

Employed, or Work-Centered Mothers (N = 12)

Most of these women live alone, too, and 9 of 12 are no longer married. But they are highly involved as workers and very satisfied with their work situations. (One-half work part time and one-half work full time.) They are very satisfied with their health status, have many different hobbies and recreational pursuits, and visit others frequently. One third of them report seeing at least one of their children every week. They tend to be younger than most other types, and free of physical disabilities and complaints. This group has shown the most change over time; in their 30s and 40s they were the lowest in energy level, but in their elderly years they are characterized by high levels of energy.

Disabled-Disengaging Mothers (N = 12)

Women in this category resemble the husband-centered wives (first category), except that they register no satisfaction in marriage. In fact, they are not very satisfied with any aspect of their lives. They are disengaging or withdrawn from their former involvement in life, and have no close friends. Relationships with their children are strained. Almost half of them have husbands who still work, and they participate in activities with their husbands, but do not enjoy them. Like the unwell-disengaged fathers, these women had health problems in their early adult years, and they continue to be highly involved with a sick role in life. The majority have several physical disabilities.

Group-Centered Mothers (N = 11)

The lifestyles of these women extend beyond their families into the areas of clubs and other formal groups, plus church and politics. They attend group meetings frequently, perform leadership roles in these groups, and are very satisfied with their group activities. Although most of them are married, the marital role is not the most important aspect of their lives, nor is being a homemaker. As parents they tend to be somewhat dominant; they give their children advice but little else. They possess the highest educational level and come from well-to-do families. They are in good health, are optimistic, and see things changing for the better. A certain remoteness and formality is typical of these women; they enjoy intimacy at a distance.

Is there any evidence that members of aging couples, married more than four decades, pattern their lifestyles in ways that seem responsive or reciprocal to their partners' own emerging lifestyles? Maas and Kuypers conclude not; they seem to develop quite independently. For example, of the 47 intact couples in their long-term longitudinal study, 19 of the men were "family-centered" but only 5 of these had wives who were "husband-centered." An equal number of the "husband-centered" wives had husbands whose hobbies and leisure-time activities were central to their lives. Maas and Kuypers note that for both men and women, the family-centered or husband-centered type is only moderate in life satisfaction. The moral of their study, for these researchers, is that those of each sex who are most satisfied with their lives are those whose lives are focused beyond—but do not exclude—their families.

These longitudinal studies are worthwhile beginnings, but they provide us little in the way of variables that distinguish between successful long-term marriages and ones that fail or continue to exist in name only. Family therapists point to the following as some of the factors that seem to make a difference:

1. Problem-solving skills, especially willingness and ability to negotiate. A study of couples married 30 to 40 years, compared with couples who divorced at midlife, done by Maggie Hayes (cited by Elias, 1984), found differences in communication and conflict patterns. When asked if their partner was easy to talk to, 83% of the persons in the still-married couples agreed, whereas only 27% of the divorced did so. The way of handling feelings of anger toward the partner is a crucial variable here; the successful marriages seem successful in deflecting negative feelings and keeping them from escalating (Goleman, 1984).
2. A sense of optimism about their future, plus a view of potential crises as positive challenges.
3. A sharing of basic values and goals, and of at least some activities and interests.
4. A feeling that the two partners love each other in roughly equal degrees (Goleman, 1984).
5. A need for intimacy. Dan McAdams, in his program of research on intimacy needs, finds people with these needs as having a preoccupation with themes of harmony, responsibility, and commitment. They also possess "positive passivity"; they are adept at listening and letting a relationship grow naturally without manipulating it.

In a nationwide study of 1,200 men and women, McAdams and Bryant (1985) found that those with stronger intimacy needs had a better sense of well-being, were happier, and felt more secure. Using the body of data on former Harvard freshmen analyzed by Vaillant (1972) and described in Volume 1, McAdams judged the relative needs for intimacy in these men when they were 30 years of age, using Thematic Apperception Test-type stories they generated, and compared these with their marital adjustment 15-20 years later. The higher their need for intimacy at age 30, the more they enjoyed their marriages and their work (Goleman, 1986).

The research of Robert Sternberg, cited earlier, also concludes that intimacy becomes more crucial, particularly for women, as successful relationships endure (Goleman, 1985).

6

Changes in Values and Attitudes

I see and know what is right, yet I do what is wrong.

Ovid

The 40, 50, or more years that comprise adulthood for most of us include an incomprehensible collection of experiences. Many of these reflect our relationships with others, and these human relationships invariably involve conflict (Langdale, 1986). It is conceivable that these happenings change our views of the world, our basic values, and our judgments of what is important in life. But do they do so in any systematic way? It is possible to say that during adulthood people generally change in a consistent fashion? Do they become more conservative, or less, more trusting—or less? Do the determinants of what people consider as moral behavior uniformly change? Do they become more restrictive in their political attitudes or social behavior? This chapter examines these issues. In doing so, it operates from a foundation of stage theories, which would hypothesize that changes in values inevitably occur at certain age periods during adulthood, but the chapter also uses a dialectical framework where appropriate.

Value

The concept of a *value* has several distinct meanings. I will refer to a value as a standard for decision making, a guide in choosing what is important or how to behave. Following the use of the term by Rokeach (1968), we may think of values as "abstract ideals, positive or negative, not tied to any specific attitude, object, or situation, representing a person's beliefs about ideal modes of conduct and ideal terminal goals" (p. 124). We are aware of at least some of our values, but others may operate at an unconscious or unaware level, but both types are reflected in the choices we make. Everyday choices—whether to go to a football game or an art museum, choosing a colorful, "outrageous" piece of clothing over an acceptable but "dull" one, telling a friend a "white lie" or telling that friend the brutal truth—show in our behavior which values determine our actions. The very fact that daily life involves hundreds of unexamined choices implies that each of us may have many competing values demanding their advocacy at any one time. The concept of a *value system* is useful here, reflecting a hierarchical organization or rank-ordering of values in terms of their importance to each of us.

Values differ from attitudes in several ways. An attitude always has an object; we possess attitudes toward every conceivable topic or object, from abortion to Zinfandel wine. Values have a broader focus; often our attitudes toward specific objects, processes, or people may derive from our values.

The measurement of values by psychologists has been a topic with isolated periods of fertile growth, but long periods during which the topic was ignored (Braithwaite & Scott, 1991). In the 1930s the operationalizing of values received a boost from the construction of an instrument titled the Study of Values (Allport & Vernon, 1931). Six values, based on Spranger's *Types of Men* (1928), were measured: theoretical, economic (or functional), aesthetic, social, political, and religious. The Study of Values became a popular measuring instrument, and was revised twice (Allport, Vernon, & Lindzey, 1960). Often, a widely used instrument can, unintentionally, color or shift the predominant theoretical definition of a construct; the wide usage of the Study of Values is an example. It conceived of values as personal goals or interests rather than as moral imperatives, being influenced by Spranger's contention that there were "types of men" who reflected different dominant interests (Robinson & Shaver, 1969).

But for the period of the 1950s and early 1960s, the measurement of values was largely ignored by psychologists; Robinson and Shaver (1969) offer two reasons:

> The first has to do with psychologists' desire to define their discipline as a part of the larger enterprise of scientific research, with its emphasis on rigorous objective methods. Patterning themselves after physicists, differentiating themselves from philosophers, many psychologists consider[ed] value judgments to be outside the boundaries of an empirical discipline. They seem to have confused making value judgments, which is incompatible with scientific objectivity, with studying objectively *how other people make them*—a phenomenon as amenable to psychological study, in principle, as other forms of human learning and choice. . . . The second major problem, once the psychological study of values is accepted as legitimate, is to find a fruitful conceptual or theoretical framework from which to initiate research. (pp. 406-407, italics in original)

The latter problem was referred to earlier in this chapter. Research on the measurement of values received a spurt in 1968 with the publication of Milton Rokeach's Value Survey. Rokeach distinguished between terminal and instrumental value—ends versus means—with respect to their place as guiding principles (the terminal values are listed in Box 6.1).

As the above paragraphs imply, there are many types of values. This chapter focuses on three types: moral values, religious values, and political ones. For each of these, after an initial description of the most useful conceptualizations, the section will describe whatever available evidence exists about changes during adulthood.

Morality and Moral Values

What determines our choices of right and wrong? Are there moral concepts of good and bad that people use to resolve conflicts? Do people agree as to the standards for moral action? During adulthood, do conceptions of morality change? Moral values reflect one type

---

BOX 6.1

Rokeach's Terminal Values

---

1. a comfortable life
2. a meaningful life
3. a world at peace
4. equality
5. freedom
6. maturity
7. national security
8. respect for others
9. respect from others
10. salvation
11. true friendship
12. wisdom

---

of value that has benefited from sophisticated psychological conceptualizations that are highly developmental in their orientation.

Kohlberg's Theory of Moral Development

With respect to the adult years, the most extended example of the developmental view is the theory of moral judgment developed by the late Harvard psychologist Lawrence Kohlberg (1958, 1963, 1980, 1981), who theorized that six stages of moral development may account for the changes in perspective on issues like justice, equality, and reciprocity experienced by people as they move from childhood through adolescence to adulthood. Kohlberg's theory reflects the general characteristics of stage theories described in Volume 1; in his theory, each stage is a step in an invariant hierarchical cognitive scheme; furthermore, each of these stages reflects a different organization of the way in which people "perceive the sociomoral world and reason about it" (Walker, 1986, p. 110). In addition, Kohlberg proposes that not all people will reach the maturity of moral development reflected in the sixth and final stage.

As they move from the first stage onward, they may become stuck at any one stage and use that as a filter through which they resolve moral dilemmas for the rest of their lives. But for those who progress through the stages, they pass from one level to a second and then a third level, at each level changing their basis for resolving moral dilemmas. In addition, like at least some stage theorists—especially Erikson—Kohlberg believes that certain types of moral reasoning are more desirable than others; specifically, he proposes that each later stage is ethically superior to the ones before.

Kohlberg and his colleagues (Colby & Kohlberg, 1987; Power, Higgins, & Kohlberg, 1989) defined moral thinking as primarily based on a concept of justice, or just resolution of dilemmas about conflicting rights. Kohlberg (1971) wrote, "A just solution to a moral dilemma is a solution acceptable to all parties, considering each as free and equal, and assuming none of them knew which role they would occupy in the situation" (p. 213). As noted by Cohen (1980), such a definition echoes the theory of justice advocated by John Rawls (1971), who capitalized on this minimal risk strategy. He saw the progression toward justice evolving in six steps. The three levels and the two stages within each level are the following:

Preconventional Level. Young children are responsive to cultur-ally determined rules and labels such as *good* and *bad,* or *right* and *wrong.* But children interpret these labels in light of the *physical* or *emotional consequences* of their actions; that is, an action that leads to being punished must, therefore, be bad, whereas those that lead to receiving favors, or otherwise getting rewarded, must have been good. Also, young children, at this level of what might be called *subnormal moral development,* interpret good or bad in light of the physical power of those who announce and enforce the rules and labels; that is, at this level, "might makes right." Young children, operating within this preconventional orientation, begin by responding at Stage 1, but as they grow older, the vast majority of them move to Stage 2 responses.

The first stage in Kohlberg's theory reflects a *punishment and obedience orientation.* To the child behaving at this stage, the consequences of an action determine the goodness or badness of the action; nothing else matters. If a child does something and does not get caught or punished for it—such as taking cookies from the cookie jar—the child concludes that the act must not have been wrong. Fear of authority is thus central to behaving "morally" at this stage.

The second stage is, in Kohlberg's terminology, the *instrumental-relativist orientation,* or *hedonistic orientation.* At this stage, what the child labels as *right* actions consists of those behaviors that satisfy one's own needs and occasionally the needs of others. Children whose behavior reflects this stage of moral development are still considered "preconventional" in their orientation because their actions are still primarily motivated by selfishness. Although acts might on first appearance seem to be unselfish—for example, a boy helps his grandmother cross a busy street—they are done by the child in an expectation that he will benefit in the long run. Human relations are viewed in the language of the marketplace: "You scratch my back and I'll scratch yours."

Although this orientation emerges in rather young children according to Kohlberg's scheme of development—perhaps at ages 4 to 6—many adults in our society may still reflect this outlook. Furthermore, parents often encourage "moral" behavior in their children by appealing to the youngster's selfish interests: "You should help your grandmother across the street because that'll cause her to give you a nice present on your birthday."

Conventional Level. According to Kohlberg, "morality," for most Americans, means either obeying the laws and rules, or behaving in a way that people expect of you. For the person operating at this conventional level, a shift occurs, and the self-centered orientation of the preconventional stages is supplanted by one that reflects an awareness of the rights, feelings, and concerns of others. That is, at this typical level of moral development, the fulfilling of the expectations of one's family, religious group, or nation is seen as valuable in its own right, regardless of the immediate consequences to the person. The orientation is not only one of conformity to the social order, but of loyalty to it. Emphasis is on actively maintaining, supporting, and justifying the social order and identifying with the persons or groups in it.

The *interpersonal concordance* or *good-boy/nice-girl orientation* is the third stage of development in Kohlberg's theory and is typically reached during high school (Candee, 1980). Moral behavior, in view of the person at Stage 3, is that which pleases, helps, or is approved of by others; maintaining the quality of interpersonal relationships is at the forefront. Intentions are important in defining morality here; the notion that someone "means well" becomes important for the first time, and one earns approval for being "nice."

The other stage (Stage 4) at this conventional level is, in Kohlberg's terminology, called the *law-and-order orientation*. Here the emphasis is on obeying laws and rules and maintaining the social order. Moral behavior thus consists of doing one's duty, showing that one respects authority, and perpetuating the given social order because *it is* the given social order (Kohlberg, 1963). Many adults never progress beyond this conventional level of moral development (Kuhn, Langer, Kohlberg, & Haan, 1977).

Postconventional Level. At the third and highest level of morality in Kohlberg's conceptualization—the *postconventional* or *principled level*—the person further internalizes the standards for determining morality. The person makes an effort to define moral values and codes of conduct apart from the authoritativeness of the groups or persons advocating these principles and apart from the person's own identification with these groups. The code of conduct reflects the emergence of a set of principles that may or may not agree with the proscriptions, rules, and laws of the groups of which the person is a member.

Kohlberg sees this as a development of adulthood. He wrote, "With regard to adult moral stages, biography and common experience indicate dramatic or qualitative changes in adulthood in moral ideology. . . . The conclusion is that there are indeed adult stages. Stage 5 and typically Stage 6 thinking is an adult development, typically not reached until the late twenties or later" (1973, pp. 188-190). He estimated that 10% to 20% of adults reflect this principled level of moral development (Kohlberg, 1980).

Different explanations exist for the impetus for changes into postconventional morality. Kohlberg (1973) posited environmental or situational factors, that is, factors outside the person. One might occur when young people leave the sheltered environment of their homes for one (especially college, though a marriage or life in a bigger city might suffice) in which their traditional values and principles are challenged by other persons. But others have emphasized that internal factors, especially continued development of one's personality, might account for the shifts. For example, Lifton (1986) writes:

> Specifically, two dimensions within an individual's total personality structure form necessary though not sufficient conditions for moral maturity. The first is a cognitive dimension, that is, being a rational, logical, unemotional individual. The second is an interpersonal dimension, that is, being concerned with persons other than oneself. As these two dimensions more and more come to characterize an individual's personality, so will his or her level of moral development increase in sophistication. (pp. 58-59).

Returning to an explication of the specific stages, we note that the *social contract* or *legalistic* orientation falls in this highest level of moral maturity and is the fifth stage of development. The persons operating at this stage realize that their internalized standards of right and wrong are at variance with the laws or norms of society. These might include, for examples, beliefs that nuclear war or execution of murderers are immoral. The person at Stage 5, although objecting to the death penalty on grounds that it violates the principle of maintaining human life, still recognizes that the death penalty is the law of the land, or at least of that state. The essence of the Stage 5 orientation is the attempt by the person to change the laws or rules through democratic means. The Stage 5 person says, in effect, "I believe the death penalty is wrong in principle, but I accept that it is the law and that the law is a representation of consensus views. Therefore I will lobby to change the law; I may write letters to the newspapers, I may circulate petitions; I may campaign for political candidates who promise to abolish the death penalty." Those persons behaving at Stage 5 feel a distance from society's consensus values but they realize that they must exist in society and work within it to change it. This fifth stage resembles the "official" morality of democratic governments and the U.S. Constitution.

The orientation of *universal ethical principles* is the sixth stage of Kohlberg's scheme. At this highest stage, what is morally right is not defined by the laws and rules of the social order but by one's own conscience, in accordance with self-determined ethical principles. Rather than being concrete moral rules, these principles are

---

BOX 6.2

An Example of Stage 6 Behavior

Jean Gump was a 60-year-old woman who served a 6-year sentence in the Federal Reformatory for Women in Alderson, West Virginia. Her crime: an assault on a Minuteman II missile silo, near Butler, Missouri, on Good Friday, 1986. She and four other protesters attacked the missile silos with sledgehammers and human blood. The attack was largely symbolic; no serious damage was done. But the action reflected Jean Gump's values; "I believe our government is involved in illegal activities that have no end; I have said 'no' to the government and their policies," she said (quoted in Uhlenhuth, 1987, p. E-1). Mrs. Gump has had a long history of working for the peace movement through what she calls "legitimate channels," including the organization of nuclear-freeze movements. But the attack on the missile silos reflected a decision to take a more radical strategy. "I have a responsibility to not only speak the truth, but to live the truth," she stated (quoted in Uhlenhuth, 1987, p. E-2).

The effect of her action on her husband's values is an example of Kohlberg's claim that growth in moral development comes as a result of our values being challenged by those of a person operating at a higher level of morality (see, e.g., Candee, 1980, p. 180, and Schochet, 1980, pp. 211-212). Her husband, about the same age as Mrs. Gump, had looked forward to the relaxed life of a retiree. But her activities led to some soul-searching on her husband's part: "Her example began to redirect my energies," Joe Gump has said, though his evolution toward protest was slower (Uhlenhuth, 1987, p. E-2). Joe Gump joined her in protest; at the last report he was awaiting trial for the charge of damaging federal property.

---

broad and abstract; they might include universal principles of justice, principles of reciprocity and equality of human rights, and respect for the dignity of every human being. For example, one's position regarding the acceptability of abortion on demand may reflect one's principles about the sanctity of human life, or, conversely, about the rights of individuals to control their own bodies. Kohlberg (1973) has found that postconventional morality (both Stage 5 and Stage 6) "is probably attainable only in adulthood and requires some experience in moral responsibility and independent choice" (p. 500). An example of a person reflecting Stage 6 morality—a 60-year-old woman—is provided in Box 6.2. Kohlberg (1981) cited Socrates, Jesus, Abraham Lincoln, and Martin Luther King as persons reflecting Stage 6 morality in their behavior.

Kohlberg has boldly claimed that "all individuals in all cultures go through the same order or sequence of gross stages of development, though varying in rate and terminal point of development" (1971, 1973). Although some have referred to this claim as an "academic conceit" (Reid & Yanarella, 1980, p. 117), the empirical studies that examine the moral-judgment levels of children, adolescents, and adults provide some general support for the hierarchical nature of the first three stages of Kohlberg's theory (Kurtines & Gewirtz, 1984, 1987, 1991; Snarey, 1985), as do the infrequent studies that assess children's moral-judgment levels and retest them 5, 10, and 20 years later (Kohlberg, 1958, 1963, 1981).

Proposing a Different View of Morality: A Woman's View

As noted earlier, Kohlberg measured the development of morality through ethical dilemmas that assumed that justice was the primary criterion. (These were considered dilemmas because no solution existed that did not carry some negative costs.) Other conceptions of morality were ignored (Langdale, 1986). Peters (1971) wrote, "How do children come to care? This seems to be the most important question in moral education, but no clear answer to it can be found in Kohlberg's writings" (p. 262). Kohlberg based his theory on the responses of boys and men; in doing so, he did little to discourage others from assuming that this conception also characterized girls' and women's development. More pointedly, Kohlberg expressed his belief that fewer women achieve the higher stages of moral development in his theory because their allegiance to their children precludes their developing abstract moral principles centered on the concept of justice. Hence, we may conclude that a more-than-implicit developmental inferiority for women exists in Kohlberg's theory. (It even extends backward to Piaget's 1932 observations of boys and girls on the playground.) Carol Gilligan (1982), a former student of Kohlberg's and later a colleague of his at the Graduate School of Education at Harvard University, objected to the male-oriented focus of his theory and its failure to be relevant to the socialization and experience of women. She has written about the "unfair paradox . . . that the very traits that have traditionally defined the 'goodness' of women are those that mark them as deficient in moral development" (Gilligan, 1982, p. 18); that is, that classify women as Stage 3 in Kohlberg's system.

Furthermore, Gilligan has developed a systematic conception of women's development that, although resembling Kohlberg's in structure, differs radically from it in content. One way in which it is structurally similar is that at an early level, persons of both sexes share an inability to distinguish the perspective of others from their own perspective. It is also structurally similar in that Gilligan proposes that women pass through three levels, and that these levels, like the men's in Kohlberg's, move from self-centeredness to an other-oriented to an autonomous conception.

The differences in the two approaches are more important than their similarities. Although Kohlberg's approach has a rules orientation, with emphasis on abstract concepts and especially the concept of justice, Gilligan proposes that women possess a responsibility orientation with emphasis on sensitivity to others and the concept of care. For women, development is understood within a context of relationships, and connected with other people. In contrast to men, whose identity is defined through their separation from others, for girls and women identity is defined through attachment (Gilligan, 1982, p. 8). And, for women, the moral dilemma results not from competing *rights,* as is the case for men, but from competing *responsibilities.* Thus, in Gilligan's words, for women it "requires for resolution a mode of thinking that is contextual and narrative rather than formal and abstract" (Gilligan, 1982, p. 19).

Like Kohlberg, Gilligan bases her theory on subjects' responses to moral dilemmas. But although Kohlberg posed his subjects some hypothetical dilemmas involving fictitious persons, Gilligan listened to the "voices" of women in the real world; she interviewed 29 females (ages 15 to 33) who were facing a real-life decision themselves, whether or not to abort a pregnancy. Some of these were unmarried, and some were still students in high school; others were married but for one reason or another were unsure that they wanted to carry the fetus to full term. (Although Gilligan is to be com-

---

BOX 6.3

**Abortion Decisions
and Moral Development Stages**

Smetana (1981) studied the reasoning of women about their decisions whether to abort a pregnancy, much as Gilligan did. She compared 48 unmarried young women who were pregnant (in an unplanned way) with a control group of 22 women who had never been pregnant. Each subject was interviewed and also completed Kohlberg's measure of moral-development stage. Clear differences emerged in regard to how the pregnant women interpreted abortion; one fourth of these women viewed it as a moral issue (i.e., considerations of life and justice were central). But about one-third saw it as a personal issue beyond the moral domain; that is, emphasis on values of autonomous choice and control of one's own body were salient.

The remaining 40% saw the decision as reflecting both moral and personal considerations. Of most interest is the relationship between this and their eventual decisions; 93% of the women who viewed abortion only as a moral issue continued their pregnancies, where 94% of those who saw both aspects as relevant were more evenly divided in their decisions. No differences in Kohlberg's moral-stage level existed between those who saw abortion as a personal decision and those who perceived it as a moral issue.

---

mended for using real-life dilemmas, research indicates that the decision to abort is influenced by other factors, too; see Box 6.3.)

Based on these detailed interviews and follow-up interviews a year later, Gilligan concluded that women may progress through three levels of moral development, but the focus is on *care* rather than *justice*. In all women, she concluded, the conflict is between obligations and responsibilities to oneself and to others. Their initial level of orientation, like Kohlberg's preconventional morality, is entirely selfish. The self is the sole object of concern in what Gilligan labels the *orientation to individual survival*. When asked what one "should" do, the only thought is what one "would" do for oneself. If there is any sense of *obligation*—seen by Gilligan as central to women's development—it is an obligation only to oneself. There is no awareness of conflict.

But some of these women move from selfishness to a sense of responsibility and a different interpretation of *obligation*. Like Kohlberg, Gilligan sees moral growth resulting from an awareness within the person of conflicting conceptions of morality. The young woman may become aware of conflicts within herself; for example, she may wish to establish a connection with another person (i.e., to have the baby and begin married life); yet she may also value her freedom and independence. The criterion for moral judgment changes and "should" and "would" begin to conflict. What one wants is not always right.

This idealization leads to Level 2, the conventional level of morality, called by Gilligan *goodness as self-sacrifice*. Morality here is defined as meeting the expectations of others and submitting to the norms of society. Primarily, concern is over not hurting others, and meeting the needs of others.

In considering whether to abort a fetus, a woman must, in Gilligan's (1982) piquant phrase, "confront the seemingly impossible task of choosing the victim" (p. 80). If she is an unmarried high school student who decides to have the baby, the victim may be herself—expelled from school, subjected to ridicule by her peers, abandoned by her boyfriend, ostracized by her parents. Or if she is a self-employed woman with little income, deciding to have the child may make the baby an instant victim of limited funds, little maternal support, and an impoverished future. For the woman at Level 2, the possible reactions by other people are salient. What will my parents think? Will my boyfriend reject me? Will another child place a burden on our family resources and cause my husband to blame me? At this level, the "right" way the dilemma is resolved is to decide in a way that hurts the others the least. But the stakes are high for the woman herself; her own needs are sacrificed in the decision, and she may soon struggle to free herself from the powerlessness of her own dependence.

And yet some women initiate their movement beyond Level 2. They begin to scrutinize the logic of self-sacrifice; the word *selfish* comes back in, but at a higher level of analysis. The woman begins to ask, "Is it selfish or responsible—moral or immoral—to include her own needs within the compass of her care and concern?"

(Gilligan, 1977, p. 498). She becomes aware of both "what other people think" and her own inner judgment. The new goal is to be honest to oneself, so the virtue of *truth* replaces that of *goodness* as a determinant of morality. In the words of the 19th-century feminist Elizabeth Cady Stanton, "self development is a higher duty than self sacrifice." This third level, then, is called by Gilligan the *morality of nonviolence*. The basic injunction is one against hurting, and this becomes a principle governing all moral judgment and action, in its condemnation of exploitation and hurt.

For example, one woman writes:

> For a lot of years I responded to the needs of my family and denied any emotional needs of my own. Now I'm learning that I am a valuable person who does not have to knuckle under to every demand made on me. But first I had to admit that I was the one who would have to change. (quoted by Boyd, 1991-1992, p. 82)

In summary, for Kohlberg and for men, the moral imperative is "to use rules in order to respect the rights of others and thus to protect from interference the rights to life and self-fulfillment" (Gilligan, 1982, p. 100). The choice, thus, is between competing *rights,* with a perspective colored by *rules.* In Gilligan's view, for women the moral imperative is to alleviate the troubles of the world. The choice is between competing responsibilities; for example, a woman would, as a victim of injustice, be much more concerned with compensation for suffering than with having that suffering "justified." If someone agrees to repair your roof and you pay in advance, and if the job is not done as promised, the masculine orientation is to seek justice via a court of law, whereas the feminine conception focuses on the violation of a trusting relationship between the parties.

For women, the right to property—or even the right to life—is not weighed in the abstract, in terms of its logical priority—as the law sees it—but "in terms of the actual consequences that the violation of these rights will have in the terms of the people involved" (Gilligan, 1982, p. 95).

As psychologists have considered these contrasting conceptions of the nature of moral behavior, recent thinking has rejected a *categorical* distinction that claims that men operate out of an ethic of justice whereas women operate out of an ethic of care (Barwick,

118   ADULT PERSONALITY DEVELOPMENT

Brabeck, & Stryker, 1990; Brabeck, 1983; Pratt & Royer, 1982). For example, Walker (1984) found no empirical evidence that supports Gilligan's claim that women score lower in Kohlberg's system than men. In general, studies lead to a conclusion that the justice orientation and the care orientation can coexist within the same individual (Lytton & Hunter, 1992).

In actuality, the nature of the dilemma may be a stronger determinant of the moral orientation than the gender of the respondent. Walker (1989) found that regardless of gender, the care orientation was elicited more often when the dilemma was a real-life one, and a rights orientation was used more frequently in dilemmas generated by impersonal relationships.

These two orientations are best seen as separate constructs (Rest, 1983), as two "conceptually distinct frameworks within which people organize their moral thinking" (Langdale, 1986, p. 16). Although each may develop in childhood as a correlate of differing sex-role orientations for boys and girls, shifts in orientation may occur in midlife, congruent with the shifting conceptions of one's sex role, described in Chapter 4. To test such ideas Lyons (1982, 1983) divided 144 subjects into three age groups—childhood (ages 6 to 12), adolescence (ages 13 to 23), and adulthood (ages 24 to 60 and above)—and presented them with four contrasting ethical dilemmas (one was a real-life dilemma, generated by the subject; the other three came from the research of Kohlberg and Gilligan, reflecting justice and care orientations).

Lyons found that 85% of the responses to these ethical dilemmas could be coded into either justice or care orientations. More females than males gave responses reflecting a care orientation, regardless of the type of dilemma, whereas more males than females gave a justice orientation for each dilemma.

Lyons did not find a statistically significant relationship between the moral orientation chosen and age in any of the dilemmas; she concluded that both orientations appear systematically across the life cycle. But we should note several qualifications to this conclusion; first, the number of subjects who were older than their mid-twenties was quite limited. Second, among the females, the percentage choosing a justice orientation in Kohlberg's original ethical dilemma increases from 37% to 48% with increasing ages. Another interesting result was the greater tendency of the females than the males to give several different orientations in response to a moral dilemma; approximately one third of the females did so, though only about 8% of males did.

Carol Gilligan's conception, like Sandra Bem's conception of psychological androgyny described in Chapter 4, has led to a roller-coaster ride of reactions. Initially it was quite popular and captured the attention of a large audience; it later has come to be described as methodologically inadequate (Broughton, 1983; Colby & Damon, 1983), an exaggeration of sex differences (Hare-Mustin & Marecek, 1988), and "narrow, anecdotal, [and] unsubstantiated," even by some feminists (Kaminer, 1991, p. 125; 1992). Gilligan's initial articles and her book served as a type of projective test, on which people could "find" what they wanted to believe. It is true that we could wish that greater conceptual clarity could have been a part of her early work (Auerbach, Blum, Smith, & Williams, 1985). For example, is the "different voice" a product entirely of socialization? Is it categorical? And one reviewer speculated that she would write *In a Different Voice* differently today (Heilbrun, 1992). However, a more recent collaborative effort (Gilligan, Ward, & Taylor, 1988) continues to overgeneralize gender differences from a subset of participants (Crawford & Unger, 1990).

Langdale (1986), in reviewing relevant findings, reaffirms the conception "that there may be critical experiences at different points in the life cycle influencing the predominance of the justice and care orientations" (p. 45). It seems appropriate to think of these orientations as two paths along which moral development progresses simultaneously. In fact, a dialectical conception may be useful; at certain periods in life, development along one path may speed up, while the other slows down. Later, the pattern may reverse.

Stages in Religious Development

Religious faith may also be thought of as developing through a set of stages. Fowler and Lovin (1980) have proposed that religious faith possesses, for different people, different basic structures. These theorists propose that a structure of faith is a set of beliefs; but more than that, it is "a way that the mind operates in reasoning or judging about whatever content it focuses on" (p. 18).

The emerging stages of religious faith, in this conception, represent a series of tasks "in which each new life challenge arises in part from the limits of previous faith solutions" (1980, p. 23); this is a conception in keeping with the stage theories previously reviewed in this book and Volume 1.

Fowler and Lovin (1980) propose six stages, as follows:

Stage 1: Intuitive-Projective Faith. At the initial stage, faith is simply an expression of the child's wishes. Children ages 3 to 7 are oriented toward fantasy and imitation, but the content of thought patterns is rather fluid. Similar to Kohlberg's Stage 1, the child here is egocentric, but is becoming aware of strong taboos against certain actions.

Stage 2: Mythic-Literal Faith. In Stage 2, persons begin to internalize the stories, beliefs, and observances that characterize belonging to a particular society. Moral rules and beliefs are quite concrete and literal. Stage 2 also reflects "an increased accuracy in taking the perspective of other persons" (1980, p. 26); reciprocal fairness and imminent justice become determinants.

Stage 3: Synthetic-Conventional Faith. At the third stage awareness of the world comes to extend beyond the family. At this point religious faith serves the function of providing a coherent orientation to the world in the midst of a more varied and complex world and synthesizing contrasting viewpoints. The authors state:

> Stage 3 typically has its rise and ascendancy in adolescence, but for many adults it becomes a permanent equilibration. It structures the ultimate environment in interpersonal terms. Its images of unifying value and power derive from the extension of qualities experienced in personal relationships. It is a "conformist" stage in the sense that it is acutely tuned to the expectations and judgments of significant others, and as yet does not have a sure enough grasp on its own identity and autonomous judgment to construct and maintain an independent perspective. While beliefs and values are deeply felt, they typically are tacitly held—the person "dwells" in them and the meaning world they mediate, but there has not been occasion to step reflectively outside them to examine them explicitly or systematically. At Stage 3 a person has an "ideology," a more or less consistent clustering of

values and beliefs, but he or she has not objectified it for examination, and in a sense is unaware of having it. Differences of outlook with others are experienced as differences in "kind" of person. Authority is located in the incumbents of traditional authority-roles (if perceived as personally worthy) or in the consensus of a valued, face-to-face group. (Fowler & Lovin, 1980, p. 27)

Stage 4: Individuative-Reflective Faith. Stage 4 reflects an internalization of beliefs. The transition from Stage 3 to Stage 4 is especially important because at this point the adolescent or young adult must accept responsibility for his or her own lifestyle, values, and commitments. At this stage, a form of "demythologizing" may take place.

Stage 5: Paradoxical-Consolidative Faith. Stage 5 responds to a crisis that often happens in midlife. Previous certainty of values is questioned by forces that in earlier years had been suppressed from consciousness or ignored. The authors of the theory speak of "opening to the voices of one's deeper self" (Fowler & Lovin, 1980, p. 29); they note "this involves a critical recognition of one's *social* unconscious—the myths, ideal images, and prejudices built deeply into the self-system by virtue of one's nurture within a particular social class, religious tradition, ethnic group, or the like" (p. 29) (see also Box. 6.4).

Stage 6: Universalizing Faith. Like the Stage 6 morality in Kohlberg's conception, the authors see this as the highest development of religious faith, but note that its occurrence is quite rare. Those persons who have achieved this perspective "have generated faith compositions in which their felt sense of an ultimate environment is inclusive of all being" (Fowler & Lovin, 1980, p. 30). They facilitate and actualize the spirit of a fulfilled human community.

Unfortunately, despite the inherent interest in theories of religious development, research on them has been "sporadic at best" (Gorsuch, 1988, p. 211), and what has been done—for example, finding that older people are more likely to hold intrinsic religious beliefs—reflects the cross-sectional approach. As Gorsuch (1988) notes, "Few advances will be made in this area until longitudinal and experimental approaches are brought into it" (p. 211). The Faith Development in the Adult Life Cycle project seeks to do this.

Political Values

Does development during adulthood have any impact on political attitudes? Some have claimed that the individual differences in moral reasoning described earlier in this chapter reflect variations in political ideology rather than moral maturity (Emler, Renwick, & Malone, 1983).

As Reicher and Emler (1984) note, a much replicated finding is that political conservatives and radicals display different levels of moral reasoning (Alker & Poppen, 1973; Candee, 1976; Fishkin, Keniston, & MacKinnon, 1973; Nassi, Abramowitz, & Youmans, 1983; Rest, 1975). Although conservatives are more likely to reason about moral dilemmas at the Stage 4 level, radicals are more likely to give responses scored as Stage 5. The usual interpretation of these differences assumes more cognitive sophistication or maturity on the part of the politically left. But Emler et al. (1983) challenged this interpretation, producing results that they interpret to mean that the above differences in moral reasoning reflect differences in ideological orientation rather than in cognitive level.

We assume that as people grow older in our society they become more "conservative" (Glenn, 1974). But is that assumption generally true, and if so, does it apply to political conservatism? And, given that conservatism is defined partly as the preservation of tradition, how does political conservatism jibe with the radical change shown in some people in midlife? Even if older age is associated with right-wing attitudes, may it best be accounted for by a cohort effect (Braungart & Braungart, 1990; Bunzel, 1988) or by age differences in income or standard of living? These are challenging questions (Himmelweit, Humphreys, Jaeger, & Katz, 1981).

Several recent reviews (Sapiro, 1990; Sears, 1990; Sigel, 1989) emphasize that political socialization occurs over the entire life span. The learning of basic identifications and affective reactions may occur in childhood, followed by acquisition of knowledge. In later childhood and adolescence the learning of political attitudes begins. But how consistent do these remain over adulthood? Sears

(1990) notes that the traditional view assumed the persistence of early-formed orientations, but a concept of lifelong openness suggests a potential for change in political orientation at any age.

Statements about age and political values are also confounded by differing meanings of political values. At one level, we could focus on broad ideologies such as the previously mentioned conservatism and liberalism (Cutler, 1983). Somewhat related to these, but still distinguishable, would be an emphasis on political alienation, cynicism, and trust. A third emphasis would be on voter participation and community involvement. Confounding these is the changing level of importance of political-party identification with age and cohort, as well as the diminished centrality of political parties in the contemporary political process.

For example, some evidence exists that older people often adopt more conservative positions on contemporary social issues such as legalization of marijuana, abortion, or school busing (Cutler, 1974), on foreign policy (Back & Gergen, 1963), and on political party preference (Crittenden, 1962).

But Cutler (1983), in an extensive review, notes that such findings need to be qualified in several ways:

1. Not all young people are on one side of an issue and not all older people are on the other side.
2. Political-party identification by the respondent may modify the relationship between age and political attitudes more for some types of attitudes than others.
3. The findings often confound age differences and cohort effects.
4. For some issues, increased age may lead to liberal rather than conservative shifts in political attitudes, specifically those, such as medical care or Social Security, that are relevant personally.

SUMMARY

A review of theory and research on moral, religious, and political values leads to a conclusion that development does take place and that older persons reflect more sophisticated and complex values than do younger persons. But most of the change appears to occur in childhood, adolescence, and young adulthood.

7

Reactions to Death and Dying

Do not go gentle into that good night. . . .
Rage, rage against the dying of the light.

Dylan Thomas*

Awareness of death is present in some undifferentiated way even in young children, and some psychiatrists have speculated that a child's early response to death affects the whole of personality development (Lifton & Olson, 1982). But for most of us, death becomes a personal issue only much later in our lives except for brief periods; for example, when a classmate dies. It was only after he suffered a stroke in 1987, for example, that Edward Koch—then the mayor of New York City—carried his musings about his own mortality to the point of preparing for his funeral and composing his own epitaph (Finder, 1987). Even for most adults, who do not dwell constantly on their own death, the issue sooner or later has an impact on their personality development. This chapter deals with various aspects of death and dying, including the role of religion and support groups, the function of bereavement, and

---

*From *Poems of Dylan Thomas*. Copyright 1952 by Dylan Thomas. Reprinted with permission of New Directions.

personality factors in adaptation. Noted here—and emphasized at several points subsequently—is the observation that although the concepts of "death and dying" are often linked together in the professional literature (even here!), they are also separate issues with respect to personality development in adulthood. For example, the death of a spouse leaves adjustment challenges for the survivor, challenges that may only very slightly overlap with the survivor's own fears of death. "Dying," as a concept present within one's thought processes, may be quite different from "death." The term *death anxiety*, as it is usually referred to in the literature, may refer to a multitude of fears, some of which deal with the finality of death and some of which deal with the process of dying (Kastenbaum & Costa, 1977).

Awareness of One's Mortality

How much do children understand about death? This is a question that seemingly is best answered either by the imprecise "It depends" or by another question: "How can we know?" But psychiatrists and social scientists have sought more precise answers (Papadatou & Papadatos, 1991; Stambrook & Parker, 1987). Lifton and Olson (1982) report awareness of death in some form by pre-school-age children; as early as age 3, the child may be able to differentiate death from sleep (Kastenbaum, 1977b). But the preschool child often conceptualizes death as possessing a property, like sleep, of being reversible or "coming back." For example, we are told that 4-year-old Cecilia Cichan, the only survivor of a Northwest Airlines plane crash that took the lives of her parents and brother, reacted to being informed by "awareness, but not really comprehension." Awareness of the inevitability of death, conclude Lifton and Olson, comes only later. "The age at which children begin to understand all this varies tremendously, but in most cases it occurs between five and nine" (Lifton & Olson, 1982, p. 75).

Two aspects of awareness of death can be distinguished: universality versus irrevocability (Troll, 1982). By the age of 10, 90% of children recognized that death happens to everyone, but only one-third said that death was final (Childers & Wimmer, 1971). When children of differing ages are sensitively interviewed about their beliefs, three stages regarding irrevocability emerge (Nagy, 1948; Safier, 1964). Children around age 4 seem to interpret life and death as a constant flux; Safier (1964) observes that for them "something goes, then it stops, then it goes again. There is an absence of the idea of absolutes" (p. 286). Nagy (1948) described this as a stage that lacked appreciation for death as final. Then, at an intermediate stage, children view death as final but, at the same time, not inevitable. Here, life and death are both caused by outside agents; "Something makes it go; something makes it stop." The children at the third stage (about age 9 or 10) could recognize that death was both inevitable and final; Safier's respondents also felt that an internal agent could cause changes; "something goes by itself; something stops by itself" (Safier, 1964, p. 286). However, age in itself is not the best guide; a Piagetian classification of a child's ability to handle different types of mental operations is a better predictor of his or her understanding of death (Koocher, 1973), and we need to recognize that social, economic, or cultural factors can influence the child's concept formation (Bluebond-Langner, 1977).

The fact that awareness in children develops slowly, in stages in keeping with Piagetian conceptions (Balleweg & Haddon, 1992), should not, however, obscure the fact that even young children have ideas about death, often built on realistic, concrete perceptions (Kastenbaum & Costa, 1977). In a review of the literature on psychological perspectives on death, Kastenbaum and Costa (1977) summarize this viewpoint as follows:

> While there remains room for disagreement on a variety of questions, it does appear that the child's development of death cognitions is intimately related to its total construction or appreciation of the world, rather than standing outside the main developmental stream as secondary or exotic process. Curiosity about impermanence and destination seems as much a part of the child's intellectual orbit as the more frequently researched questions of permanence and origins. We believe that developmental psychology has overemphasized the processes through which the child comes to appreciate and acquire stability and equilibrium. Real children seem just as interested in disappearances, inconsistencies, and disequilibriums. This perhaps is another way of saying that loss, endings, and death are core concerns from childhood onward. (p. 232)

But when, if ever, do these attitudes become personalized? Do we ever really internalize the realization of our own finiteness? Kübler-Ross, Becker, and other experts doubt that we do. The suicide experts Shneidman and Farberow (1957) tell us that many people who "successfully" commit suicide do not really intend to end their lives; they are unable to imagine their own death (Troll, 1982). Again, three stages developing throughout life may be distinguished. First, after children develop some object constancy, they may be able to appreciate irrevocability as an abstract concept. Second comes a more internalized level of awareness. The gerontologist Munnichs (1966) called this the awareness of finitude, and he viewed it as separating youth from old age, as it reflects a shift in focus and a related adjustment. Like Kohlberg's stages of moral development, it is hard for persons at less advantaged stages to appreciate the more advanced ones. Yet some people can tell you the exact moment that they internalized this awareness of their personal mortality. Kastenbaum (1977b) quotes the playwright Ben Hecht: "I can recall the hour in which I lost my immortality, in which I tried on my shroud for the first time and saw how it became me. . . . The knowledge of my dying came to me when my mother died" (p. 148).

Likewise, one of the most dramatic sections of Gail Sheehy's *Passages* (1976) describes her instant awareness:

Without warning in the middle of my thirties, I had a breakdown of nerve . . . I was talking to a young boy in Northern Ireland where I was on assignment for a magazine when a bullet blew his face off. That was how fast it all changed. . . . When I flew home from Ireland, I couldn't write the story, could not confront the fact of my own mortality. . . . Some intruder shook me by the psyche and shouted: *Take stock! Half your life has been spent . . . You have been a performer, not a full participant.* And now you are 35. To be confronted for the first time with the arithmetic of life was, quite simply, terrifying. (pp. 2, 4, italics in original)

One manifestation of this shift at the second stage is more emphasis on "subjective life expectancy" or greater awareness of the "number of years left" (Lieberman & Caplan, 1970). Although previously the person was aware that he or she would not live forever, still there was not any emphasis on thoughts like "I have 70 years left" or "I've already lived 20% of my life." At this second stage, the finite quality of life comes to the fore.

Lifton and Olson (1982) describe this stage this way:

> On the life watershed of middle age, one becomes aware that life is not unbounded at the far end. The boundary of one's death is suddenly no more distant than the boundary marked on the other end by one's birth. One is in the middle. Of course, one has always "known" that one would die, but now this knowledge becomes a compelling individual reality. One's life is suddenly felt to be limited, finite. It also becomes apparent that one cannot finish everything; there will not be time for all one's projects. (p. 78)

Here, the ages at which one's parents died, or the general longevity of one's family, intrude into one's thoughts more frequently. Marshall (1975) interviewed U.S. citizens between ages of 64 and 96 about their expectations. He discovered that many of his interviewees used a formula to estimate their own life expectancies that was based on the relative length of life in their family members. One man said, "Up to now no men in my family have lived past 70. But a brother is going to be 72. But both parents died at 70. They say you die according to when your parents died." In Marshall's sample, only about one third of those respondents who had already lived longer than both their parents expected to live at least 5 more years, whereas 92% of those younger than the age of their parents' deaths expected to live 5 more years.

But finitude of death sometimes may extend to another stage, at which it becomes even more personal. At the last stage the shift seems to be away from shock and rejection at the thought of one's own death, toward some dealing with the actuality. Whether such is fully contemplated is impossible to know, of course; Freud believed that none of us can image our own death, and Kübler-Ross (1969) has written that "in our unconscious, death is never possible in regard to ourselves" (p. 2). But clearly new emphases take place; for example, pondering what one's life has added up to. This process of "life review" apparently cannot fully operate before this stage.

Death Anxiety

Existential theorists have proposed that the fear of death is the central human anxiety (May, 1973; Troll, 1982). At some deep unconscious level this may predominate; interestingly, when asked directly, most interviewers report they fear the deaths of others more than they fear their own (Geer, 1965; Schoenrade, 1986). As Volume 1, Chapter 9 reported, George Vaillant's (1977) subjects, former Harvard students reinterviewed in their 40s, feared the death of their spouses more than their own death. (See also Box 7.1 for a contemporary example of a research concept that empirically tests the unconscious fear of death.)

The term *death anxiety* has been used to refer to this dread that supposedly underlies most of the other of life's fears. However, the term requires elaboration. When asked what they fear about death, different respondents give a variety of fears: pain, mutilation, loss of dignity, for example (Troll, 1982). Some fear abandoning their loved ones, especially their children, and others fear being abandoned by others. Those with certain kinds of religious values may fear punishment in afterlife, and others may fear the unknown. Death anxiety thus can refer to either fear of dying or fear of the event of death itself (Lonetto & Templer, 1986).

Age and Death Anxiety

Does the aging process increase levels of death anxiety? Troll (1982) notes that some investigators conclude that older people, presumably because they are nearer their own deaths or deaths of loved ones, have less fear of death than do younger adults (Kastenbaum & Aisenberg, 1972; Munnichs, 1966).

Richard Kalish (1976), another distinguished observer of the aging process, takes a more detailed perspective. He offers three reasons for older people admitting to less fear of dying than do younger adults:

1. Older people put less value on their own lives, because society tends to view them as "over the hill," "used up," and discarded.

BOX 7.1

Death Fears and
Terror Management Theory

Ernest Becker (1971, 1973) proposed that people systematically deny personal mortality and this fear of death is repressed to an unconscious level.

Contemporary social psychologists Jeff Greenberg, Tom Pyszczynski, and Sheldon Solomon (1986; Solomon, Greenberg, & Pyszczynski, 1991) have used Becker's ideas and those of others to develop the concept of *terror management theory;* that is, that culture provides us with positive self-evaluations that shield us against the terror or anxiety we would feel if we remained consciously aware of our mortality. The theory holds, as an example, that "a culture's very concept of reality, its model of 'the good life,' and its moral codes are all intended to protect people from the terror of death" (Goleman, 1989, p. 19).

A series of empirical studies test the hypothesis that thinking about death motivates defense of, and adherence to, one's internalized cultural worldview. For example, Rosenblatt, Greenberg, Solomon, Pyszczynski, and Lyon (1989) found that when subjects were made more aware of their mortality, they evaluated more harshly those who transgressed against moral codes; by punishing law violations, subjects defended their standards. (Mortality salience was manipulated by asking subjects to write responses to two open-ended questions: what emotions they would experience when they thought about their own death and what would happen to them as they physically died.) Similarly, Greenberg et al. (1990) showed that when one's mortality was more salient, the person evaluated more favorably those who were in the person's in-group or who praised one's culture; subjects under the mortality-salience manipulation had more negative reactions to out-group members and those highly critical of one's culture. Burling (1993) sought support for a hypothesis that when subjects' mortality was made more salient, those subjects who were quite religious or quite concerned with status would accentuate those values. He found that the manipulation did increase status concerns but had no significant effect on religiosity as measured by the "interactional" and "internal" scales of Batson and Ventis (1982). The general conclusion of this innovative program of research is that thinking about one's death, even briefly, in a laboratory experiment, has at least some temporary effect on one's personality.

2. The internalized life expectancy, mentioned previously in this chapter, plays a role. If an older person has surpassed the age at which his or her parents died, the survivor may feel blessed, and hence less apprehensive about dying.

3. The greater number of deaths of family and friends experienced by older people gives them an opportunity to "rehearse"—or at least to become accustomed to—the unavoidability of dying. A dissonance-reduction process also seems possible; "I'm going to die so I'll fear it less" (Schoenrade, personal communication, October 7, 1987). Consider, for example, the situation of a healthy 75-year-old who lives in a retirement home of 100 or 200 residents. This person encounters the loss of acquaintances more often than even an equivalent-aged person who lives alone. Death never becomes "routine" but it is likely that the frequent confronting of it that is forced on some elderly people moderates their own death anxiety.

One study, done in Great Britain (Cartwright, Hockey, & Anderson, 1973) supports the latter conclusion. Persons who had recently suffered the loss of a loved one were studied; the proportion of bereaved people who needed assistance because of shock or distress or who reported trouble sleeping decreased with age. But as Troll (1982) asks, does this mean that the older people were really less bereaved? Or have they learned to suppress their anxieties as a result of their greater experience with death? For example, other researchers (Templer, Ruff, & Franks, 1971), after administering a death-anxiety scale to respondents of varying ages, found no major age differences past adolescence. Probably the safest conclusion is that reactions to death are too complex and too embedded at deeper levels of awareness ever to expect a consistent, straightforward relationship with age. Growing older may heighten fears in some, whereas others may—with age—experience reactions that reduce anxiety. It would be more profitable to explore how other determinants interact with age to affect death anxiety. Religion is one such variable, and to it we turn.

Religion and Death Anxiety

What role do one's religious beliefs play in determining one's feelings about death? And if they are a factor, does this relationship change with increasing age? Batson and Ventis (1982) state that religious beliefs are present in "whatever we as individuals do to come to grips with the questions that confront us because we are aware that we and others like us are alive and will die" (p. 7).

Methodological Issues

Unfortunately, much of the research done to answer these questions has used narrowly defined populations, thus creating doubt about the propriety of applying these findings to other populations (Lester, 1967). Among these specific groups were patients in mental hospitals (Feifel, 1959), older persons (Swenson, 1961), older persons who were also patients in mental hospitals (Christ, 1961), college undergraduates (Alexander & Adlerstein, 1959), theology students (Magni, 1970), and medical school students (Siegman, 1961). The diverse nature of these samples accounts for some of the conflicting findings about how extensive is the fear of death. But even from samples of apparently similar nature, conflicting results can emerge. For instance, Feifel (1955) concludes, on the basis of interviewing a mentally ill population, that old age is the time of life when people most fear death and childhood the period when they are least afraid. But Swenson (1961) found that death attitudes of a fearful or negative nature were not acknowledged by his elderly sample, and Christ (1961), interviewing older psychiatric patients, found that 87% of them said that they never had talked about death or dying before. Such conflicting findings can partially be clarified by the use of common measures, whether they be interviews, or questionnaires, or depth measures.

But at present the measurement techniques are another problem in drawing answers to these questions (Petzel, 1988). Direct questioning, which has been used in most of the studies, may be inappropriate for reaching the real feelings of respondents, even though good rapport has been established (Kastenbaum & Costa, 1977). As Munnichs (1961) notes, it is difficult to give a real answer to the sudden question, "Are you afraid to die?" Because many people have given little or no previous reflection on a conscious level to the thought of death, their replies are likely to be negative as defenses against a direct question. Also possible is their assumption that they are not afraid because they do not think about it much (P. A. Schoenrade, personal communication, October 7, 1987).

Instead of using direct questions, Jeffers, Nichols, and Eisdorfer (1961) suggest that projective techniques and depth methods may be more fruitful. The latter types, although often subjective in their scoring and interpretation, may be more valid because they probe into feelings that are much deeper than the superficial responses elicited by direct questions and true/false attitude statements. Another type of fruitful method, pioneered by Alexander, Colley, and Adlerstein (1957), is the use of the galvanic skin response and other physiological arousal measures to show that death-related words elicit more autonomic arousal than do neutral words (Templer, 1971). This is a particularly relevant, though problematic method, because on direct measures, there are "relatively rare expressions of high manifest death concern despite widespread acceptance among researchers of the belief that death anxiety is universal" (Kastenbaum & Costa, 1977, p. 234).

The supposed validity of the measurement techniques in this area is often pragmatically determined; if a measure "works" (i.e., if its findings are in line with theoretical predictions), it is declared valid. Using this criterion, some direct methods appear to be more useful than others. For example, Sarnoff and Corwin (1959) constructed a Fear of Death Scale, responses to which show relatively good differentiation between greater and lesser fear of death. From a larger pool of items, five items were selected by the use of item analysis. (A sample item is "I tend to worry about the death toll when I travel on the highways.") In a test of predictions from psychoanalytic theory, Sarnoff and Corwin found that scores on the scale were related to the extent of castration anxiety reported by the subjects. But other simple, direct measures have not been as productive in confirming theory-driven hypotheses.

Another factor that needs to be given more consideration in research studies is the amount of contact with death that the respondent has experienced. It seems quite plausible that the person who has recently encountered the loss of a loved one will have thought about death much more than the person whose environment has not been so affected. This is an example of a factor that could interact with the person's age in determining death-anxiety levels.

A third type of limitation in at least the early studies was that religion was treated too broadly. Religion is now seen as a multidimensional construct (Batson & Ventis, 1982; Schoenrade, 1986) with many measurable components. One recent strategy–to be discussed in detail subsequently–is to relate specific death-related religious beliefs, such as a belief in an afterlife, to death anxiety (Schoenrade, 1989).

The Role of One's Philosophy of Religion

In relating extent of fears of death to religious attitudes, we need to give attention to the role of death in different religious philosophies. As Schoenrade (1986) notes, the issue of death is often a basic focus of major religious teachings. In Buddhism, "salvation ultimately means transcending death in a very radical way, by being taken out of the stream of existence into a transcendent realm" (Smart, 1968, p. 115). In Christianity, "the resurrection of the dead" may be more literal in the beliefs of some denominations than others, but it always has relevance for the individual believer (Schoenrade, 1986). In the fundamentalist denominations of Protestantism, death is seen as a doorway to either a better or worse condition. The religion the person follows often guarantees the person the reward of eternal life as a result of faith or works. Sometimes one's trust in an afterlife with God reaches the extent that, like the apostle Paul, the person might prefer to leave this life to enter that land beyond. Whether or not one's confidence reaches this peak, it does seem that the person who believes in an afterlife has less reason to fear death than one who does not. Furthermore, it would seem that the more religious a person is and the greater claim the person has to "eternal life," the less he or she should feel anxiety concerning impending death. So at least goes the reasoning of many philosophers and social scientists (Becker, 1973; James, 1902; Kübler-Ross, 1969; Lifton, 1979; Schoenrade, 1986).

But Feifel (1959) has reasoned differently. He argued that certain people who fear death strongly may resort to a religious outlook in order to cope with their fears concerning death. He further concluded that the religious person, when compared to the less religious individual, is personally more afraid of death. For the nonreligious person, the emphasis is a philosophical one–on fear of discontinuance of life on earth rather than what will happen after death. The stress on the religious person is seen as coming from two sources: essentially, religious concerns with afterlife matters such as "I may go to Hell," or "I have sins to expiate yet," as well as the philosophical concern with the cessation of present earthly experiences. Feifel's data indicated that even the belief that one is going to Heaven is not sufficient to do away with the personal fear of death in some religious persons.

Apparently the only other study to support this conclusion is that of Faunce and Fulton (1958), who reported that "emotional responses suggesting either fear of death or of the dead were more frequent among spiritually oriented than among temporally oriented individuals" (p. 208). But in both these studies absolutely no statistical techniques were employed. Feifel based his conclusions on his observations of questions asked in an interview, whereas Faunce and Fulton reached their interpretation by examination of responses to a sentence-completion task.

A few studies have found that religious feeling makes no difference in the way one views death (Feifel, 1974; Kalish, 1963; Templer & Dotson, 1970). Even when death anxiety is compared with the specific variable of nature of beliefs about an afterlife, sometimes no relationship emerges (Aday, 1984).

But a greater number of studies have shown that religious belief serves as a means of reducing anxiety about death. Jeffers et al. (1961) state, "No fear of death includes a tendency to read the Bible oftener, more belief in a future life, and reference to death with more religious connotation" (p. 43). Alexander and Adlerstein (1959), on the basis of several empirical measures, reached a similar conclusion, as did studies by Lester (1970), Magni (1970), Templer (1972), and Swenson (1961), who used a sample of older persons.

Schoenrade (1989) observed that the studies described previously did not *activate* a concern with death, other than to ask the respondents for their reactions to it. What if an individual were confronted *directly* with the prospect of his or her death? Then the role of religious beliefs might be more apparent. For example, Berman (1974) interviewed a small number of persons who shared the experience of having almost died. Those who strongly believed in an afterlife did not remember any less fear at the time, but those who were active religiously were more likely to report having prayed at the time of the near-death experience.

Osarchuk and Tatz (1973) tested these ideas in a laboratory set-ting; they confronted undergraduates with the (artificially inflated) probability that people of the subject's ages would die in automo-bile accidents. The results suggest that the death confrontation increased their belief in afterlife in those subjects who were al-ready so predisposed, that this is one means of dealing with death (Schoenrade, 1986).

Schoenrade's (1989) careful study of undergraduates found a similar result: Among those subjects who already possessed rela-tively strong beliefs about afterlife, forcing them to confront their deaths through a laboratory manipulation enabled them to embrace a positive view of death and to accept its negative implications. For those subjects who lacked strong beliefs in afterlife, the confronta-tion did not affect their attitudes toward death.

In an effort to deal with methodological limitations of some earlier studies, Martin and Wrightsman (1965) administered a variety of instruments to 58 members of three churches. Ages of the subjects ranged from 18 to 75; the mean age was 44. Two different measures of religious values were given, one assessing extent of participation in religious activities (church services, Sunday school, personal prayer, and reading of religious materials) and the other measur-ing two factors of religious attitude, a "nearness to God" dimension and a "fundamentalism-humanism" dimension (Broen, 1957). Three measures of fear of death were included; two of these were tradi-tional Likert-type attitude scales, including Sarnoff and Corwin's Fear of Death Scale, but the third was a sentence-completion mea-sure of concern over death constructed for that study. In all, 13 incomplete sentences were constructed by the authors to tap death concern or death involvement. Each statement included some word or phrase that served as a death cue, such as "cemetery," "ambu-lance siren," or "airplane crash." In addition, a measure of nearness of death in the respondent's family was collected. In general, reli-gious participation was negatively correlated with concern over death; in one of the churches two of these correlations were –.73 and –.70. That is, the more religious activity a person reported, the less he or she feared death. But the responses to Broen's Religious Attitude Inventory did not significantly correlate with measures of death anxiety. Religious participation, but not religious attitude, seemed to serve as a means of comfort.

There was no clear-cut relationship between age of the respondents and the extent of their fear of or involvement with death. More of the correlations were negative than positive; thus the trend in the results went against Feifel's (1955) claim that "old age is the time when people most fear death" (p. 375). In two of the three congregations, older churchgoers reported less concern over death.

Since this study was done, the thinking about attitudes toward death has become more sophisticated (Feifel, 1990). (One example is presented in Box 7.1.) Reactions to one's own eventual death are now considered to be more complex than a simple fear/no fear dimension; that is, it is now possible to hold several different—even seemingly contradictory—perspectives on death (Schoenrade, 1986, p. 12). Kastenbaum and Costa (1977) suggest that:

> it is possible that the focus on "fear" or "anxiety" has led to the neglect of other orientations toward death. The total human interpretation of death is too complex to be subsumed under concepts most favored by research. Sorrow, curiosity, and even a sense of joyous expectation are among the orientations that have been observed in non-research contexts. (p. 236)

In a study that rectifies this lack, Spilka and his colleagues (Minton & Spilka, 1976; Spilka, Stout, Minton, & Sizemore, 1977) constructed a death perspective questionnaire, which includes eight subscales: Death as Pain and Loneliness, Failure, Forsaking Dependents Plus Guilt, Unknown, Natural End, Courage, Afterlife of Rewards, and Indifference. Each of the subscales contains four to six statements. In contrast to the earlier assessment of a single dimension, Spilka's scale allows for positive, negative, and neutral views of death within the same individual. As Schoenrade (1986) observes, "If religious beliefs do function to highlight the positive implications of death, it is not a logical necessity that they also diminish the negative implications. Indeed, when death is confronted, awareness of both positive and negative implications might increase, the former helping the individual to accept the latter" (p. 13). A study that looks at age differences in the relationship of religion to these different reactions to death apparently has not yet been done, but is a likely next step.

Reactions to the Death of a Loved One

More than half of the women over 65 years of age and 12% of men that age in the United States have been widowed (Stroebe, Stroebe, & Hansson, 1988). Previous references to reactions to the death of one spouse highlight its importance to a chapter on developmental factors in reactions to death and dying. Researchers and health-service delivery workers agree that the experience of losing one's spouse or significant other person may be related to increases in the occurrence of depression and physical illness, and even a greater vulnerability to death in the survivor (Pellman, 1991, 1992; Raphael, 1983; Stroebe & Stroebe, 1983; Stroebe & Stroebe, 1987), although specific reactions may depend on cultural and temporal factors (Stroebe, Gergen, Gergen, & Strobe, 1992), as well as individual values and worldviews (Adler, 1991).

A comprehensive review of the rapidly accumulating literature on this topic (Stroebe & Stroebe, 1983) has been organized around sex differences rather than age differences in bereavement, and such a focus is congenial with a major theme of this book.

Distress and Depression

Integral to the feeling of grief are responses reflecting distress and depression; thus such responses are considered normal and should be distinguished from the depression that is a part of chronic psychological disorder (Averill, 1968; Averill & Nunley, 1988). For example, one woman from New York writes, "My husband died three years ago, but the pain doesn't get better with the passing of time. I find evenings and nights the worst for me. Although I go to a support group and try to keep busy, nothing really helps" (quoted by Boyd, 1991, p. 72). One study (Bornstein, Clayton, Halikas, Maurice, & Robbins, 1973) interviewed 65 women and 27 men shortly after the death of their spouse and again between one year and 20 months later. At one month, 35% were depressed; a year later, 17% were depressed. So no simple conclusion emerges; the rejection of a neat label for the processes of widows and widowers also comes from the longitudinal study of 70 surviving San Diego spouses (Shuchter, 1986).

Another longitudinal study (Parkes & Brown, 1972; also described in Glick, Weiss, & Parkes, 1974) has two distinctive qualities; it compared the widowed spouses with matched controls of married persons, and, more relevant for our purposes, all the widowed subjects were under the age of 45 (49 widows and 19 widowers). A summary of this important study is as follows:

> The women showed more overt distress than the men after bereavement, and a year later their social and psychological adjustment was poorer than that of the widowers. However, the same adjustment measures also revealed large differences between married men and women in the matched control group, and "when this was taken into account it seems that the widowed women showed no greater *decline* in adjustment that the widowed men: moreover, at a follow-up two to four years after bereavement, it was the men who were found to have taken longer to recover than the women" (Parkes, 1972, p. 149). After 14 months the control women scored almost as high on the depression score as the bereaved men and much higher than the control men. . . . The longer term follow-up showed a steady decline in depression, and by the third year the difference between the bereaved and the controls was slight. Pertinent here is the fact that, though the widows had higher depression scores than widowers 1 year after bereavement, at the later follow-up the widows were no more depressed than married women. Widowers, on the other hand, remained significantly more depressed than married men. (Stroebe & Stroebe, 1983, pp. 285-286)

Although studies with large samples, of varying ages, and with appropriate control groups are limited in number, the pattern of results indicates that adjustment to the loss of a partner requires several years, and that men may remain more depressed for longer times than women.

The length of time before recovery is dependent on many factors, of course, although one review concludes that in general, "after twelve to eighteen months most bereaved begin to recover and ultimately show little sign of psychological or physical damage" (Stroebe & Stroebe, 1987, p. 121). In keeping with this conclusion is a longitudinal study by McCrae and Costa (1988) that traced 14,000 respondents, ages 25 to 74, over a 10-year period. Widowed persons showed little or no difference from married on measures of psychological well-being and personality, leading McCrae and

Costa to emphasize the quality of resilience in the ability to adapt to major life stresses.

The findings for other psychiatric reactions, especially those requiring hospitalization, are generally similar to those for depression. Of the 17 cross-sectional studies reviewed by Gove (1972), all find higher rates of mental illness for the widowed, both males and females, than for their counterparts (Stroebe & Stroebe, 1983). Most of these cross-sectional studies, however, found that the difference between being married and being widowed is greater for men than for women. Widowed men had higher rates of mental illness than had widowed women. But, as we saw, the pattern of results from longitudinal studies is less consistent.

Physical Health and Illness

Bereavement has long been associated with a marked deterioration not only in mental health but also in physical health (Sanders, 1988). Those who have lost their partners consult physicians more often, consume more drugs, and have higher incidence of symptoms and illness rates than do controls (Stroebe & Stroebe, 1983; Stroebe & Stroebe, 1987).

Here, the evidence from longitudinal studies is consistent with the findings on previous aspects: "If there is any sex difference at all, bereavement affects the physical health of men more severely than of women" (Stroebe & Stroebe, 1983, p. 290).

Of more relevance to our developmental focus is the conclusion that the effects of loss are greatest in the younger widows and widowers, and physical health effects are less pronounced among those who are older when they lose their spouses. An important study here is that by Heyman and Gianturco (1973), whose subjects were 41 elderly persons (14 men and 27 women), all over age 60, who were participants in a longitudinal aging project at Duke University. They were examined both before and after the death of their spouses. In this older sample, there was no general health deterioration as a result of bereavement, a finding in contrast to studies of younger widowed. Heyman and Gianturco (1973) concluded that the elderly are better prepared psychologically to expect and accept the death of a spouse.

Mortality

Mortality rates are higher for widowed than for still-married people of the same age, but the excess risk is much greater for men than for women. Consistent with the earlier findings, loss of spouse has more dire effects on men than on women.

Causes of widowers' death with excessively high rates include homicide, cirrhosis of the liver, and suicide (Stroebe & Stroebe, 1983, p. 291). Also, for widowers, there is an excessively high death rate, especially from heart disease, during the first 6 months after the spouse's death. Causes of widows' deaths with excessively high rates are accidents (other than automobile accidents), suicide, and arteriosclerotic heart and coronary disease. In contrast to men, the period of highest risk of death for widows seem to be in the second year of bereavement rather than in the first 6 months or year.

Suicide

The rate of suicide among the elderly has increased, even before publicity about doctor-assisted suicides; for example, during the decade of the 1980s the rate increased by 21% (Snider, 1991).

Ever since the publication of Durkheim's groundbreaking work in 1897, social scientists have known that the rate of suicide is higher among the widowed than among the married. Men commit more "successful" suicides than do women, but the ratio is even greater for those who have lost a spouse. The widowed-to-married suicide ratio for men is more than twice that for women.

Suicide rate is specially high in the first year or two after the spouse's death (Bojanovsky & Bojanovsky, 1975, cited by Stroebe & Stroebe, 1983; MacMahon & Pugh, 1965).

Interestingly, like the earlier mortality-rate difference, for males suicide rate was highest in the first 6 months of bereavement, whereas for females, the peak suicide rate came in the second year (Bojanovsky & Bojanovsky, 1975, cited by Stroebe & Stroebe, 1983).

Explanations for Reactions to Bereavement

In summary, there are consistent sex differences in the effects of loss of a spouse. Less clear but a general trend is the indication that loss of a spouse has more devastating effects on relatively younger adults than on the elderly. A number of explanations have been offered for these differences. Although these concepts are primarily oriented to explaining the sex differences, they also provide insight into the developmental changes.

Stress theory, one of these, assumes that stressful life events play an important role in the causes of various somatic and psychiatric disorders (Dohrenwend & Dohrenwend, 1981; Holahan & Holahan, 1987). Clearly bereavement is stressful (Parkes, 1988). But why do men seem to suffer more from bereavement than do women? Why younger adults more than older adults? There are no clear-cut answers. Some physiologists (e.g., Ramey, 1987) argue that the male of every species is more fragile than the female, and there is evidence that the human male is considerably more vulnerable to a variety of diseases than the female (Gove & Hughes, 1979; Hamburg & Lunde, 1966). But these would not seem to account for all the differences (Stroebe & Stroebe, 1983; Stroebe & Stroebe, 1987). Recent work on immune system differences (Laudenslager, 1988) may provide part of the answer; recent work links marital disruption to altered immune status (Kiecolt-Glaser et al., 1987; O'Leary, 1989).

Role theory, in contrast, assumes that the roles played by persons in different marital statuses may differentially expose them to risk (Hansson, 1986). Gove (1972, 1973) attributes the better health of married people than single people to the fact that "single men and women tend to lack close interpersonal ties and are relatively isolated" (p. 35). Therefore, greater strain is present in the single role. But, Gove proposes, being married is less advantageous to a woman than to a man. Gove's argument centers around the "captive state" of the woman as a housewife/homemaker—in some cases, her only role—whereas the man can enjoy gratification from two roles, that of household head and breadwinner. With the changing role of women in the workforce, this explanation appears less applicable. But the flip side still seems valid; when a two-career married couple splits up, the man must adjust more to two roles (launderer, house cleaner, cook, and so on) than the woman because even among two-career couples the woman continues to do the majority of maintenance tasks in the home.

A third explanation, *interpersonal protection theory*, extends one of Gove's role-theory ideas. It proposes that close interpersonal relationships buffer individuals against the negative impact of stressful life events (Markides & Cooper, 1989). Three types of social support have been identified (by Stroebe, Stroebe, Gergen, & Gergen, 1982):

1. material and task support, or the provision of material aid by the partner; examples would be doing the laundry, yard work, generating income;
2. validational support, or playing a role as a reference person in helping the partner to evaluate and structure his or her social environment; examples would be acting as a critic, a "sounding board," or best friend;
3. emotional support; that is, contributing to the partner's feeling of self-worth and positive self-regard.

It has been found that if a person experiences many stressful life events but has a high level of social support, the usual physical effects are less likely to occur. The death of a spouse not only removes this protective screen of social support that was provided by the partner but it may also leave the surviving partner worse off than if she or he had never married (Dykstra, 1990). The person, in a good marriage, has lost a major source of emotional and validational support and is likely also to have lost material support. Women are more able than men to obtain alternative or substitute sources of social support (Blieszner & Adams, 1992; Day, 1991; Lopata, 1988). They can also admit to feelings of loneliness and needs for companionship (Stroebe & Stroebe, 1983). Also, men are more isolated from social contacts outside their work environment, and husbands often leave it to their wives to establish contacts with the neighborhood and maintain contacts with friends and relatives (Bock & Webber, 1972). Further, they seem more likely to rely exclusively on their spouses as confidants (Fischer & Phillips, 1982). Partly for such reasons, and partly because there are fewer widowers than widows, surviving husbands have fewer community-based support groups available than do widows (Silverman & Cooperband, 1975).

All of this makes sense. Stroebe and Stroebe (1983), after reviewing evidence for the three approaches, conclude:

> Interpersonal protection theory offers a reasonable account for the pattern of health findings reported in this paper. Furthermore, there is empirical evidence to support the protection theory assumptions about the processes which mediate the relationship between marital status and health. There is evidence that social support buffers individuals against deleterious effects of life stress (e.g., Berkman & Syme, 1979; Brown & Harris, 1978; Eaton, 1978; Surtees, 1980) and that widows can draw on more extensive social support. There can be no doubt, therefore, that at present there is more empirical support for an interpretation of marital health differentials in terms of protection rather than role theory. (p. 299)

8

The Use of
Personal Documents in Understanding
Adult Personality Development

*If we want to know how people feel—what they experience
and what they remember, what their emotions and motives
are like, and the reasons for acting as they do—why not ask
them?*

Gordon W. Allport

Who knows us better than ourselves? Some would say that such a
question is easily answered, but only a few psychologists, regretta-
bly, follow Allport's admonition quoted at the beginning of this chapter. Instead, various—even devious—methods have been developed
to determine persons' personalities without directly asking them.

Yet some psychologists do seek examples of the subject's written
or oral expression as indications of personality. The purpose of this
chapter is to describe the use of personal documents in furthering
our understanding of the concepts and processes presented in
earlier chapters of Volume 1 and this book.

Types of Personal Documents

Gordon Allport (1942) defined personal documents as "any self-revealing record that intentionally or unintentionally yields information regarding the structure, dynamics, and functioning of the author's mental life" (p. xii). He limited the term to first-person documents; the restriction has continued. Generally, the term *personal documents* refers to autobiographies, memoirs, oral histories, diaries, collections of letters, and similar materials. Note that all of these "intentionally" (to rely on Allport's definition) tell the reader about the author. But given that Allport includes "unintentional" revelations of personal information, the term *personal documents* could be broadened to include the products of novelists, painters, poets, songwriters, and even architects and clothes designers. It could be argued that the clothes we wear, the kinds of cars we drive, and the places we live unintentionally—if not intentionally—reveal information about our mental lives. However, most analyses of personal documents have restricted their sources to the narrower conception—autobiographies, diaries, letters—and that is the focus of this chapter.

Just as the topic of personality development in adulthood was neglected by psychologists for many years, so too has the methodology of the analysis of personal documents. It is not much of an exaggeration to claim that the "state of the art" regarding the use of personal documents in psychology has not—until the past decade—advanced beyond that summarized in Allport's (1942) monograph review published more than 50 years ago.

It is especially regrettable that personal documents were for so long overlooked as sources of data, because each type of personal document is congenial with a contrasting theory of adult personality development. For example, diaries, daily personal records, and collections of letters are more relevant to a dialectical theory, because they represent an ongoing, but continuously changing, production of raw material. Volume 1, in describing the collection of letters by Jenny Masterson (Allport, 1965), demonstrated the utility of dialectical theory in understanding this long-running expression of personal information. What you write in your diary today may reflect concern with a different problem from your diary entry of 3 months before or 3 months in the future. Diary entries and letters to friends may also be useful in identifying how one works through a critical period or crisis in adulthood, as emphasized in stage theories. In contrast, autobiographies are retrospective; we describe what has happened to us in the past. I would argue that analysis of an autobiography, as a personal document, is most congenial with life script theory, because it is usually the case that in writing an autobiography we succumb to strong pressures to fit everything within a certain theme. "Some autobiography tries to be honest, but at the very least a process of selection is involved" (Glendinning, 1988, p. 57). As George Kelly would remind us, we cannot view our own lives completely and objectively. An autobiography is not just a random collection of memories. We pick and choose what to remember, and what is chosen is partly determined by the constructs we apply to ourselves and our own lives.

Much more methodological work has been devoted to an analysis of autobiographies than to letters and diaries; therefore the focus of this chapter will be on that type of personal document. However, Box 8.1 cites some examples of the diary as another source for analysis.

The History of Autobiography

Have people always written autobiographies? No; generally it is a relatively recent phenomenon. With a few exceptions (including St. Augustine's "Confessions" in A.D. 400) writing one's own life story is a phenomenon of the 19th and 20th centuries.

A listing of 7,000 British autobiographies indicated that 90% of them were written in the 19th or 20th centuries. Only 200 had been written in the 17th century and 400 in the 18th century. Why this rapidly accelerating trend over the past 400 years? In earlier times the concept of "the self" was unknown or little acknowledged; neither individuality nor introspection was valued. Weintraub (1978) writes:

During the millennium from 800 B.C. to 200 A.D., the conditions of ancient life neither stimulated nor promoted the growth of autobiography. The ancients did not put a premium on the life devoted to settling the quandary: Who am I? How did I become what I am? In

---

BOX 8.1

Diaries as Keys to Understanding

Diaries are the most private of personal documents, especially if one assumes, as Allport (1942) did, that the intended audience is only the author himself or herself. Experts from the perspective of history or literature have devoted more attention than psychologists to diary-keeping as a topic of study; Thomas Mallon's (1984) book contains a typology of motivations for diary keeping, but psychologists have begun to examine the diaries of prominent persons, including Samuel Pepys and Vera Brittain (Stein, 1977; Stewart, Franz, & Layton, 1988), to draw conclusions about personality development. Furthermore, a recent, useful study interviewed a variety of people about their experiences in keeping a diary (Wiener & Rosenwald, 1993), and another has employed diary entries to test theories of grief (Rosenblatt, 1983).

---

what sense am I a distinctive personality? And what complex interplay of external forces and internal characteristics accounts for my specific configuration? There was no need to use autobiography as a basic quest for the self, or as a tool for self-clarification. (p. 13)

Thus, during the Middle Ages and up through the 15th or 16th century, it was not considered appropriate to introspect about oneself or consider oneself to be unique. Individual differences were apparent but the causes for them were seen to be external.

The autobiographical movement got its impetus in the 17th century (Olney, 1980), although the term *autobiography* did not appear until about 1795 (Buckley, 1984). This was a period that experienced a transformation—actually a breakdown—in traditional social customs. When this outer framework, or social structure, falls apart, people turn inward for understanding of what is happening. Protestant England in the 17th century was an especially fertile ground. Religious groups shared their testimony through some of their memoirs, capitalizing on the adventurous exploratory spirit. The journal of George Fox, the founder of the Religious Society of Friends (Quakers), was published about this time.

Reasons for Writing an Autobiography

Why write your autobiography? It is easy to do. There are no rules, no structure that is uniform. Furthermore, it is an ego trip. Hence many people have.

But certainly members of some occupational groups do so more than others. Among American autobiographers, ministers traditionally have been most prolific. Also, many journalists, writers, doctors, scientists, entertainers, and politicians have prepared their memoirs. In contrast, there are relatively few from businesspeople or farmers.

The above distinctions imply that some personal characteristics seem necessary or relevant to the decision to report one's life story. For example, an autobiography is more likely to emerge if the person is introspective or self-reflective. Also, if the person is self-confident and has positive self-regard, such will be the result. That is, showing a certain kind of *chutzpah,* the person says, "I am important in my own right" (Reefer, 1990). In ancient Greece and Rome, the gods determined one's fate. In the early Middle Ages, self-expression was little done because people's lives derived from kinship relations; that is, "I am X, child of Y, grandchild of Z." Autobiographers are more likely to have some belief in their own uniqueness, or at least being different and seeing oneself as different. They resonate to a credo that "every life is something extraordinary, full of particular drama and tension and surprise, often containing unimagined degrees of suffering or heroism, and invariably touching extreme moments of triumph and despair, though frequently unexpressed" (Holmes, 1985, p. 208). In addition, a sense of an internal locus of control leads to autobiographical writing; some degree of belief that one is the cause of one's own outcomes in life would seem to be a requirement.

Motives for Writing One's Autobiography

Peter Davison (1992), who has edited a number of autobiographies, writes, "Memoirs (like first novels) have a tendency to paint self-portraits in those colors the author deems most flattering" (p. 92). Psychologists, however, have sought to develop classifications of the reasons for publishing one's memoirs.

As one example, Krueger and Reckless (1931) claimed that all personal documents were either *confessional* or *detached*. In contrast, Clark (1935) offered a fourfold typology:

1. appeal for sympathy
2. need for self-justification
3. desire for appreciation
4. need for artistic communication

Gordon Allport's early but still influential monograph provides the most detailed and comprehensive listing. Allport (1942) first makes the basic distinction between authors who spontaneously create their products and those who provide a product at the instigation of some outsider. But he notes that "valuable documents have been secured under both types of instigation" (p. 69). Combining several of these and other earlier classifications, Allport distinguished about a dozen different motives.

Special Pleading

The motivation of the autobiographer here is to prove that he or she is more sinned against than sinning. Such autobiographers may blame others for failure to understand them. Politicians want vindication; much of the thrust of President Lyndon Johnson's memoirs reflects this motivation. Several years ago Mary Cunningham, who rapidly moved up the managerial ranks at the Bendix Corporation, was accused in the media of using an alleged personal relationship with her boss to achieve these promotions. Her autobiography was an attempt literally to prove that she had been more sinned against than sinning. Donald Trump's (1990) autobiography was met with reviews that described it as self-serving and lacking in real self-revelation. Playwright Arthur Miller's (1987) book "reflects a massive desire to make things right with himself" (Kazin, 1987, p. 150).

One special aspect of this motivation is to counter interpretations by biographers and others who have written about the person's life. Henry Adams stated in his autobiography that setting the record straight was "a shield of protection in the grave." More recently, Geraldo Rivera told a reporter he wrote his memoirs as something of a preemptive strike; "There were two unauthorized biographies in the works and I didn't want people to scoop me on my own story" (quoted by Donlon, 1991, p. 3D). Alfred Kazin (1979) wrote, "So that is why I write, to reorder an existence that man in the mass will never reorder for me" (p. 88).

Furthermore, as Barrett Mandel (1980) notes:

> Writing an autobiography ratifies the form one has given to one's life. The ongoing activity of writing discloses the being's ratification of the ego's illusion of the past, thereby solidifying it. The acceptance of the illusion, occurring in the present where meaning is possible, is what makes an autobiography capable of telling the truth. . . . Autobiography is a passage to truth because, like all genuine experience, it rises from the ground of being that transcends one's memories, petty lies, grand deceptions, and even one's desire to be honest. (p. 64)

Exhibitionism

Some autobiographers seek always to display themselves in as vivid a light as possible (Allport, 1942). "Sins as well as virtues may be exposed with such relish and satisfaction that we are likely to dismiss the author as hopelessly narcissistic" (Allport, 1942, p. 70). The autobiographies of some movie stars seem to reflect this motivation; Shelly Winters's (1980) book, for example, seems to take pleasure in revealing her intimate relationships with other named celebrities. For example, she wrote, "I told Marlon [Brando] to hurry and get all his clothes together and go up on the roof because I didn't know whether Burt [Lancaster] would come back up the elevator or run up the stairs" (p. 287). Likewise, in *Bittersweet,* actress Susan Strasberg (1980) tattles about her adolescent affair with Richard Burton; and Margaret Trudeau, then the wife of the Canadian prime minister, wrote in *Beyond Reason* (1979) about her nervous breakdown and her fights with her husband.

Perhaps their model was Mae West, whose 1959 autobiography, *Goodness Had Nothing to Do With It,* reflected not only one of her most famous lines in the movies but also her personal philosophy. This book almost reads like a telephone book, listing man after man she was involved with during her long life (Mae West was born in 1893 and died in 1980).

Literary critics have been less than kind to exhibitionistically motivated autobiographies. W. H. Auden (1962) has written that "literary confessors are contemptible, like beggars who exhibit their sores for money, but not so contemptible as the public that buys their books" (p. 99). But they remain a frequent type.

Desire for Order

There are people who are desirous of keeping their lives as tidy as their rooms. In an effort to do so, they record their daily experiences and keep meticulous records. Such may be grist for the mill of an autobiography. B. F. Skinner, the leading recent behavioral psychologist, completed three volumes of his autobiography (Skinner, 1976, 1979, 1983). The first volume, *Particulars of My Life,* was aptly named, for it is an incredibly specific compendium of the daily life and development of the author from his birth up to the age of 24. Skinner was able to recall details of such matters as how horse whips were made, how coal stoves were fired, how certain boyhood games were played. And he tells the reader all, absolutely without evaluation or interpretation. The book is not a diary; it is an autobiography, although an extreme case in its absence of self-aggrandizement, justification, or virtually any emotion. Even when recalling the death of his only sibling, a brother, Skinner reports that he was "far from unmoved." Skinner's goal, in keeping with his psychological theory, is description without subjective distortion. Reviewers have taken note of its unusual flavor; Paul Zimmerman (1976) wrote:

> Rarely has an autobiography seemed less motivated by self-justification or rancor, less clouded by sentiment or illusions of what might have been, more ruthlessly matter-of-fact about personal limitations. But Skinner's objectivity—a constant fix upon externals that is consistent with his general theory of conditional behavior—also deprives his narrative of a crucial emotional dimension. (p. 83; from NEWSWEEK, April 5, 1976. Copyright © 1976, Newsweek, Inc. All rights reserved. Reprinted by permission.)

Allport (1942), in describing this type of reason for writing an autobiography, concludes that it often leads to a product that "is dull and uneventful, but much of it, because of its very lack of dramatic accentuation, is true to life" (p. 71). Skinner's books reflect both aspects of this observation.

Literary Delight

Writing is an aesthetic art, at least to some of those proficient and experienced at it. For a writer of fiction, the challenge of writing about one's own life may be met through an expression of the writer's characteristic motivations. Allport (1942) notes, "The narrowly aesthetic motive can be traced in innumerable literacy biographies wherein personal experience is revealed in a delicate and pleasuring way. Symmetry, perfection of expression, artistic form, are obviously intended by the author" (p. 71).

But the aesthetic motive may extend beyond professional writers. Bette Midler's autobiography, titled *A View From a Broad* (1980), seems to be motivated by a combination of aesthetic and exhibitionistic needs; she writes, "I never know how much of what I say is true. If I did, I'd bore myself to death."

Securing a Personal Perspective

As Erikson has told us, a manifestation of the later years is a need to take stock of one's life. H. G. Wells gave this as the driving force for the writing of his *Experiment in Autobiography* (1934). Stern (1925), in his writings on life history, poses an interesting research hypothesis: That periods of change and transition are the periods when personal documents are more likely to be produced. Stern did not believe that an autobiography can be produced at any arbitrary point in a person's life; rather, the stress of change brings forth a desire for stock taking and planning new ways to respond.

For example, Mary Catherine Bateson (1989) wrote that her book "started from a disgruntled reflection of my own life as a sort of desperate improvisation in which I was constantly trying to make something coherent from conflicting elements to fit rapidly changing settings" (quoted by O'Reilly, 1989, p. 7).

Buckley (1984) sees autobiography as an attempt to establish a meaningful continuity—a connectedness of the self—and to establish or reaffirm one's identity by working through memories of past events (Swogger, 1984).

The ideal autobiography presents a retrospect of some length on the writer's life and character, in which the actual events matter far less than the truth and depth of his [or her] experience. It describes a voyage of self-discovery, a life-journey confused by frequent misdirections and even crises of identity but reaching at last a sense of perspective and integration. It traces through the alert awakened memory a continuity from early childhood to maturity or even to old age. It registers a commitment to the unity and mystery of the self or soul, both alone and among other human beings. And as a work of literature it achieves a satisfying wholeness. Yet it is never complete since the writer's life is necessarily still in process. (Buckley, 1984, pp. 39-40)

Certainly some autobiographies are generated by the desire to answer one's own question: "How do I know what I feel until I hear what I say?" And by taking Allport's label, "securing personal perspective," we can see the breadth of this motive. For example, Mandel (1980), commenting on Rousseau's *Confessions,* writes, "We see Rousseau, struggling to believe the very words he writes, but find them pulling him toward conflicting interpretations of his own past experiences. Rousseau's *Confessions* is a masterpiece of the genre because it allows these conflicting truths to manifest themselves, creating a complex unit" (p. 71).

Relief From Tension

Peter Davison (1992) observes, "Autobiography depends not only on the nature of the subject but also on the audience imagined for it, to which the editor must be sensitive indeed" (p. 93).

Sometimes autobiographies are written for others; sometimes, as the preceding Desire for Order and Securing a Personal Reflection reflect, for oneself. Perhaps the ultimate in this type is the autobiography written in order to gain relief from mental tension. Krueger (cited by Allport, 1942, p. 71) claims that catharsis is the underlying motivation when a person writes a confessional document. Certainly John Stuart Mill's autobiography reflects this goal; he shed tears, discovered new possibilities for himself, and emerged from a period of depression.

Redemption and Social Reincorporation

Following from the previous motivation, the autobiography may reflect a plea for forgiveness and social acceptance. Confession is, after all, a precondition for absolution or forgiveness. Alfred Kazin (1979) observes, "For the nonfiction writer, as I can testify, personal history is directly an effort to find salvation, to make one's own experience come out right" (p. 79). Kitty Dukakis (1990), in her autobiography, revealed for the first time her long-time addiction.

Many autobiographies by religious persons are not simply affirmations of faith, but dramatic accounts of a loss of faith and a period of suffering before spiritual rebirth occurs.

Many of the memoirs and autobiographies by President Nixon's associates who were involved in the Watergate burglary cover-up reflect this motivation, but none is more pervasive in its emphasis on redemption than Charles W. Colson's *Born Again* (1976). Colson, formerly Nixon's White House "hatchet man," became a born-again Christian in the midst of the Watergate investigations. He served a prison term and decided to devote the rest of his life to prison reform. *Born Again* may be read as an entirely credible account of a man who came to realize that he was experiencing a spiritual crisis (translation: nervous breakdown) while at the pinnacle of success, achievement, and influence.

Monetary Gain

Autobiographies have become popular reading material. "Instant celebrities," especially, are tempted to write their autobiographies, or assist someone else who "ghostwrites" it, in order to capitalize on their newfound fame. Although this is probably not the only motivation for the rash of "kiss-and-tell" autobiographies recently, it certainly contributes to their profusion. For example, General Norman Schwarzkopf signed a contract to write his memoirs for a reported $5,000,000 (Cohen, 1991), and Barbara Bush earned $889,000 in royalties from the sales of *Millie's Book*, a "celebrity autobiography" that she had ghostwritten for her dog (Carlson, 1992).

Certainly Harry Truman had a number of reasons to write his two volumes of memoirs after he left the presidency. But according to his biographer David McCullough (1992), a prominent reason was his need for money. Back in those days, ex-presidents received no pension; Truman had no assets, had to borrow money to pay for the move back to Missouri from Washington, D.C., and received only about $100 a month from his army pension.

Assignment

Allport (1942) notes that autobiographies are sometimes written as a requirement, either for a class in school or as a part of an application for admission to graduate school or a professional school.

Assisting in Therapy

Similar to the above type in its original instigation being outside the author is the example of an autobiography written by a patient or client in psychotherapy as a part of diagnosis or treatment.

Scientific Interest

Allport (1942) uses this category, "scientific interest," to refer to persons who "will frequently offer their diaries or their candid autobiographies to psychologists interested in problems of personality" (p. 73). Each is sure that his or her life experiences are unique, that he or she "has suffered what others have not suffered, that scientists may find his [or her] story novel and significant" (p. 73). Allport may be uncharacteristically condescending here; psychologists' understanding has benefited from the availability of such personal documents.

Allport does not mention a resource that has provided a valuable collection of brief autobiographies for scientific analysis. In the 1920s psychologist Carl Murchison began to compile the autobiographies of prominent psychologists. Eight volumes of these have now been published (Murchison, 1930, 1932, 1936; Boring, Langfeld, Werner, & Yerkes, 1952; Boring & Lindzey, 1967; Lindzey, 1974, 1980, 1989). The series contains autobiographies of 86 psychologists, mostly North American and mostly men. The autobiographies average about 25-30 pages in print (although Carl Seashore found it necessary to spend 75 pages on his!). Although the emphasis is on professional development and contributions, some of the accounts (especially those by Henry Murray, Sidney Pressey, and Karl Dallenbach) reveal intimate personal matters. Another psychologist, T. S. Krawiec (1972, 1974), has compiled 23 psychologists' autobiographies in two volumes. As with the Murchison-initiated series, the contributors here were selected on the basis of their distinguished achievements in the field of psychology. Between the two series, after removing duplications, there are autobiographies of 105 psychologists, written at the height of their career. Few of the psychologists in these volumes were women, but Benjamin (1980) has compiled a bibliography of approximately 100 sources of biographical and autobiographical material on women who have contributed significantly to psychology, and O'Connell and Russo (1993) collected reminiscences of eminent women in psychology. Another set of volumes collects the autobiographies (averaging about 20 pages in length) of 180 eminent scientists (Gibson, 1978; Lederberg, 1990; Luck, 1965).

Public Service and Example

Allport observes that there are autobiographies written for the express purpose of achieving a reform, or offering a model to help others through their difficulties. Clifford Beers (1928) wrote about his experiences as a mental patient in order to improve the lot of the insane. Likewise, Booker T. Washington wished to assist Black people, and Jane Addams the slum dweller.

Desire for Immortality

Allport's last motive is perhaps the most elusive and maybe the most general. Marie Bonaparte (1939), a psychoanalyst, wrote that personal documents were a part of humankind's "battle against oblivion" because "to be forgotten is to die a second and more complete death." But rarely do the authors of autobiographies express the desire for immortality as their motive.

Ways of Classifying Autobiographies

The rather extended classification of motives in the previous section is not the only way to subdivide autobiographies.

James Olney (1972), a professor of English, classifies writers of autobiographies into two types: Those whom he called "autobiographers of the single metaphor" (p. 39) include Charles Darwin, George Fox, and John Stuart Mill. In contrast, the autobiographers Carl Jung, T. S. Eliot, and Michel de Montaigne (author of *The Essays*), among others, are "autobiographers of the double metaphor." The essential distinction seems to be a certain kind of single-mindedness present in the single-metaphor group. Olney (1972) calls it a "daimon," or "a personal genius and guardian spirit, a dominant faculty or function or tendency that formed a part of his whole self and from which there was no escape, even had he wished it" (p. 39). As I try to translate this into psychological language, it seems to me that Olney is proposing that single-metaphor autobiographers fixate on an idea at a relatively early age and henceforth fail to grow. For example, Olney claims that George Fox's development ceased at about the age of 11. Olney bases this conclusion on the Quaker religion founder's *Journal* and other evidence from his life; Olney (1972) writes:

> Once the single light of the Lord had shown in and onto him, Fox was set for life, and though he performed many actions and provoked many reactions, these were all repetitions, more or less, of his first witness to the light; they were not done from any essentially new basis in personality. (pp. 40-41)

Likewise, Charles Darwin reached a clearly defined, self-labeled end point in development—what Olney says is a specific date beyond which there was no change, but only more of the same. This occurred well before the completion of his autobiography; there Darwin wrote:

> I have now mentioned all the books which I have published, and these have been the milestones in my life, so that little remains to be said. I am not conscious of any change in my mind during the last thirty years, excepting in one point presently to be mentioned (the curious and lamentable loss of the higher aesthetic tastes); nor indeed could any change have been expected unless one of general deterioration. (Darwin, 1958, p. 136)

The idea that some people "rigidify" in development at a relatively early age, even despite their influential contribution to society, is a provocative one, and clearly of relevance to various theories of adult development. It may have merit, but relying on only the autobiography (as opposed to further information from work products, letters, observations of contemporaries, and so on) as evidence for the distinction is not sufficient. Some autobiographers—perhaps including George Fox and Charles Darwin—can be too harsh on themselves.

The concept of rigidity emerges also in another distinction between two types of autobiography: Gunn (1982) contrasts efforts in which the autobiographer attempts to make everything explicit and comprehensible within some ideology, with those that recognize and allude to life experience but see it as still in the process of being discovered or elaborated. "Autobiography can exhibit a compulsion toward wholes in two ways: either by assuming . . . the self as an already complete entity which simply unfolds, acorn-to-oak fashion, in the autobiographical process; or by aiming towards an idealized selfhood, freed from the contingencies of historical time and space" (Gunn, 1982, p. 120).

Are Autobiographies Fact or Fiction?

That autobiographers are too harsh on themselves is seldom considered, but the general accuracy of autobiographies is a matter of great concern. Is an autobiography, "a biography of oneself," even possible? Dostoyevsky wrote in *Notes From the Underground* that:

> Every man has reminiscences which he would not tell to everyone, but only to his friends. He has other matters in his mind which he would not reveal even to his friends, but only to himself and that are secret. But there are other things which a man is afraid to tell even to himself, and every decent man has a number of such things stored away in his mind. . . . A true autobiography is almost an impossibility. . . . Man is bound to lie about himself. (quoted by Kazin, 1979, p. 74)

Literary critics struggle a great deal over the distinctions, if any, between autobiography and fiction. Mandel (1980) writes, "After all, as James Joyce knew so well, any human verbalizing is a process that by its very nature fictionalizes the experience. . . . [Both fiction and autobiography are] a pretense, a construction, an illusion" (p. 53). The reasons for this blurred line between autobiography and fiction are the focus of a book-length review of autobiographies by Timothy Adams (1990). For example, Sherwood Anderson wrote three works he labeled as autobiography; in these:

> one finds a dizzying confusion as to names, dates, and events: some-times his mother was of Italian origin, a bit more colorful than her real German background. And, what about the Anderson legend that one day he walked out of a factory he managed and gave him-self over to literature? Anderson admitted it was a legend. (Reefer, 1990, p. 14)

And if autobiography truly is so unrepresentative of reality, of what use is it in understanding human development in adulthood? As Adams (1990) notes, what we choose to misrepresent may be as telling as what actually happened.

Allport's (1942) classic monograph dealt with some of these troubling issues. He noted the following limitations of autobiographies in particular, and personal documents in general, as sources of data for psychological theorizing and research:

1. the unrepresentativeness of the sample
2. the writer's possible fascination with style rather than sincerity and fact
3. nonobjectivity

Allport (1942) notes here that "by definition personal documents are subjective data" (p. 126), and hence are not in keeping with the prevailing American scientific emphasis on objectivity. (Taking a long view over the past 100 years, one might say a dialectic has been present in psychological science, shifting from the subjectivity of introspection to the objectivity of laboratory manipulation but then a modest shift back toward the richness of personal experience.)
And finally:

4. deception

Box 8.2 reflects one view of the frequency of deception and self-deception. But many types of deception exist. One is blindness to one's own motives: "A person of fifty in writing of himself at nineteen may ascribe motives to his conduct that are, in reality, only appropriate to him at the time of the writing" (Allport, 1942, p. 133).

BOX 8.2

Can an Autobiographer Acknowledge Distortion Even if He or She Does Not Recognize It?

In a review of Patrick White's (1982) autobiography, *Flaws in the Glass: A Self-Portrait*, reviewer Humphrey Carpenter (1982) wrote:

Autobiography is probably the most respectable form of lying. No one expects the whole truth; in any case how could it be revealed, since the person we know least is likely to be ourself? The worst autobiographies are those that exploit it. This one, by Patrick White, the Nobel laureate, is in the second group. This title, "Flaws in the Glass," is a declaration at the onset that the mirror by means of which the self-portrait is drawn is at least a faulty device. In one of the many houses where the Whites lived during the author's childhood, there was a "Long Room" with at one end a "great gilded mirror, all blotches and dimples and ripples." A lesser writer might have labored this image again and again throughout the book; Mr. White allows the single use of it to suffice. (p. 9)

SOURCE: Carpenter, 1982, p. 9. Copyright © 1982 by The New York Times Company. Reprinted by permission.

Another is oversimplification. Allport (1942) observes that "in response to his [or her] drive for consistency the writer may soften the contradictions, join together the incompatible features of his [or her] life, and produce a shipshape structure in which all parts fit" (p. 134). As noted earlier, this tendency is more likely in an autobiography than in a diary or set of letters.

We may add another aspect—the general rule that autobiographical writing seems to be preoccupied with conflict and turmoil, whereas happy peaceful periods in the person's life are passed over in silence or with little comment.

Also, success seems less interesting and worthy of comment than failure. Critic Joseph Epstein (1981) wrote:

Certainly, the confession of imperfections makes for interesting reading: and it is undeniably true that autobiography generally becomes dull exactly at that point when the author arrives at success, where only acquaintance with the famous or a taste for vengeance through paying off old scores seems to enliven an autobiographical work. No, the trick in much modern autobiography is somehow to display oneself as a failure or a swine, but emerge at the end an attractive failure or charming swine. (p. 7; copyright © 1981 by Joseph Epstein. Reprinted by permission of Georges Borchardt, Inc. for the author.)

The above quotation meshes with my impression (not empirically verified) that the last halves of autobiographies are not as interesting as the first halves are; they are not on the cutting edge.

In keeping with this difference is the observation that autobiographies have a lot of trouble ending themselves, because the autobiographer is still alive when the final words are written (Davison, 1992).

A final type of self-deception is the betrayal of one's memory. At a party honoring Leonard Bernstein's 62nd birthday, the composer Aaron Copeland was telling listeners the problems in writing his autobiography. "I have no trouble remembering everything that happened 40 or 50 years ago—dates, places, faces, music. But I'm going to be 90 my next birthday, November 14, and I find I can't remember what happened yesterday or last month." Then one listener politely pointed out, "Mr. Copeland, you're going to be 80 this year" (quoted by Wallis, 1980, p. 57).

In a different kind of example, George Bush, during the 1988 presidential election campaign, published two campaign autobiographies (one written with Victor Gold and one written with Doug Wead) that contained divergent accounts of his experience when his torpedo bomber was shot down over the South Pacific on September 2, 1944, and he had to ditch the plane (Blumenthal, 1992). In one version one of the other crew members also parachuted out of the plane; in the other, neither of the other crew members were able to escape.

The Inevitability of "Distortion"

Allport was concerned with autobiographers' *implicit conceptualization,* or his term for what George Kelly would call the individual's construing of his or her world. Selection of materials requires implicit interpretation. The selection may take place on the basis of the writer's own conceptual or diagnostic biases. Although the autobiographer's use of an implicit conceptualization can be seen as a limitation, it validates George Kelly's claim that personal constructs are inevitable. Even before Kelly developed his theory, Allport recounted an experience that shows the dangers of forcing people into a conceptual framework foreign to their own:

> In one study the investigator secured fifty topical autobiographies, forcing all writers to tell about radicalism and conservatism in their lives. Having forced his cases into this mold, the investigator was tempted to "discover" that each case could be rated on the radical-conservative continuum according to his self-revealed nature; this suggested to him further that radicalism-conservatism constitutes one of those first-order variables of which all personalities are compounded. But the circularity of this reasoning became evident in time to save him. A closer reading of the fifty documents convinced him that in most lives the concept of radicalism-conservatism was wholly irrelevant. The lives were organized according to *other* principles, and the foci or centers of organization were different in each life. (Allport, 1942, pp. 137-138, italics in original)

Mandel (1980), a literary critic, observes, "In my experience most autobiographies are honest (that's the whole point of the genre) with occasional distortions, honest evasions, and discrete pockets of noncommunication. An honest autobiography puts its illusion of the past forward in good faith, not suspecting that it is but one angle of perception" (p. 66).

In truth, every source of information on adult development has its limitations. If it is the case that many autobiographers are self-deceptive, the task of writing about someone else's life has perils of its own. For example, it is exceedingly difficult for biographers to remain open-minded about their subjects. This point will be elaborated on in Chapter 9, one theme of which is that the process of writing about one's own life and that of writing about someone else's life are not as different as you might first assume.

And these are not the only psychological research methods free of limitations. Consider the methods used to develop the knowledge reported in the earlier chapters of this book. Interviews and questionnaires are subject to response biases such as acquiescence response set and the desire to look good. Clinical judgments are subjective and often are limited in their predictive accuracy. Laboratory experimentation may deal with responses far removed from the real world. No approach is valid, used alone.

Personal Documents
and Adult Personality Development

Within the decade of Allport's 1942 monograph, there had been a fertile development of the personal documents approach. Charlotte Buehler (1935), Else Frenkel-Brunswik (Frenkel, 1936; Frenkel-Brunswik, 1939), John Dollard (1935), Henry A. Murray (1938), Jerome Bruner (Allport, Bruner, & Jandorf, 1941), Alfred Baldwin (1940, 1942), and other prominent psychologists used diaries, life histories, and other autobiographical material to understand responses to catastrophe, mechanisms of self-deception, and changes over the life cycle, among other matters. After World War II, interest dwindled. There were exceptions, of course: Robert White's (1975) continuing interest in the growth of personality; the intensive case analyses of a small number of adult males by Smith, Bruner, and White (1956), done in an attempt to understand how opinions are developed and maintained; and the analysis of Theodore Drieser's writings by Seymour Rosenberg and Russell Jones (1972) in order to understand Drieser's implicit personality theory.

It has only been in the past decade or so that a resurgence of interest in these materials has occurred. In 1986 the Social Science Research Council, which sponsored Allport's 1942 monograph, announced its plans to appoint a committee on "personal testimony" (Crapanzano, Ergas, & Modell, 1986). The American Council of Learned Societies is cosponsoring this committee, reflecting the less formidable barriers between the social sciences and the humanities.

Chapter 3 of Allport's 1942 monograph listed and annotated 21 different purposes for the use of personal documents; these are listed in Box 8.3. Looking at these purposes through the filter of 50 intervening years, we can note several salient characteristics (Wrightsman, 1993):

(Text continued on page 168)

BOX 8.3

Allport's List of Purposes for Psychologists' Use of Personal Documents

---

1. Phenomenological investigations

   Definition: "interest in complex phenomenal states" (1942, p. 37).

   Example: Galton's accounts of the imagery of his correspondents.

2. The study of religious experience

   Example: Several investigators have analyzed diaries and autobiographies from the point of view of religious experience.

3. Study of psychological effects of unemployment

   Example: Zawadski and Lazarsfeld (1935) analyzed autobiographies of unemployed writers in Poland, leading to a grouping into four types.

4. Mental life of adolescents

   Rationale: G. Stanley Hall and others have argued that personal documents are the *best* means of studying adolescence because the "experiences peculiar to adolescence are inaccessible to adults whose later encounters with love and life have the effects of recasting totally the nascent and turbulent groping of adolescents in their struggle to come to terms with physical reality and social responsibility" (quoted by Allport, 1942, p. 39).

   Example: Norman Kiell, in 1964, collected a set of autobiographical materials prepared by adolescents in an effort to demonstrate that the internal and external agitations of the adolescent are present in every part of the world and hence only partly determined by culture.

5. Didactic uses

   Rationale: It has been claimed that practice in writing self-reports increases insight, powers of observation, and self-control in adolescents.

(Continued)

BOX 8.3 (Continued)

6. Practical use of experience records

    Rationale: Social progress may result from the analysis of vivid stories about one's personal experiences.

    Example: Clifford Beers's *A Mind That Found Itself* (1928).

7. Autoanalysis

    Purpose: Autobiographical outpourings that aim at catharsis may be useful as teaching devices, or as an aid in evolving a theory of personality.

    Example: W. E. Leonard's *Locomotive God* (1927).

8. Historical diagnoses

    Purpose: To shed light on the personalities of writers, artists, and other gifted people.

    Examples: Bragman's (1936) studies of Rossetti, Squires's (1937) study of Dostoyevsky.

9. Supplement to psychiatric examination

    Purposes: In addition to providing new leads for diagnosis, there may be a therapeutic value, "initiating and helping to guide the course of treatment" (Allport, 1942, p. 44).

10. The subject's verification and validation

    Purpose: A "rebuttal" by a subject to another's analysis of him or her.

    Example: John Dewey responded to his expositors and critics in a series titled *The Library of Living Philosophy* (1904).

11. Mental effects of special physical conditions

    Purpose: Autobiographical materials may help "to keep the influence of physical factors in perspective" (p. 45).

12. Light on creative processes and the nature of genius

    Purpose: to study creativity.

    Example: Willa Cather's (1927) account of her conception and writing of *Death Comes for the Archbishop*.

13. The psychologizing of the social sciences

Purpose: The application of "psychohistory" and "psychobiography" to historical or cultural phenomena. (These terms were generated later than Allport's 1942 monograph.)

14. The psychologizing of literature

Purpose: The probing of motivation by literary critics and biographers.

Example: Robert Sears's (1979) comparison of Mark Twain's letters and his novels to identify periods of depression in his life.

15. Illustration

Purpose: "Perhaps the commonest use of documents is to provide illustrative material for authors who wish to exemplify some generalization already in mind" (Allport, 1942, p. 48).

16. Induction

Purpose: To derive general principles for raw material, or particulars.

Example: Charlotte Buehler's *Lebenspsychologie* (1935), based on 200 life stories.

17. Occupational and other types

Purpose: The derivation of types, or clustering cases according to similarities.

Example: Donley and Winter's (1970) scoring of U.S. presidential inaugural addresses in order to classify them on strength of achievement, affiliative, and power motives.

18. Interpersonal relations

Purpose: "The possibility of using exchanges of letters between two persons as a means of studying the dyadic relations of friendship, of marriage, of the parent-child bond seems almost overlooked by social psychologists" (Allport, 1942, p. 50).

(Continued)

BOX 8.3 (Continued)

---

19. First step in the construction of tests and questionnaires

    Purpose: To provide insights for generating items in standardized tests and questionnaires.

20. Reinforcement and supplementation

    Purpose: "Often the personal document merely falls into place as one of several methods in a battery. It serves no other purpose than adding credibility to the total picture developed through interviews, tests, ratings, institutional reports, or other methods" (p. 51).

    Example: Thomas and Znaniecki's (1918) study of Polish peasants.

21. Methodological objectives

    Purpose: Social scientists may use personal documents "simply in order to find out how they may be used to the best advantage" (p. 51). There is an allusion here to theory development; focus is not so much on the individual or on general laws of behavior, as it is on "the *process* by which the significance of behavior becomes known and evaluated" (p. 51).

    Example: Allport's derivation of an empirical-intuitive theory or understanding from the reactions of students in reading Leonard's *Locomotive God* (1927).

---

1. The list reflects a surprising hodgepodge of purposes, a cataloging that lacks an overarching organization.

2. Some of the uses have become routine ones; for example, analyzing collections of letters in order to understand the personality of the letter writer, or asking a psychiatric patient to prepare a brief autobiography.

3. In contrast, other purposes identified by Allport have been largely ignored; for example, Number 19, as a source for generating questionnaire items, has not often been utilized.

4. Some of the purposes lead to creative ideas reflecting innovative applications of personal documents. Number 18 mentions exchanges

of letters; the use of advertisements in a lonely hearts column of a newspaper has more recently been used by social psychologists to study self-presentation and social needs. In one such study, Harrison and Saeed (1977) content analyzed more than 800 such advertisements, concentrating on differences in the ads placed by men and women. Women were more likely to describe themselves on the basis of their physical attractiveness, while men were more likely to specify this quality as something they wanted. Men more often mentioned financial security as one of their attributes; women were more likely to seek it. Deaux and Hanna (1984) used a similar set of documents and analyzed the content of advertisements placed by homosexual and heterosexual men and women, concluding that both the advertiser's gender and his or her sexual preference were related to both self-identified attributes and needs in a comparison.

5. The list of purposes in Box 8.2 reflects a surprising lack of emphasis on theory testing. In contrast, I would expect that contemporary psychologists, if asked about the value of personal documents, would list as their premier value their clarification of theory. For example, Swede and Tetlock (1986) observe that controversy surrounds many aspects of the construct of *implicit personality theory*. How many basic dimensions underlie an individual's trait perceptions? Is it appropriate to divide implicit theories into separate dimensions? Not only does disagreement exist over the answers to these questions, but also theories and models that provide a good fit with regard to group data may not be supported by data from separate individuals (Kim & Rosenberg, 1980). Swede and Tetlock (1986) point to the idiographic analyses of individual respondents as a way of producing inductive generalizations on this topic.

6. Allport was primarily concerned with the reliability of personal documents and deception, whether conscious or unconscious. More recently, a shift has been toward the *process* involved; for example, what were the determinants of the process of writing the personal document or narrating an event? Also, what are the perceptual and interpretive processes of the social scientist who analyzes and interprets the documents ("The Uses of Personal Testimony," 1981)? Allport was concerned that oversimplification and arbitrary conceptualizations could limit the value of personal documents. Now, however, there is:

an acceptance . . . that these filtering processes are an inherent and meaningful part of any communication about the world. A scientist or humanist should not seek to eliminate the filters but rather be conscious of them and account for them as a part of the research or creative process. ("The Uses of Personal Testimony," 1981, p. 21)

At the same time, other issues about the use of personal documents have surfaced (Cohler, 1993). These include the extent to which we can generalize from a particular life or lives to a larger group (Runyan, 1982, 1988; Stewart, Franz, & Layton, 1988) and what unit to use in analyzing personal documents (Cohler, 1993)— issues reflecting the idiographic-nomothetic distinction from Chapter 1.

In keeping with a recurring theme in this book, psychologists and scholars are beginning to examine the differences in the auto-biographies of women and men. Jill Ker Conway (1992), a scholar of women's history, concludes that men's memoirs portray them as active agents who shape the world and overcome obstacles, whereas women—until recently—portray themselves as having lives shaped more by fate and destiny, even though these women, in actuality, have planned their lives just like the men (Manning, 1993). Psychologist Mary M. Gergen (1992a) has analyzed the similarities and differences between the autobiographies of men and women, and recently has focused on *embodiment*, or how the body is invested with meaning in the recent memoirs of men and women (Gergen, 1992b; Gergen & Gergen, 1993). She writes:

[In their autobiographies] . . . men have very little to say about their physical beings, except to note how effective their bodies were in attaining their goals. . . . [M]en display little emotion when making these descriptions. The body is virtually an absent figure in their reminiscences. Women's stories tend to be far more embodied. Beginning with the early years, women include greater detail in the descriptions of the body, and they are often emotional in describing their embodied lives. (Gergen, 1992b, p. 5)

Box 8.4 summarizes some contemporary types of studies that use personal documents.

BOX 8.4

**Contemporary Types of
Studies Using Personal Documents**

---

1. Rosenberg and Jones (1972): The implicit personality theory of
   Theodore Dreiser

   In a study whose methodology has served as a guide for subsequent
   work, Seymour Rosenberg and Russell Jones applied content analysis and factor analysis to determine the implicit personality theory
   of one person: Theodore Dreiser, the author of *Sister Carrie* and
   An American Tragedy. Dreiser was chosen because his book, *A
   Gallery of Women*, published in 1929, contained detailed character descriptions. The book consists of 15 different stories, each a
   portrayal of a different woman known by Dreiser. Thus each
   person is described in 20 to 50 continuous pages, and a variety of
   people are so described. By listing each character mentioned in
   any of these stories and each trait ascribed to him or her, Rosenberg and Jones identified 241 characters and 6,761 descriptive
   units from the book.
       Statistical analysis sought to determine what traits clustered
   together. (It is trite but true to observe that these analyses could
   not have been completed when Allport's 1942 monograph was
   published.) Results indicated that traits associated with women
   were quite different from those associated with men. Furthermore,
   the dimension of conformity versus nonconformity emerged as
   an important construct in Dreiser's descriptions of people, but
   conformity was not associated only with the female sex, as the
   usual stereotype would have predicted.
       The detailed, quantitative analysis of literacy and other written
   materials has been used in some of Rosenberg's more recent work
   and served as a model for Swede and Tetlock's (1986) recent
   analysis of Henry Kissinger's implicit personality theory.

2. DeWaele and Harre (1979): Assisted autobiography as a psychological method

   In a very useful, original, and detailed book chapter, DeWaele and
   Harre (1979) described procedures for the creation of an "assisted

---

(Continued)

BOX 8.4 (Continued)

---

autobiography," which is "really a continuous process of negotiated autobiographical reconstruction" (p. 193). Then they provide a means for analysis of the contents of the autobiography. The chapter includes a 15-page appendix that serves as a checklist of various aspects of the content of the life story. Although the chapter is not relevant to advances in statistical analysis, it provides a "fresh look" at methodology in the broad sense and reflects a humanistic perspective that assumes that research is a negotiated cooperative interaction between the investigator and the research subject.

3. Tetlock (1981): A comparison of preelection and postelection statements by 20th century U.S. presidents

Philip Tetlock coded public statements and addresses by presidents from McKinley through Carter for integrative complexity. Statements made prior to election were compared with statements made in the first month, the second year, and the third year in office. In addition to repeated measures of variance, Tetlock used (more conservative) quasi-F-ratios to evaluate the data, by considering some effects (time period and paragraph sampling unit) as random, not fixed, effects. Results indicated that except for Herbert Hoover, presidential policy statements became more complex after assuming office.

Similarly, Suedfeld and Rank (1976) demonstrated that the long-term success of revolutionary leaders was related to the cognitive

---

Several of these purposes are relevant to adult personality development. Volume 1, Chapter 7 described how the analyses of autobiographies of psychologists could be used to understand the prevalence of the mentoring process. As mentioned earlier, Chapter 8 of Volume 1 illustrated the use of *Letters From Jenny* (Allport, 1965) to illustrate dialectical changes in major issues during adulthood. Chapter 5 of Volume 1 reported on Robert Sears's (1979) ingenious use of several types of personal documents in order to demonstrate how Mark Twain's experiences affected both his personal documents and his fictional writing.

complexity of their public statements. Equally important is the content analysis of speeches and interviews of Soviet Politburo members, to aid in understanding their personal characteristics, done by Margaret Hermann (1980). She has also applied this content analysis to President Reagan's public statements.

4. Berman (1985): Analysis of the diary of an older person

Harry J. Berman of Sangamon State University, Springfield, Illinois, is developing a methodology for examining the diaries and journals of older people in order to understand how they deal with the events of late adulthood. The analysis is driven by concepts from psychoanalytic theory and Daniel Levinson's stage theory of adult development (1978). This is a useful approach in the sense that the experiences of older people are distinct from those of younger ages.

5. A. J. Stewart and Healy (1985): The study of adaptation to stress and life change

The explosion of interest in adult psychological development that we have witnessed in the past decade has driven renewed interest to the study of autobiographies. Daniel Levinson and his colleagues (Levinson, Darrow, Klein, Levinson, & McKee, 1977) elicited autobiographies from their subjects as part of their investigation of stages in men's development. Abigail Stewart and Joseph Healy have analyzed autobiographies in identifying reactions to stressful events and adaptation to life changes.

As we search for an understanding of the process of personality development during our adult lives, we should not ignore these materials, as they not only provide illustrations of how other people have changed, but they urge us to explore our own lives.

9

The Idiographic Approach
to Personality Development

*It must always be foul to tell what is false and it can never
be safe to suppress what is true.*

Robert Louis Stevenson

Chapter 1 made the distinction between the nomothetic and idiographic approaches to the study of personality, and Chapter 8
examined the use of personal documents in the study of the single
case. The purpose of this chapter is to examine other methods by
which we understand an individual's personality, including oral
histories, biographies, and case studies.

Sources of Information
About an Individual Life

When we concentrate our study on the single case, we have a
variety of sources from which to choose. We can arrange these on
a continuum from self-generated materials (i.e., chosen by the sub-

ject being studied) to those chosen and initiated by the investigator. For example, diaries, letters, and memoirs, the topic of Chapter 8, reflect sources of information generated by the subject under study, generally created without any generalizable constraints.

Oral histories and "as told to" autobiographies fall closer to the middle of the continuum. Certainly the mass of raw information comes from the subject under study, but the interviewer/researcher does determine, at least to some degree, what questions are asked, thus reducing the hazards of presenting inaccurate or uncritical information.

At the same time, recent "autobiographies" of, for example, popular athletes or movies stars permit the coauthor great latitude. The subjects tell their tales into a tape recorder and then excuse themselves (Weisman, 1992). What appears may or may not be what the subject intended–or remembered. NBA basketball star Charles Barkley was so upset by passages in his own autobiography, when they were excerpted in a local newspaper, that he tried to block the publication of his own book, claiming he had been "misquoted" by his coauthor or ghostwriter.

Slightly removed from the oral history and "as told to" autobiography is the authorized biography. The biographer is responsible for the organization and shaping of the finished product, but the subject severely controls what materials are available for the biographer to use. Usually the subject, or representatives of the subject's best interests, have veto power over what appears in print.

At the end of the continuum are the unauthorized biography, the investigative biography, and the case study. Here the biographer/investigator determines what materials are to be used, as well as the content of the finished work.

"Unauthorized biography" covers a wide spectrum; most biographies, in actuality, are unauthorized in the sense that the subject or members of the subject's family do not actively cooperate in the endeavor. Of a different nature from the majority of biographers– which aspire, at least, to be objective–are those unauthorized biographies that pride themselves on the adversarial nature of the relationship between author and subject.

The investigative biography is a special category (Weinberg, 1992). Many of the authors of these books–in contrast to academic historians–were trained as journalists, and they are willing to take on powerful living subjects such as Henry Kissinger, Fidel Castro, Hugh Hefner, and Nancy Reagan. Investigative biography requires an aggressiveness and even rudeness, when dealing with their subjects, that academic historians lack. In his review of two recent biographies of Lyndon Johnson, Nicholas Lemann commented that someone with journalist Robert Caro's background:

> can now attempt a magisterial multivolume political biography of Johnson that concedes no ground to professional historians. . . . There is a substantial difference in feel between [Professor Robert] Dallek's Johnson and Mr. Caro's, but it springs from the way in which the two authors handle their material, not from a great disparity in the basic information they have at their disposal. (quoted in Weinberg, 1992, pp. 2-3)

In subsequent sections we examine some of the implications of these different methods for the understanding of personality development in adulthood. Each has something to provide in our quest for a full picture.

The Oral History

Each society has its set of oral documents preserved through memory and passed down from generation to generation. Perhaps the best-known account based on an oral tradition is Alex Haley's *Roots* (Peterson, 1988). Although some historians have doubted the accuracy of Haley's work, part of *Roots* derived from sources of oral tradition that were later verified in written documents; for example, the name of Haley's great-great-great-great-grandfather and that of his slaveholder were taught to Haley, when he was a child, by his grandmother (Hoopes, 1979).

Sometimes oral history is our main source of information about individuals; for example, even though some Blacks were literate during the period of slavery in the United States, much of our information comes from first-person oral accounts, or slave narratives (Gates, 1987). Another approach is to use folktales as a way of re-creating the physical and emotional texture of slave life; an example is Charles Joyner's *Down by the Riverside* (1984).

Oral-history interviewing is of particular value with older persons, producing a life-review that aids in achieving resolution of Erikson's last stage. In rare cases (see Blauner, 1989) oral histories have been used in longitudinal studies; Blauner collected reminiscences from 50 Afro-Americans in the 1960s and reinterviewed them twice, 10 and 20 years later, demonstrating a turning inward by Black Americans over the past 15 years.

Defining Oral History

In a classic book on the topic, historian Jan Vansina (1965) defines the oral tradition as "a chain of testimonies" (p. 19). The use of a legal simile is revealing, because in those societies without written documents, storytellers had the responsibility to remember and recount experiences accurately. Obviously, oral history is not a new kind of history, but it does serve as a new type of source of knowledge about persons' lives (Seldon & Pappworth, 1983). It offers unique advantages, some of which are listed in Box 9.1.

Our contemporary society is not an illiterate one, but the ease of the telephone and electronic mail have led to a decrease in the use of diaries, intimate letters, and private correspondence (Peterson, 1988), or in general, what Allan Nevins (1966) called "methodical, reflective writing" (p. 78). Historians have thus developed oral history as a methodology in order to obtain a more thorough record of participation in contemporary political, economic, and cultural life (Seldon & Pappworth, 1983).

Problems and Limitations

Despite its great need and value, oral history as a methodology is not without its problems and controversies. I have relied on Peterson's (1988) comprehensive review to summarize some of these; *By Word of Mouth,* by Seldon and Pappworth (1983) contains extensive practical advice for the resolution of these challenges.

The Role of the Interviewer

Who controls the interview? Some historians argue that once the interview starts, it is essential for the interviewer to take charge

---

BOX 9.1

Advantages of Oral History

---

1. Facts not recorded in documents

   A. Events
   B. Personalities
   C. Personal and organizational relationships

2. Interpretations of personalities and events

   A. Relationship and personal roles
   B. Relative significance of different issues

3. Interpretation of documents

   A. Overall grasp of documents
   B. Clarification of factual confusions
   C. Gaps in documentation

SOURCE: Adapted from Seldon & Pappworth, 1983.

---

and remain in control of the interview. This "hard-line approach" to interviewing includes asking tough questions, probing for responses, and not avoiding "bombshells" such as "Why didn't you destroy the tapes, Mr. Nixon?" From this perspective, an accurate representation of the person under study is achieved only if provocative questions delve into sensitive areas (Hoopes, 1979; Metzler, 1977).

Others let the subject determine the tone and tempo. Sherna Gluck (1980) asserts that by allowing the process to unfold according to the subject's rhythm, the interviewer obtains a validation of the resulting oral-history document.

This latter approach reflects more of a collaboration than an adversarial relationship; it is reflected in various views—that the interviewer should have "gemütlichkeit" (Nevins, 1966, p. 33) or "rapport" (Cutler, 1970, p. 82). The assumption is that a "warm and friendly atmosphere conducive to frank conversation" (Cutler, 1970, p. 82) will discourage dishonesty or reticence.

Yet it should be recognized that the collaboration reflects the purchase of a friendship. Janet Malcolm (1990), a journalist and interviewer, has written about the artificial relationship reporters establish with their sources or subjects, what she refers to as a manipulative relationship done in order to get sources to disclose information.

Procedures in Collecting an Oral History

Historians generally agree that before an interview takes place, the interviewer should conduct a significant amount of background research (Peterson, 1988). Being well informed about the person to be interviewed will assist the investigator in identifying responses that are too simplistic or misleading, and possibly will cultivate a rapport that could generate unexpected insights (Hoopes, 1979).

The results of collecting an oral history are quite susceptible to the way its questions are phrased and posed (Seldon & Pappworth, 1983), so interviewers should be aware of their personal biases and try to prevent these from intruding into the process either through spoken language or body language. If, for example, an interviewer raises an eyebrow in response to something said, this gesture could be interpreted by the respondent as disapproval, thus discouraging the subject from disclosing further information (Peterson, 1988).

Procedures. The person interviewed—variously called the interviewee, respondent, subject, or oral author—should be provided an oral history release form, for he or she has the option of placing any restrictions on the use of the material. Generally, the restrictions have to do with confidentiality, and the interviewee may want to specify a period of time, or other restrictions, before the material can be disseminated.

Oral histories with certain types of people require special sensitivity. The past decade has seen a heightened interest in the Holocaust, and this has led to a greater effort to collect reminiscences from Holocaust survivors (Wyman, 1991). A book by Lawrence L. Langer (1991) relies on interviews with 300 survivors; it reminds us of problems from the perspective of the interviewee: Many of these Holocaust victims are certain that those who did not go through these terrible experiences cannot understand or even *believe* them.

A procedural issue deals with the method of recording information. Although a small minority of oral historians prefer to take notes, the overwhelming majority of interviews are conducted with a tape recorder (Peterson, 1988). (Many interviewers take notes while also recording.) Many advantages accrue: The respondent's voice tone and style are captured, and the distracting nature of excessive note taking is avoided. Perhaps most important is that it provides a record of the content of the interview in order to substantiate the conclusions drawn (Moss, 1985).

For example, Studs Terkel (1970, 1974, 1980, 1984, 1988), universally recognized for his unpretentious, bemused interviewing skills in eliciting oral histories from everyday (what he calls "noncelebrated") people, has been criticized for his failure to provide evidence via recordings (Peterson, 1988).

The major concern about the use of tape recording an oral history has been that the awareness of the recorder might inhibit the respondent, but in recent years that concern has been reduced.

Ethical Issues

The interviewer has multiple motives and responsibilities in collecting an oral history. These may cause ethical dilemmas. For example, what if the subject becomes quite indiscreet and reveals embarrassing information? Does the interviewer stop and suggest prudence, even while knowing that the salacious disclosures will make the interviewee's material more publishable, more popular, or more profitable?

Furthermore, does the respondent have a right to review the edited version of the oral history? Clearly, ethical issues that require high degrees of sensitivity abound (Winkler, 1980).

Biographies

Biographies serve as the most popular way to depict the lives and personalities of individuals; they stimulate our imagination and add richness to our perspective on our own lives. Pachter (1979) sees the nature of the biographer as "the near-missionary drive to save, if not a soul then a personality for the company of future generations" (p. 4).

Biographies—if far-sighted—can ask questions about their subjects that those subjects seldom ask themselves. Doris Kearns (1979), the biographer of Lyndon Johnson, afterward stated, "The real question, the one I wished I had asked him from the start—was whether the effort required to reach the top so distorts most personalities that they lose those human qualities that are necessary to a proportionate exercise of power" (p. 94).

Of course, most biographers do not seek to make explicit the personality development of their subject, but personality is so central to a person's life and character that it can be readily discerned from most biographies.

Yet, as a genre, biography has been, until recently, accorded inferior status as a field of study. "Biography is going through one of its bouts of being boosted as a serious activity," writes Robert Skidelsky (1988, p. 1), "yet there's something inescapably second-rate that seems to cling to biography and its practitioners: 'gossip-writers and voyeurs calling themselves scholars' was how W. H. Auden described them." George Eliot—who was the subject of 26 different biographies—concluded that biographers are "generally the disease of English literature" (quoted by Holroyd, 1988, p. 100).

The scholarly analysis of biographies has been detailed and provocative, although most of it has been generated by the perspective of literary studies and not psychology. Although still an infrequent development, the contributions from the field of psychology are noteworthy. Book-length contributions by Erik Erikson on Luther and on Gandhi and Freud's analysis of Leonardo da Vinci were the subject of Volume 1, Chapter 5. Other psychologically based analyses include Henry Murray's (1967) exploration of the life of Herman

Melville, David McClelland's (1964) interpretation of the French writer André Gide, and Rae Carlson's (1988) demonstration of the application of life analyses of Nathaniel Hawthorne and Eleanor Marx to theory development. But as Elms (1988) notes, most personality psychologists have not seen themselves as biographers, and only the past decade or two has witnessed a growing acceptance of the biographical approach by psychologists (McAdams, 1990).

History of Biography

The origin of biography came much earlier than that of autobiography (see Chapter 8). The earliest biographers, such as the Greek Plutarch and the Roman Suetonious, chose as their subjects model human beings, those individuals superior by reason of character or position (Whittemore, 1988). Plutarch's (1935) *Lives* of Greek and Roman nobles, written around A.D. 100, established a tradition in which the accounts of the private self were subordinated to the emphasis on public acts and achievements. Plutarch "was not disposed to be objective [about his subjects], or to plumb the depths of that mysterious entity, character" (Whittemore, 1988, p. 11).

With James Boswell's biography of Samuel Johnson (1791/1953), the focus of biography shifted to what the subject, Johnson, called "the minute details of private life." No longer was selectivity a virtue; as the biographer of biographers Reed Whittemore (1988) notes, 17th century biographers set out to write whole lives, not pure ones. In contrast (in his opinion), in current times:

> No other literary form has been so plagued by the obligation to include. . . . Monster biographies keep appearing that their authors do not even think of as reading matter. They are reference books, and if *everything* about their unlucky subjects is not in the pages *somewhere*–and discoverable via the index–then woe. (p. 10, italics in original)

Just one example: In answer to the question what was new in his biography of F. Scott Fitzgerald, the third since 1954 in English, Matthew J. Bruccoli (1988) replied, "More facts" (quoted by Nadel, 1984, p. 210). Meyers (1985), in similar fashion, is critical of such biographies as Carlos Baker's *Ernest Hemingway: A Life Story*

(1969) and Bernard Crick's *George Orwell, a Life* (1981) as encyclopedic accumulations of facts that "fail to present a convincing and meaningful pattern in the author's life" (Meyers, 1985, p. 2).

In the development of the genre, Thomas Carlyle's biography of Frederick the Great (1858-1865) broke new ground by tracing the roots of the ruler's character to his childhood trauma, thus presaging contemporary efforts to link early experiences to later behavior. About the same time, Freud's analysis of Leonardo da Vinci was the first overt psychobiography.

Despite these products of that period, Victorian-period biography focused mostly on those subjects deserving of praise because of their public benefactions. "Their lives were written as models for emulation by prize-winning school children; their characters and private affections were displayed as moral tales to emphasize the connection between virtue and achievement" (Skidelsky, 1988, p. 2). When a person of great achievement (e.g., Lord Nelson's triumph over the Spanish) also possessed a glaring moral discrepancy (his love affair with Lady Hamilton), it was simply concealed in Victorian-period biographies.

But Lytton Strachey is given credit for initiating the "warts-and-all" approach to biography (Weinberg, 1992); his stated goal was "to lay bare the facts of the case as he [sic] understands them" (quoted by Pachter, 1979, p. 13). The purpose of his monumental *Eminent Victorians* (1918/1933) was to expose major figures as humbugs or prisoners of false values (Skidelsky, 1988). (*Eminent Victorians* included biographies of Florence Nightingale, General "Chinese" Gordon, Cardinal Manning, and Dr. Thomas Arnold.)

About this time—around World War I—biographers began to pay more attention to motives. Victorian biographers, obsessed with moral character, had been relatively incurious about motives (Skidelsky, 1988). The psychoanalytic movement changed all that. The shift toward interpretations gave less emphasis to "facts" per se; recent biographers followed Pirandello's definition: "A fact is like a sock which won't stand up when it's empty. In order that it may stand up, one has to put into it the reason and feeling which have caused it to exist" (quoted by Nadel, 1984, p. 10).

Marc Pachter (1979) expresses the modern view: "A life taken only at its own crafted word is imperfectly and even unjustly rendered. Fine biography challenges the pose to find the personality"

BOX 9.2

Giving Salience to the Individual

When we consider attributions of cause, both biographies and autobiographies share the possible fault of giving the individual subject too much credit for outcomes. The expert on biography A. O. J. Cockshut (1974) wonders if the subjects of 19th century biographies were as strongly willed as they are in their biographies.

The following quotation concentrates on biography, but the same critique could be made of autobiography:

> The essence of conventional biography is that one takes an individual out of the mass and sets him in a spotlight, fixes him in the arc of light behind the boat. The spotlight effect—the total concentration on one person that biography exacts—throws all the peripheral characters into shadow. These secondary characters may be more significant in historical terms, but they can only be partially accounted for, in so far as they impinge on the subject's life. The result is distortion. . . . It is false in the first place to take any one person as central in any scheme of things. (Glendinning, 1988, p. 60)

(p. 10). Despite the fact that modern biographies run the gamut from the exhaustive to the fragmentary, the scrupulously honest to the libelously scandalous, some agreement has emerged over the tasks of the biographer: to convey information and detail, to generate a mood or atmosphere, and to establish a sense of character and personality of the subject (Nadel, 1984). Box 9.2 provides an elaborated perspective.

The Ideal Biography

Given that the development of the field of biography has been a long but uncertain one, and given that a dazzling variety of biographies still confront us, what should be the criteria for a desirable biography?

Marc Pachter (1979) proposes that at the heart of a great biography is selectivity: "The eye of the fine biographer, like that of the portrait painter, sculptor, or photographer, catches the special gleam of character" (p. 3). Others specify this task: "The governing principle of selection is that it must honestly illustrate and never distort" (Tuchman, 1979, p. 145).

William Zinsser (1986) argues that "a biographer must have the insouciance of a psychiatrist or priest—a talent for being unruffled by quirky behavior—and the patience of a detective" (p. 10). Barbara Tuchman (1979), the noted historian, proposes that those biographies that stand the test of time "are mostly written by friends, relatives, or colleagues of the subject" (p. 141).

It is acknowledged that such biographers have a unique intimacy with their subjects—though perhaps not an objectivity—but personal relationship as a criterion excludes the possibility of writing an exceptional biography of someone afar. Are there not other possibilities, and other criteria?

Ann Thwaite (1988), a contemporary biographer, notes some straightforward characteristics: a need for curiosity, an ability to tell a story, a need to understand another person's life. Biographers need to see their subjects *in context;* "the biographer will, of course, look at the subject's life with late 20th century eyes; yet it is also essential for the biographer to see . . . how the life was as it was lived" (Thwaite, 1988, p. 32).

Leon Edel (1979) extends this imperative: The biographer's responsibility "entails the ability to interpret . . . facts in the light of all that the biographer has learned about his subject" (p. 18). And Robert Blake adds: "In reality the facts do not speak for themselves. A biographer who tries to avoid interpreting them is abdicating from his central task. . . . What is sure to kill a biography is to make no interpretation at all" (1988, p. 76).

Meyers (1985), writing about literary biographers, provides a set of goals that are applicable more generally:

> The . . . biographer must utilize original research that casts new light on the subject; have a thorough mastery of the material; give a complete and accurate synthesis of all the facts about the private as well as the public life: friendships, conversation, dress, habits, tastes, food, money. He should make a selection—not merely a collection—of significant and convincing details and possess a lively and narrative style. He should form a sympathetic identification with the subject, and

present a perceptive interpretation of character. He must create a dramatic structure that focuses the pattern of crises in the life, and effectively portray the social and political background. He ought to provide a sensitive evaluation of the subject's achievement—which is the justification of the book. (p. 3)

Perhaps the most succinct summary is critic Desmond MacCarthy's admonition that "a biographer is an artist under oath" (quoted by Glendinning, 1988, p. 54).

The Relationship of Biography to Autobiography

Meyers's list of criteria presents a challenging task to the aspiring biographer, who first must learn all the details about *another* person's life, and then fashion them together in the form aspired to in the above paragraph.

How different the biographer's task seems, at first, from that of those of us who decide to write about *our own* lives. As mentioned in Chapter 8, anyone can write an autobiography; no rules exist as to form or content; and, in a sense, every autobiography is a document of inherent value because it is an expression of how a person views his or her own life.

But on some important dimensions, I will argue that biographies and autobiographies are not that different. With respect to four characteristics, the two methods can be compared, and in some particular examples, a given biography may not differ from a given autobiography. The four dimensions are:

1. The motives for writing it.
2. The theme of the book.
3. Attributes of cause for events in the life.
4. The relationship of the writer to the subject.

Each is described in subsequent paragraphs.

The Motives for Writing a Biography or Autobiography

Chapter 8 listed a multitude of reasons for writing the story of one's own life, including understanding, redemption, self-actualization, and financial gain. Certainly a number of motives exist for writing about *another's* life; the question is: To what degree do they overlap with the autobiographer's motives?

To a remarkable degree, they are similar. The autobiographer is ego-involved in his or her own life, obviously. But consider the commitment that biographers make to their subjects. For instance, Robert Caro, in order to do his multiple-volume biography of Lyndon Johnson, moved with his wife to a house on the edge of the Hill Country in Texas and lived there for parts of 3 years (Zinsser, 1986).

Seemingly, the unique quality of any autobiography is, to coin a phrase, its own uniqueness. No one else but you can write an *autobiography* of your life. But for some biographers, an equivalent need to be unique exists. Biographer Ann Thwaite (1988) writes, "I have no interest in writing the life of someone, even someone I am extremely interested in, where a recent biography already exists" (p. 22). Although biographers are out there who choose as their subjects persons who have been written about before, even these biographers seek a unique key to understanding the subject; thus individuality is a motive that is common to both methods.

Geoffrey Wolff (1979) notes that with regard to both autobiography and biography as genres critics have distinguished between the Romantic and Augustan conventions. The Augustan is "exemplary"; it is archival, even "archeological"; it perpetuates and memorializes. The approach is reflected in books—whether biographies or autobiographies—that seek to make a record of one's life.

In contrast, Wolff (1979) writes, the Romantic approach—whether biography or autobiography—"celebrates the member rather than the species, investigates the particular case" (p. 64). Biographies of this type are "fundamentally autobiographical"—perhaps an exaggeration, and probably some biographers immerse themselves in other people's lives as "a way of obliquely investigating their own" (Glendinning, 1988, p. 54). Yet can we deny Wolff's fundamental point that without the style of the biographer the work becomes artless and servile? For example, books like Richard Holmes's *Footsteps* (1985) show how the interaction between a biographer and his or her subject "can be exploited successfully, becoming indeed the true topic of the book" (Glendinning, 1988, p. 51).

In addition, the writer—whether recounting his or her own life or someone else's—must come to terms with the role of facts (Nadel,

1984). Both an autobiography and a biography are complex narratives as well as a record of an individual's life, "a literary process as
well as a historical product" (Nadel, 1984, p. 1). A biographer does
not have control over the facts but is allowed to imagine their form
(Edel, 1979).

We recognize how a biographer may be motivated to play fast and
loose with the facts, but so too may an autobiographer. Leon Edel
(1979) notes how Henry David Thoreau in *Walden Pond* presented,
in actuality, a rationalization of his actions in getting away from the
slavery of civilization. He writes:

> Thoreau's hut, we learn, did not stand in great loneliness; he did not
> plant it in a wilderness. He planted it on Emerson's land on the shores
> of Walden with Emerson's consent. This made it easy for him to
> criticize those who had to pay rent or mortgages. The railway lay
> within easy distance. His mother's house was one mile down the road
> and, said the Boston hostess, Annie Fields, in her diary, David Thoreau
> was a *very* good son, "even when living in his retirement at Walden
> Pond, he would come home every day." Others have told us that he
> raided the family cookie jar while describing how he subsisted on the
> beans he grew in his field. (p. 28)

Both types of writers must confront the facts and inevitably give an
interpretation to them.

The Theme of the Book

With very few exceptions, autobiographers have a theme to their
book. By *theme*, I generally mean an expression of the relationship
between the person and his or her world. It may be a trait, as in the
example of Sir Laurence Olivier's (1982) autobiography in which
he describes his lifelong tendency of lying. Or it may reflect a sense
of justice, of how the world has unfairly treated the person. Or the
central theme may be luck or fortuitous circumstance. The decision
whether to focus the book on the person's life or on his or her work
is related to the theme, for it reflects what the author's criterion
of biographical worth is—fulfillment or achievement (Skidelsky,
1988).

For most biographers, so too is a theme almost inevitable. To be
sure, the biographer is a step away, in the interpretive process, from

the autobiographer, who has lived the process. But each has a theory of the life at hand. Virginia Woolf (1916/1973), writing a biography of Roger Fry, asked, "How can one cut loose from facts, when there they are, contradicting my theories?" (p. 281).

Robert Blake (1988) expresses it this way:

> In a sense any biographer starts with some sort of interpretation in his mind before he begins to look at the mass of material which constitutes his sources of information. It is not wrong to have a preconceived notion about one's subject. If one has no ideas at all about the person one would probably never embark on the task. (p. 77)

In fact, biographers will leave things out, just as autobiographers do, and these omissions will be revealing—"perhaps more so since, if the biographer is any good, they are more likely to be unconscious" (Brogan, 1988, p. 106).

Attributions of Cause for Events in the Life

It is almost inevitable that when we consider the behavior of ourselves and others, we offer explanations focusing on the causes of this behavior. The pervasiveness of the phenomenon links together those who write about their own lives with those who write about others.

Several psychological concepts are relevant to the individual differences. Gestalt psychology taught us about the figure and the ground; how we focus on what is central. Both biographies and autobiographies can vary with respect to how much the subject is figure and not ground; for instance, how much attention is given to intellectual, political, or geographical forces of the times as influences on the subject's life.

The body of literature on attribution theory (Heider, 1958; Jones & Davis, 1965; Kelley, 1967) offers a framework for classifying a variation in causes. In inferring causes for a person's actions, attribution theory proposes that we distinguish between internal and external causes, that we attribute the cause either to something within the person or to the environment (Heider, 1958).

More specifically within the construct of *internal attributions of cause,* both autobiographers and biographers must decide what weight to give heredity and childhood experiences (Tozzer, 1953). How much account is given of the social and economic world? Is the story of a life organized in a chronological order, implying a determinant role for the above, or is the focus on a phenomenological or contemporaneous search for meaning? Doris Kearns (1979), the aforementioned biographer of Lyndon Johnson, is candid about this dilemma:

> If I had it to do over again, . . . I would have written the book backwards rather than forwards, starting with his last years on the ranch, then going back to the Senate and House years, and finally to the sources of his character in childhood: In other words, following the tale in the order he presented it to me. It might have meant a loss of analytical details, since I couldn't have built up the patterns of traits shown in his childhood and early adulthood and later his leadership. And it might have made the narrative telling more personal and difficult. But it would have allowed me to accompany Johnson on his search for his own past, to go with him, backwards in time, as he tried, in the last years of his life, to understand who and what he was. (pp. 102-103)

The debate over the so-called great man theory of leadership can be seen as a phenomenon similar to internal versus external attributions of cause. In its boldest form, the theory hypothesizes that major events in national and international affairs are influenced by the specific individuals who hold leadership positions. A sudden act by a powerful leader could change the fate of a nation . . . and the world. Thus, according to the "great man" theory, Germany became overtly nationalistic and belligerent in the 1930s solely because Adolf Hitler was in power; had there been no Hitler, neither would there have been a World War II. Implicit in the great man theory is an internal attribution of cause, an assumption that leaders possess personality characteristics or a charisma that facilitates the accomplishment of their goals, even in the face of great obstacles.

Both types of attributions are relevant because both biographers *and* autobiographers may use either one of them. Writing about one's own life does not necessarily lend itself to an internal attribution of cause. Laurence Olivier (1982), arguably the best actor of this century, played no role in deciding to become a thespian; it was entirely his father's decision that he go to acting school. Some autobiographies by scientists attribute their groundbreaking discoveries to their being "at the right place at the right time." Writing about another's life does not necessarily lead to an explanation that portrays the subject as a "victim of circumstances."

The Relationship of the Writer to the Subject

As we brush our teeth in the morning, we face ourselves in the bathroom mirror. How do we view ourselves? How do others view us? Of all the dimensions, the relationship of the writer to the subject should reflect the greatest potential difference. After all, a biographer is writing about someone else, while autobiographers are describing their own lives. Yet, in the broadest sense, they are alike in that they operate out of the same within-culture expectations and assumptions. As just one example of the moderating influence of modern culture, the frame of interpretation for both autobiographies and biographies has changed, as ours is "a century distrustful of exemplary lives in the heroic sense" (Homberger & Charmley, 1988, p. xi). We thus see more autobiographies in the form of confessions and more biographies in the form of exposés.

But even in the case of autobiographies, authors may have differing relationships with themselves as subjects. Some autobiographers may stress objectivity, whereas others are completely self-serving. Some may be exhaustive, others selective. Some may organize their narrative chronologically; others may reflect a more idiosyncratic organization.

Another similarity is the degree of ego involvement and commitment of the author to his or her topic. Biographer Ronald Steel noted, "I often felt I hardly had any life outside that of Walter Lippmann" (1986, p. 125). And no autobiography and no biography can hence be definitive (Homberger & Charmley, 1988).

Sometimes the cost is too great. Justin Kaplan, author of prizewinning biographies of Mark Twain and Walt Whitman, spent 5 months exploring the life of Ulysses S. Grant before deciding to abort the project. "I didn't have the stamina to live for five or six years with Grant" he explained (quoted by Silver, 1981, p. 11).

In keeping with the intensity of the relationship, it is very difficult for biographers to remain open-minded about their subjects. Doris

Kearns (1979) has said, "One cannot live with and worry about a
subject for years without alternating feelings of anger, admiration,
aggression, and affection" (p. 91). And biographer Ann Thwaite
(1988) writes:

> My own indignation is a measure of how much I am already identifying
> with [her subject A. A.] Milne [the author of *Winnie the Pooh*]. I try
> to keep an objective attitude toward my subjects, but in practice I
> find, as I get to know them really well, I become more and more
> sympathetic. I feel particularly close to Edmund Gosse, poet *manqué*,
> biographer, family man, cat lover. I shared his feelings about friend-
> ship and his longing to be liked. I sympathized particularly with his
> doubts that anyone would remember him after he was gone. (p. 31)

Amalgamation of two identities is reflected in Ronald Steel's comment:

> In my own case I felt drawn to Lippmann for a great many reasons,
> not all of them intellectual by any means. And I think I was often
> severely judgmental of him because I saw so many of his follies and
> his foibles and his rationalizations and his self-delusions in myself.
> (1986, p. 126)

Steel took 9 years to write his biography of Walter Lippmann.

William Zinsser (1986) asks, "Can the biographer trust his [or
her] objectivity after years of round-the-clock living with a saint
who turns out to be only human?" (p. 18). Biographer Jean Strouse
(1986) recalls that at one point she got terribly mad at her subject,
Alice James, the sister of novelist Henry James and psychologist
William James. When asked by an interviewer if she *liked* her
subject, Strouse (1986) replied:

> Sometimes yes and sometimes no. My reactions to her were extremely
> complex and interesting, and at one point during the writing I got so
> mad at her that I just got completely stuck. Alice was in her late
> twenties and early thirties, and she was systematically closing down
> every option that might have led her away from a life of invalidism.
> She wasn't doing any intellectual work, although she had some that
> she could have been doing. She was being awful to every man who
> approached her and wasn't even very nice to her female friends. She

was turning into a tyrannical invalid who collapsed in order to get people to take care of her. And I hated it. I really got so mad that I couldn't continue writing. It was amazing, because I had known all along that that's how the story was going to come out. That's why I hesitated at the beginning—because the story seemed too depressing. But I had decided to go ahead, and thought I'd dealt with the problem—until, at this point in the process of writing, I just got too furious at her to go on. What I did was take a month off. And I remembered that Erik Erikson had had a similar problem when he was writing his biography of Gandhi. He had been writing about this saintly man and then found out how awful Gandhi was to his family, and he was horrified. I think he actually sat down and wrote out all his objections in a letter to Gandhi—who wasn't around anymore to receive it, of course—but that was Erikson's way of working out the problem. In my case, I didn't write it out, but I had long conversations with Alice and Henry in my head. (p. 192)

An even greater threat to a biographer's objectivity is his or her discovery that the subject of the biography has been duplicitous. Robert Caro (1986) began his biography of President Lyndon Johnson with admiration and respect for Johnson's efforts to benefit the Blacks and the poor. But gradually he uncovered Johnson's lifelong habit of lying and betrayal. He recalls, "I still can remember my feeling, which was: 'God, I hope this doesn't mean what I think it does' " (p. 217). But it did, and Caro was forced to tell a story as sordid as he had feared it to be.

Case Studies

If the biography may lack objectivity, the goal of the case study is to be an objective, albeit qualitative investigation of a single subject. The unique quality of this approach is that multiple sources of evidence are used (Yin, 1989), in contrast to the oral history, the autobiography, the experiment, or the survey. Among the sources of evidence for a case study are documents, archival records, interviews, direct observation, participant observation, and physical artifacts (Yin, 1989). Different skills and methodological procedures are required for each source. Thus the intensive study of the single case may at times provide more meaningful information than that obtained from the traditional experimental method, which studies large samples (Chassan, 1969).

The case study approach has had a long and fruitful history in psychoanalysis, although Freud did not use all of the sources of evidence advocated by the contemporary case-study method. But, he seemed to assume that a single case confirmed the hypotheses he sought to apply to the general population (McAdams, 1990).

In the United States, psychologists at Harvard University have been among the most influential in the development of the case-study method. Henry Murray (1938) in *Explorations in Personality* initiated a set of procedures used later by George Vaillant in the longitudinal study of Harvard freshmen described in Volume 1, Chapter 9, and by Robert W. White (1975, 1981) in *Lives in Progress*. Murray and his co-workers used more than 20 different procedures in studying each individual, including interviews, an autobiography, and a variety of ability and personality tests. Ratings of each subject on a variety of variables were done by several staff members, and all the information was integrated into a separate case study on each person.

Gordon Allport (1961), also at Harvard, encouraged the use of case studies to test generalizations derived from nomothetic approaches, like laboratory experiments, as he sought to identify the unique pattern of qualities within each person.

Despite its unique features, the case-study method has been stereotyped as a "weak sibling" among social science methods (Yin, 1989) because of its supposed lack of precision and rigor. But in recent years greater attention has been devoted to concerns of reliability and validity—both internal and external—and book-length expositions of the procedure are now available (cf. Bromley, 1986; Yin, 1989). For example, the internal validity can be tested through the use of *pattern-matching,* which compares a predicted pattern of responses with the obtained pattern. A method of structured, focused comparisons requires specific predictions to be made.

Furthermore, a procedure called the multiple-case study has been reviewed by Rosenwald (1988); here, the persons who are the subjects of individual case studies are brought into "conversation" with one another, hoping to clarify the meaning of each life.

A special type of case study with promise is Representative Case Research (Gordon & Shontz, 1993), which has as its purpose to learn how individual persons experience and deal with significant life events. (Examples of significant events would include experiencing a religious conversion, falling into—or out of—love, developing a terminal illness, or creating a work of art.) The goal is to elucidate what the experience means to the person studied; revelation is distinguished from explanation. Like other case studies, multiple sources of data are consulted (and data are collected relevant to several levels of functioning), but here the criterion for validity, in addition to plausibility, is acceptance by the person of the insights generated. The subject is granted "expert status" (Gordon & Shontz, 1990) and is a true collaborative investigator in the study, reflecting the suggestions of Rae Carlson (1971b) who felt that "the person" was being left out of personality research.

For example, Colletti (1991) carried out a Representative Case Study with a man diagnosed as having the AIDS virus. The "subject" was considered a coinvestigator, an expert on his own experience; the purpose of the investigation was to arrive at an understanding of his experiences, not to change his life or his reality.

Mangione (1984, 1993) studied one artist intensively over a period of several weeks, in order to better understand the highly individualized process that is creativity. A different type of study, but still Representative Case Research, is reflected in Spotts and Shontz's (1980, 1987) studies of chronic drug users.

Representative Case Research is not free of criticisms; in fact, its commitment to collaborative research puts it methodologically "beyond the pale" in the eyes of some personality researchers. But it is a fitting topic with which to end this book, because it emphasizes both the traditional scientific need to analyze, to dissect human experience, and also the need to connect, to synthesize finding and ideas. The development of personality in adulthood is too complex, too multileveled, too value-laden to be studied without the use of multiple modes of knowing.

References

Adams, B. (1979). Mate selection in the United States: A theoretical summarization. In W. Burr, R. Hill, I. Nye, & R. Reiss (Eds.), *Contemporary theories about the family: Research-based theories* (Vol. 1). New York: Free Press.

Adams, T. D. (1990). *Telling lies in modern American autobiography*. Chapel Hill: University of North Carolina Press.

Aday, R. H. (1984). Belief in afterlife and death anxiety: Correlates and comparisons. *Omega: Journal of Death and Dying, 15,* 67-75.

Adler, J. (1993, April 26). Sex in the snoring '90s. *Newsweek,* pp. 55-57.

Adler, T. (1991, October). "World view" shapes bereavement pattern. *APA Monitor,* pp. 20-21.

Adler, T. (1992, February). Study links genes to sexual orientation. *APA Monitor,* pp. 12-13.

Alexander, I. E., & Adlerstein, A. M. (1959). Death and religion. In H. Feifel (Ed.), *The meaning of death* (pp. 271-283). New York: McGraw-Hill.

Alexander, I. E., Colley, R. S., & Adlerstein, A. M. (1957). Is death a matter of indifference? *Journal of Psychology, 43,* 277-283.

Alker, H. A., & Poppen, P. J. (1973). Personality and ideology in university students. *Journal of Personality, 41,* 652-671.

Allport, G. W. (1942). *The use of personal documents in psychological science.* New York: Social Science Research Council.

Allport, G. W. (1961). *Pattern and growth in personality.* New York: Holt, Rinehart & Winston.

Allport, G. W. (1965). *Letters from Jenny.* New York: Harcourt Brace.

Allport, G. W., Bruner, J. S., & Jandorf, E. M. (1941). Personality under social catastrophe: An analysis of German refugees' life histories. *Character and Personality, 10,* 1-22.

Allport, G. W., & Ross, J. M. (1967). Personal religious orientation and prejudice. *Journal of Personality and Social Psychology, 5,* 432-443.

Allport, G. W., & Vernon, P. E. (1931). *A study of values.* Boston: Houghton-Mifflin.

Allport, G. W., Vernon, P. E., & Lindzey, G. (1960). *Study of values: Manual and test booklet* (3rd ed.). Boston: Houghton-Mifflin.

197

Associated Press. (1987, March 21). Growing number of older men shift direction, enter seminaries. *Lawrence Journal-World,* p. 8A.

Associated Press. (1987, June 29). Pollster says divorce rate is 13 percent. *Lawrence Journal-World,* p. 10B.

Associated Press. (1992, January 4). More than half of U.S. teens have had sex, survey finds. *Kansas City Star,* p. A-5.

Astin, H. S. (1984). The meaning of work in women's lives: A sociopsychological model of career choice and work behavior. *Counseling Psychologist, 12,* 117-126.

Auden, W. H. (1962). *The dyer's hand and other essays.* New York: Random House.

Auerbach, J., Blum, L., Smith, V., & Williams, C. (1985, Spring). On Gilligan's *In a different voice. Feminist Studies, 11*(1), 149-161.

Averill, J. (1968). Grief: Its nature and significance. *Psychological Bulletin, 70,* 721-728.

Averill, J. R., & Nunley, E. P. (1988). Grief as an emotion and as a disease: A social-constructionist perspective. *Journal of Social Issues, 44*(3), 79-95.

Babchuk, N., & Bates, A. P. (1963). The primary relations of middle-class couples: A study in male dominance. *American Sociological Review, 8,* 377-384.

Back, K. W., & Gergen, K. J. (1963). Apocalyptic and serial time orientations and the structure of opinions. *Public Opinion Quarterly, 27,* 427-442.

Bailey, J. M., & Pillard, R. C. (1991). A genetic study of male sexual orientation. *Archives of General Psychiatry, 48,* 1089-1096.

Bakan, D. (1966). *The duality of human existence: Isolation and communion in Western man.* Boston: Beacon.

Baker, C. (1969). *Ernest Hemingway: A life story.* New York: Scribner.

Baldwin, A. L. (1940). The statistical analysis of the structure of a single personality. *Psychological Bulletin, 37,* 518-519.

Baldwin, A. L. (1942). Personal structure analysis: A statistical method for investigating the single personality. *Journal of Abnormal and Social Psychology, 37,* 720-725.

Balleweg, B. J., & Haddon, D. V. (1992, August). *Teaching cognitive development by examining children's literature on death.* Paper presented at the meetings of the American Psychological Association, Washington, D.C.

Baltes, P. B. (1987, August). *Toward a psychological theory of wisdom.* Invited address presented at the meetings of the American Psychological Association, New York City.

Baltes, P. B., & Smith, J. (1990). Toward a psychology of wisdom and its ontogenesis. In R. J. Sternberg (Ed.), *Wisdom: Its nature, origins, and development* (pp. 87-120). New York: Cambridge University Press.

Barker, R. G., & Wright, H. F. (1951). *One boy's day: A specimen record of behavior.* New York: Harper.

Barringer, F. (1989, June 9). Doubt on "trial marriage" raised by divorce rates. *New York Times,* pp. 1, 23.

Barringer, F. (1993, April 15). Sex survey of American men finds 1% are gay. *New York Times,* pp. A1, A9.

Barwick, C., Brabeck, M., & Stryker, S. (1990, August). *Gender differences in ethical sensitivity to care and rights issues.* Paper presented at the meetings of the American Psychological Association, Boston.

Basow, S. A. (1992). *Gender stereotypes and roles* (3rd ed.). Pacific Grove, CA: Brooks/Cole.

Basseches, M. (1980). Dialectical schemata: A framework for the empirical study of dialectical thinking. *Human Development, 23,* 400-421.

Bateson, M. C. (1989). *Composing a life.* Boston: The Atlantic Monthly Press.

Batson, C. D. (1976). Religion as prosocial agent or double agent. *Journal of the Scientific Study of Religion, 15,* 29-45.

Batson, C. D., & Ventis, W. L. (1982). *The religious experience: A social-psychological perspective.* New York: Oxford University Press.

Baucom, D. H. (1987). Attributions in distressed relations: How can we explain them? In D. Perlman & S. Duck (Eds.), *Intimate relationships: Development, dynamics, and deterioration* (pp. 177-206). Newbury Park, CA: Sage.

Beard, G. M. (1874). *Legal responsibility in old age.* New York: Russell Sage Foundation.

Becker, E. (1971). *The birth and death of meaning* (2nd ed.). New York: Free Press.

Becker, E. (1973). *The denial of death.* New York: Free Press.

Beers, C. W. (1928). *A mind that found itself: An autobiography* (5th ed.). Garden City, NY: Doubleday, Doran.

Begley, S. (1987, November 23). All about twins. *Newsweek,* pp. 58-69.

Belkin, L. (1992, June 17). The less-traveled road to medical school. *The New York Times,* pp. A1, C19.

Bell, A. P., & Weinberg, M. S. (1978). *Homosexualities: A study of diversity among men and women.* New York: Simon & Schuster.

Bem, S. L. (1974). The measurement of psychological androgyny. *Journal of Consulting and Clinical Psychology, 42,* 155-162.

Bem, S. L. (1977). On the utility of alternative procedures for assessing psychological androgyny. *Journal of Consulting and Clinical Psychology, 42,* 155-162.

Bem, S. L. (1979). Theory and measurement of androgyny: A reply to Pedhazur-Tetenbaum and Locksley-Colten critiques. *Journal of Personality and Social Psychology, 37,* 1047-1054.

Bem, S. L. (1981). Gender schema theory: A cognitive account of sex typing. *Psychological Review, 88,* 354-364.

Bem, S. L. (1982). Gender schema theory and self-schema compared: A comment on Markus, Crane, Bernstein, and Siladi's "Self-schemas and gender." *Journal of Personality and Social Psychology, 43,* 1192-1194.

Bem, S. L. (1983). Gender schema theory and its implications for child development: Raising gender-aschematic children in a gender-schematic society. *Signs: Journal of Women in Culture and Society, 8,* 598-616.

Bem, S. L. (1985). Androgyny and gender schema theory: A conceptual and empirical integration. In T. B. Sonderegger (Ed.), *Nebraska Symposium on Motivation, 1984: Psychology and gender* (Vol. 32, pp. 179-226). Lincoln: University of Nebraska Press.

Bem, S. L. (1987). Gender schema theory and the romantic tradition. In P. Shaver & C. Hendrick (Eds.), *Sex and gender* (pp. 251-271). Newbury Park, CA: Sage.

Benjamin, L. T., Jr. (1980). Women in psychology: Biography and autobiography. *Psychology of Women Quarterly, 5,* 140-144.

Berkman, L. F., & Sume, L. S. (1979). Social networks, host resistance, and mortality: A nine-year follow-up study of Alameda County residents. *American Journal of Epidemiology, 109,* 186-204.

Berman, A. L. (1974). Belief in afterlife, religion, religiosity, and life-threatening experiences. *Omega: Journal of Death and Dying, 5,* 127-135.

Berman, H. J. (1985, March). *On the brink: Elizabeth Vining's "Being seventy."* Unpublished paper presented at the Conference on "Humanistic Perspectives on the Aging Enterprise in America," Center for the Study of Aging, University of Missouri, Kansas City.

Bernard, J. (1973). *The future of marriage.* New York: Bantam.

Berzins, J. I., Welling, M. A., & Wetter, R. E. (1975). *The PRF ANDRO scale user's manual.* Unpublished manual, University of Kentucky, Lexington.

Betz, N. E., & Fitzgerald, L. F. (1987). *The career psychology of women.* Orlando, FL: Academic Press.

Blake, R. (1988). The art of biography. In E. Homberger & J. Charmley (Eds.), *The troubled face of biography* (pp. 75-93). New York: St. Martin's.

Blauner, B. (1989). *Black lives, White lives.* Berkeley: University of California Press.

Blieszner, R., & Adams, R. G. (1992). *Adult friendship.* Newbury Park, CA: Sage.

Block, J. H. (1973). Conceptions of sex roles: Some cross-cultural and longitudinal perspectives. *American Psychologist, 28,* 512-526.

Block, J. H. (1984). *Sex role identity and ego development.* San Francisco: Jossey-Bass.

Bluebond-Langner, M. (1977). Meanings of death to children. In H. Feifel (Ed.), *New meanings of death* (pp. 47-66). New York: McGraw-Hill.

Blum, D. (1989, May 1). A process larger than oneself. *The New Yorker,* pp. 41-74.

Blumenthal, S. (1992, October 12). War story. *New Republic,* pp. 17-20.

Blumstein, P., & Schwartz, P. (1983). *American couples: Money/work/sex.* New York: William Morrow.

Bock, E. E., & Webber, I. L. (1972). Suicide among the elderly: Isolating widowhood and mitigating alternatives. *Journal of Marriage and the Family, 34,* 24-31.

Bojanovsky, J., & Bojanovsky, A. (1975). Zur Risikozeit des Selbstmordes bei Geschiedenen und Verwitweten. *Nervenarzt, 47,* 307-309.

Bonaparte, M. (1939). A defense of biography. *International Journal of Psycho-Analysis, 20,* 231-240.

Boring, E. G., Langfeld, H. S., Werner, H., & Yerkes, R. M. (Eds.). (1952). *A history of psychology in autobiography* (Vol. 4). Worcester, MA: Clark University Press.

Boring, E. G., & Lindzey, G. (Eds.). (1967). *A history of psychology in autobiography* (Vol. 5). New York: Appleton-Century-Crofts.

Bornstein, P. E., Clayton, P. J., Halikas, J. A., Maurice, W. L., & Robbins, E. (1973). The depression of widowhood after thirteen months. *British Journal of Psychiatry, 122,* 561-566.

Boswell, J. (1953). *Life of Johnson.* New York: Oxford University Press. (Original work published 1791)

Botwinick, J. (1967). *Cognitive processes in maturity and old age.* New York: Springer.

Botwinick, J. (1978). *Aging and behavior* (2nd ed.). New York: Springer.

Bouchard, T. J., Lykken, D. T., McGue, M., Segal, N. L., & Tellegen, A. (1990). Sources of human psychological differences: The Minnesota Study of Twins Reared Apart. *Science, 250,* 223-228.

Boyd, M. (1991, October-November). Alone, not lonely. *Modern Maturity,* p. 72.

Boyd, M. (1991, December-1992, January). Resolve to be happy. *Modern Maturity,* p. 82.

Brabeck, M. (1983). Moral judgment: Theory and research on differences between males and females. *Developmental Review, 3,* 274-291.

Bragman, L. J. (1936). The case of Dante Gabriel Rosetti. *American Journal of Psychiatry, 92,* 1111-1122.

Braithwaite, V. A., & Scott, W. A. (1991). Values. In J. P. Robinson, P. R. Shaver, & L. S. Wrightsman (Eds.), *Measures of personality and social psychological attitudes* (pp. 661-753). San Diego, CA: Academic Press.

Braungart, M. M., & Braungart, R. G. (1990). The life-course development of left- and right-wing youth activist leaders from the 1960s. *Political Psychology, 11,* 243-282.

Broderick, C. B. (1982). Adult sexual development. In B. B. Wolman & G. Stricker (Eds.), *Handbook of developmental psychology* (pp. 726-733). Englewood Cliffs, NJ: Prentice Hall.

Broen, W. E. (1957). A factor-analytic study of religious attitudes. *Journal of Abnormal and Social Psychology, 54,* 176-179.

Brogan, H. (1988). The biographer's chains. In E. Homberger & J. Charmley (Eds.), *The troubled face of biography* (pp. 104-112). New York: St. Martin's.

Bromley, D. B. (1986). *The case study method in psychology and related disciplines.* New York: John Wiley.

Brooks, G. R. (1991). Men's studies and psychotherapy: A current perspective on the status of the men's movement. *Psychotherapy Bulletin, 26*(2), 19-22.

Brooks, L. (1990). Recent developments in theory building. In D. Brown, L. Brooks and Associates (Eds.), *Career choice and development* (2nd ed., pp. 364-394). San Francisco: Jossey-Bass.

Broughton, J. M. (1983). Women's rationality and men's virtues: A critique of gender dualism in Gilligan's theory of moral development. *Social Research, 50,* 597-642.

Brown, G. W., & Harris, T. (1978). *Social origins of depression: A study of psychiatric disorders in women.* London: Tavistock.

Brown, J. W., & Shukraft, R. C. (1971). *Personal development and professional practice in college and university professors.* Unpublished doctoral dissertation, Graduate Theological Union, Berkeley, CA.

Bruccoli, M. J. (1981). *Some sort of epic grandeur: The life of F. Scott Fitzgerald.* New York: Harcourt Brace Jovanovich.

Buckley, J. H. (1984). *The turning key: Autobiography and the subjective impulse since 1800.* Cambridge, MA: Harvard University Press.

Buehler, C. (1935). The curve of life as studied in biographies. *Journal of Applied Psychology, 19,* 405-409.

Bulcroft, K., & O'Conner-Roden, M. (1986, June). Never too late. *Psychology Today,* pp. 66-69.

Bunzel, J. H. (Ed.). (1988). *Political passages: Journey of change through two decades, 1968-1988.* New York: Free Press.

Burling, J. W. (1993). Death concerns and symbolic aspects of the self: The effects of morality salience on status concern and religiosity. *Personality and Social Psychology Bulletin, 19*, 100-105.

Burros, M. (1988, February 24). We bet you can guess who's making dinner. *Kansas City Star*, pp. A1, A6.

Buss, A. H. (1988). *Personality: Evolutionary heritage and human distinctiveness.* Hillsdale, NJ: Lawrence Erlbaum.

Buss, D. M. (1989). Conflict between the sexes: Strategic interference and the evocation of anger and upset. *Journal of Personality and Social Psychology, 56*, 735-747.

Candee, D. (1976). Structure and choice in moral reasoning. *Journal of Personality and Social Psychology, 34*, 1293-1301.

Candee, D. (1980). The moral psychology of Watergate and its aftermath. In R. W. Wilson & G. J. Schochet (Eds.), *Moral development and politics* (pp. 172-189). New York: Praeger.

Candy, S. (1977). *A comparative analysis of friendship functions in six age groups of men and women.* Unpublished doctoral dissertation, Wayne State University.

Cantor, N., & Kihlstrom, J. F. (1985). Social intelligence: The cognitive basis of personality. *Review of Personality and Social Psychology, 6*, 2-32.

Carlson, P. (1992, July 26). When Henry met Zsa Zsa. *The Washington Post Magazine*, pp. 8-24.

Carlson, R. (1971a). Sex differences in ego functioning. *Journal of Consulting and Clinical Psychology, 37*, 267-277.

Carlson, R. (1971b). Where is the person in personality research? *Psychological Bulletin, 75*, 203-219.

Carlson, R. (1988). Exemplary lives: The uses of psychobiography for theory development. In D. P. McAdams & R. L. Ochberg (Eds.), *Psychobiography and life narratives* (pp. 105-138). Durham, NC: Duke University Press.

Carlyle, T. (1858-1865). *History of Frederick the Great* (8 vols.). New York: Scribner.

Caro, R. A. (1986). Lyndon Johnson and the roots of power. In W. Zinsser (Ed.), *Extraordinary lives: The art and craft of American biography* (pp. 197-231). New York: Book-of-the-Month Club.

Carpenter, H. (1982, February 7). Patrick White explains himself. *The New York Times Book Review*, pp. 9, 41.

Cartwright, A., Hockey, L., & Anderson, J. S. (1973). *Life before death.* London: Routledge & Kegan Paul.

Cather, W. (1927). A letter from Willa Cather: A short account of how I happened to write *Death comes to the archbishop. Commonwealth, 7*, 713-714.

Chaplin, W. F. (1990). Personality: Beyond the big five and biology. *Contemporary Psychology, 35*, 940-941.

Chassan, J. B. (1969). Statistical inference and the single case in clinical design. In P. D. Davidson & C. G. Costello (Eds.), *N = 1: Experimental studies of single cases* (pp. 26-45). New York: Van Nostrand Reinhold.

Cherlin, A. (1979, October). Cohabitation: How the French and Swedes do it. *Psychology Today*, pp. 18-24.

Childers, P., & Wimmer, M. (1971). The concept of death in early childhood. *Child Development, 42*, 705-715.

Chodorow, N. (1978). *The reproduction of mothering: Psychoanalysis and the sociology of gender*. Berkeley: University of California Press.

Christ, A. E. (1961). Attitudes toward death among a group of acute geriatric psychiatric patients. *Journal of Gerontology, 16,* 44-55.

Church, G. J. (1987, September 7). The work ethic lives! *Time,* pp. 40-42.

Clance, P. R. (1985). *The impostor phenomenon*. Atlanta: Peachtree Publishers.

Clark, A. M. (1935). *Autobiography: Its genesis and phases*. Edinburgh: Oliver & Boyd.

Clayton, V. P., & Birren, J. E. (1980). The development of wisdom across the lifespan: A re-examination of an ancient topic. In P. B. Baltes & O. G. Brim (Eds.), *Life-span development and behavior* (Vol. 3, pp. 103-135). San Diego, CA: Academic Press.

Cockshut, A. O. J. (1974). *Truth to life: The art of biography in the nineteenth century*. New York: Harcourt Brace Jovanovich.

Cohen, A. M. (1980). Stages and stability: The moral development approach to political power. In R. W. Wilson & G. J. Schochet (Eds.), *Moral development and politics* (pp. 69-84). New York: Praeger.

Cohen, D. (1977). *Creativity: What is it?* New York: M. Evans.

Cohen, R. (1987, October 5). Why Elizabeth Dole should not have resigned. *The Washington Post National Weekly Edition*, p. 29.

Cohen, R. (1991, June 24). Schwarzkopf gets $5 million-plus deal for autobiography. *The New York Times*, pp. B1, B2.

Cohler, B. J. (1993). Describing lives: Gordon Allport and the "science" of personality. In K. H. Craik, R. Hogan, & R. N. Wolfe (Eds.), *Fifty years of personality psychology* (pp. 131-146). New York: Plenum.

Colby, A., & Damon, W. (1983). Listening to a different voice: A review of Gilligan's *In a different voice. Merrill-Palmer Quarterly, 29,* 473-481.

Colby, A., & Kohlberg, L. (1987). *The measurement of moral judgment*. New York: Cambridge University Press.

Coleman, J. (1974). *Blue-collar journal: A college president's sabbatical*. Philadelphia: J. B. Lippincott.

Colletti, J. (1991). *Living and dying with the AIDS virus: A representative case*. Unpublished master's thesis, University of Kansas, Lawrence.

Collins, G. (1987, December 2). Two-career couples: A delicate balance. *The New York Times*, pp. 19-20.

Colson, C. W. (1976). *Born again*. New York: Bantam.

Constantinople, A. (1973). Masculinity-femininity: An exception to a famous dictum? *Psychological Bulletin, 80,* 389-407.

Conway, J. K. (Ed.). (1992). *Written by herself: Autobiographies of American women, an anthology*. New York: Vintage.

Craik, F. I. M. (1992). Memory changes in normal aging. In I. Kostavic, S. Knezevic, H. Wisniewski, & G. Spilich (Eds.), *Neurodevelopment, aging, and cognition*. Boston: Birkhauser.

Crapanzano, V., Ergas, Y., & Modell, J. (1986, June). Personal testimony: Narratives of the self in the social sciences and the humanities. *Items, 40*(2), 25-30.

Crawford, M., & Unger, R. K. (1990). Hearing voices, seeing differences. *Contemporary Psychology, 35,* 950-952.

Crick, B. (1981). *George Orwell, a life*. London: Secker & Warburg.

Crittenden, J. A. (1962). Aging and party affiliation. *Public Opinion Quarterly, 26,* 648-657.

Crosby, F. J. (1987). *Spouse, parent, worker: On gender and multiple roles.* New Haven, CT: Yale University Press.

Cruver, D. (1986, July 14). Most husbands say "I'd marry her again." *USA Today,* p. 1D.

Cuber, J. F., & Harroff, P. B. (1965). *The significant Americans: A study of sexual behavior among the affluent.* New York: Appleton-Century-Crofts.

Cutler, N. E. (1974). *The impact of subjective age identification on social and political attitudes.* Paper presented at the meetings of the Gerontological Society, Portland, OR.

Cutler, N. E. (1983). Age and political behavior. In D. S. Woodruff & J. E. Birren (Eds.), *Aging: Scientific perspectives and social issues* (2nd ed., pp. 409-442). Pacific Grove, CA: Brooks/Cole.

Cutler, W. (1970). Accuracy in oral history interviewing. In D. J. Dunaway & W. K. Baum (Eds.), *Oral history* (pp. 79-85). Nashville: American Association for State and Local History.

Dacey, J. (1982). *Adult development.* Glenview, IL: Scott, Foresman.

Dacey, J. S. (1989). *Fundamentals of creative thinking.* Lexington, MA: Lexington Books.

Daly, C. B. (1993, May 22-28). Homosexuality: Is it mainly in the genes? *The Washington Post National Weekly Edition,* p. 38.

Dan, A. J., & Bernhard, L. A. (1989). Menopause and other health issues for midlife women. In S. Hunter & M. Sundel (Eds.), *Midlife myths: Issues, findings and practice implications* (pp. 51-66). Newbury Park, CA: Sage.

Darwin, C. (1958). *Autobiography* (N. Barlow, Ed.). London: Collins.

Davis, B., Sommers-Flanagan, R., & Kessi, A. M. (1990, August). *New woman vs. traditional: Preferences of singles ads readers.* Paper presented at the meetings of the American Psychological Association, Boston.

Davison, P. (1992, October). To edit a life. *Atlantic Monthly,* pp. 92-100.

Day, A. T. (1991). *Remarkable survivors: Insights into successful aging among women.* Washington, DC: Urban Institute Press.

Deaux, K., & Hanna, R. (1984). Courtship in the personal column: The influence of gender and sexual orientation. *Sex Roles, 11,* 363-375.

Deaux, K., Kite, M. E., & Lewis, L. (1985). Clustering and gender schemata: An uncertain link. *Personality and Social Psychology Bulletin, 11,* 387-397.

Denney, N. W. (1982). Aging and cognitive changes. In B. Wolman & G. Stricker (Eds.), *Handbook of developmental psychology* (pp. 807-827). Englewood Cliffs, NJ: Prentice Hall.

Dennis, W. (1958). The age decrement in outstanding scientific contributions: Fact or artifact? *American Psychologist, 13,* 457-460.

Dennis, W. (1966). Creative productivity between the ages of 20 and 80 years. *Journal of Gerontology, 21,* 1-8.

Devine, P. G. (1989). Stereotypes and prejudice: Their automatic and controlled components. *Journal of Personality and Social Psychology, 56,* 5-18.

DeWaele, J.-P., & Harre, R. (1979). Autobiography as a psychological method. In G. P. Ginsburg (Ed.), *Emerging strategies in social psychological research* (pp. 177-224). New York: John Wiley.

Dewey, J. (1904). *The library of living philosophy*. Chicago: University of Chicago Press.

Dohrenwend, B. S., & Dohrenwend, B. P. (Eds.). (1981). *Stressful life events and their context*. New York: Neal Watson.

Dollard, J. (1935). *Criteria for a life history*. New Haven, CT: Yale University Press.

Donley, R. W., & Winter, D. G. (1970). Measuring the motives of public figures at a distance: An exploratory study of American presidents. *Behavioral Science, 15,* 227-236.

Donlon, B. (1991, September 9). Geraldo is poised to expose his more respectable side. *USA Today*, p. 3D.

Douvan, E. (1979). Differing views of marriage 1957 to 1976. *Newsletter, Center for Continuing Education of Women, University of Michigan, 12*(1), 1-12.

Dukakis, K. (with J. Scovell). (1990). *Now you know*. New York: Simon & Schuster.

Dykstra, P. A. (1990). *Next of (non)kin: The importance of primary relationships for older adults' well-being*. Lisse, the Netherlands: Swets & Zeitlinger.

Eaton, W. W. (1978). Life events, social supports, and psychiatric symptoms: A re-analysis of the New Haven data. *Journal of Health and Social Behavior, 19,* 230-234.

Edel, L. (1979). The figure under the carpet. In M. Pachter (Ed.), *Telling lives: The biographer's art* (pp. 16-34). Washington, DC: New Republic Books/National Portrait Gallery.

Elias, M. (1984, October 19). What keeps couples together? *USA Today*, pp. 1D, 2D.

Elms, A. C. (1988). Freud as Leonardo: Why the first psychobiography went wrong. In D. P. McAdams & R. L. Ochberg (Eds.), *Psychobiography and life narratives* (pp. 19-40). Durham, NC: Duke University Press.

Elo, A. F. (1965). Age changes in master chess performance. *Journal of Gerontology, 20,* 289-299.

Emler, N., Renwick, S., & Malone, B. (1983). The relationship between moral reasoning and political orientation. *Journal of Personality and Social Psychology, 45,* 1073-1080.

Epstein, J. (1981, February 15). Confessions of an Australian charmer. *The New York Times Book Review*, pp. 7, 30.

Erber, J. T., Szuchman, L. T., & Rothberg, S. T. (1990). Everyday memory failure: Age differences in appraisal and attribution. *Psychology and Aging, 5,* 236-241.

Faunce, W. A., & Fulton, R. L. (1958). The sociology of death: A neglected area of research. *Social Forces, 3,* 205-209.

Feifel, H. (1955). Attitudes of mentally ill patients toward death. *Journal of Nervous and Mental Diseases, 122,* 375-380.

Feifel, H. (1959). Attitudes toward death in some normal and mentally ill persons. In H. Feifel (Ed.), *The meaning of death* (pp. 114-130). New York: McGraw-Hill.

Feifel, H. (1974). Religious conviction and the fear of death among the healthy and the terminally ill. *Journal for the Scientific Study of Religion, 13,* 353-360.

Feifel, H. (1990). Psychology and death: Meaningful rediscovery. *American Psychologist, 45,* 537-543.

Finder, A. (1987, September 15). Koch writes epitaph in musing on mortality. *The New York Times*, p. 21.

Fischer, C. S., & Phillips, S. L. (1982). Who is alone? Social characteristics of people with small networks. In L. A. Peplau & D. Perlman (Eds.), *Loneliness: A source-*

book of current theory, research, and therapy (pp. 21-39). New York: John Wiley.

Fisher, H. E. (1992). Anatomy of love: The natural history of monogamy, adultery, and divorce. New York: Norton.

Fisher, K. (1989, July). Psychologist explores realms of the ordinary. APA Monitor, p. 11.

Fishkin, J., Keniston, K., & MacKinnon, C. (1973). Moral reasoning and political ideology. Journal of Personality and Social Psychology, 27, 109-119.

Fitzgerald, L. F., & Betz, N. E. (1984). Astin's model in theory and practice: A technical and philosophical critique. Counseling Psychologist, 12(4), 135-138.

Fitzgerald, L. F., & Crites, J. O. (1980). Toward a career psychology of women: What do we know? What do we need to know? Journal of Counseling Psychology, 27, 44-62.

Fitzpatrick, M. A. (1988). Between husbands and wives: Communication in marriage. Newbury Park, CA: Sage.

Forrest, L., & Mikolaitis, N. (1986). The relational component of identity: An expansion of career development theory. Career Development Quarterly, 35, 76-88.

Fowler, J. W., & Lovin, R. W. (1980). Trajectories in faith. Nashville, TN: Abingdon.

Freedman, S. A., & Frantzve, J. L. (1992, August). Sextyping and gender schematicity: A tenuous relationship. Paper presented at the meetings of the American Psychological Association, Washington, D.C.

Frenkel, E. (1936). Studies in biographical psychology. Character and Personality, 5, 1-35.

Frenkel-Brunswik, E. (1939). Mechanisms of self-deception. Journal of Social Psychology, 10, 409-420.

Gallagher, W. (1993, May). Midlife myths. The Atlantic Monthly, pp. 51-68.

Galton, F. (1869). Hereditary genius: An inquiry into its laws and consequences. London: Macmillan.

Galton, F. (1875). The history of twins as a criterion of the relative powers of nature and nurture. Journal of the Anthropological Institute, 6, 391-406.

Garnets, L., & Pleck, J. H. (1979). Sex role identity, androgyny, and sex role transcendence: A sex role strain analysis. Psychology of Women Quarterly, 3, 270-283.

Gates, D. (1993, June 14). The case of Dr. Strangedrug. Newsweek, p. 71.

Gates, H. L. (Ed.). (1987). The classic slave narratives. New York: New American Library.

Gedo, J. E. (1990). More on creativity and its vicissitudes. In M. A. Runco & R. S. Albert (Eds.), Theories of creativity (pp. 35-45). Newbury Park, CA: Sage.

Geer, J. (1965). The development of a scale to measure fear. Behavior Research and Therapy, 3, 45-53.

Gergen, M. M. (1992a). Life stories: Pieces of a dream. In G. Rosenwald & R. Ochberg (Eds.), Storied lives: The cultural politics of self-understanding. New Haven, CT: Yale University Press.

Gergen, M. M. (1992b, August). Socially constructing the body in the popular autobiography. Paper presented at the meetings of the American Psychological Association, Washington, DC.

Gergen, M. M., & Gergen, K. J. (1993). Narratives of the gendered body in popular autobiography. In R. Josselson & A. Lieblich (Eds.), The narrative study of lives (pp. 191-218). Newbury Park, CA: Sage.

Gibson, W. C. (1978). *Autobiographical memoirs of eminent scientists* (Vol. 2). Palo Alto, CA: Annual Reviews.

Gilbert, L. A. (1984). Understanding dual-career families. In J. C. Hansen & S. H. Cramer (Eds.), *Family therapy collections: Perspectives on career development and the family* (Vol. 10, pp. 56-71). Rockville, MD: Aspen Systems.

Gilbert, L. A. (1985). *Men in dual-career families: Current realities and future prospects*. Hillsdale, NJ: Lawrence Erlbaum.

Gilbert, L. A., & Davidson, S. (1989). Dual-career families at midlife. In S. Hunter & M. Sundel (Eds.), *Midlife myths: Issues, findings, and practice implications* (pp. 195-209). Newbury Park, CA: Sage.

Gilbert, L. A., Hanson, G. R., & Davis, B. (1982). Perceptions of parental role responsibilities: Differences between mothers and fathers. *Family Relations, 31,* 261-269.

Gilligan, C. (1977). In a different voice: Women's conception of self and morality. *Harvard Educational Review, 47,* 481-517.

Gilligan, C. (1982). *In a different voice: Psychological theory and women's development*. Cambridge, MA: Harvard University Press.

Gilligan, C., Ward, J. V., & Taylor, J. McL. (Eds.). (1988). *Mapping the moral domain: A contribution of women's thinking to psychological theory and education*. Cambridge, MA: Harvard University Press.

Gindick, T. (1985, October 8). Romance is back, love experts say. *Kansas City Times,* p. B-5.

Gladwell, M. (1990, April 23-29). Over the hill at twenty something. *The Washington Post National Weekly Edition,* p. 38.

Glendinning, V. (1988). Lies and silences. In E. Homberger & J. Charmley (Eds.), *The troubled face of autobiography* (pp. 49-62). New York: St. Martin's.

Glenn, N. D. (1974). Aging and conservatism. *Annals of the American Academy of Political and Social Science, 415,* 176-186.

Glick, I., Weiss, R. S., & Parkes, C. M. (1974). *The first year of bereavement*. New York: John Wiley.

Gluck, S. (1980). What's so special about women, women's oral history. In D. J. Dunaway & W. K. Baum (Eds.), *Oral history* (pp. 221-237). Nashville, TN: American Association for State and Local History.

Goldberg, L. R. (1990). An alternative "description of personality": The big five factor structure. *Journal of Personality and Social Psychology, 59,* 1216-1229.

Goldsmith, H. H. (1990). Adopting a behavior-genetic approach to development. *Contemporary Psychology, 35,* 752-754.

Goleman, D. (1984, December 6). Perspectives on love. *Kansas City Times,* pp. C-1, C-2.

Goleman, D. (1985, September 12). Affairs of the heart: Changes occur as relationships bloom. *Kansas City Times,* pp. B-5, B-7.

Goleman, D. (1986, July 22). Psychologists pursue irrational aspects of love. *The New York Times,* pp. 17, 20.

Goleman, D. (1987, June 23). In memory, people re-create their lives to suit their images of the present. *The New York Times,* pp. 17, 20.

Goleman, D. (1989, December 5). Fear of death intensifies moral code, scientists find. *The New York Times,* pp. 19, 22.

Goleman, D. (1990, March 27). Studies offer fresh clues to memory. *The New York Times,* pp. B5, B6.

Good, G. E., & Mintz, L. B. (1990). Gender role conflict and depression in college men: Evidence for compounded risk. *Journal of Counseling Development, 69,* 17-21.

Gordon, J., & Shontz, F. C. (1990). Representative case research: A way of knowing. *Journal of Counseling and Development, 69,* 62-66.

Gordon, J., & Shontz, F. C. (1993). *A way to know persons: Representative case research.* Unpublished manuscript, University of Kansas, Lawrence.

Gorsuch, R. L. (1988). Psychology of religion. *Annual Review of Psychology, 39,* 201-221.

Gottfredson, L. S. (1981). Circumscription and compromise: A developmental theory of career aspirations. *Journal of Counseling Psychology, 28,* 545-579.

Gottman, J. M. (1993). *What predicts divorce? The relationship between marital processes and marital outcomes.* Hillsdale, NJ: Lawrence Erlbaum.

Gove, W. R. (1972). The relationship between sex roles, marital roles, and mental illness. *Social Forces, 51,* 34-44.

Gove, W. R. (1973). Sex, marital status and mortality. *American Journal of Sociology, 79,* 45-67.

Gove, W. R., & Hughes, M. (1979). Possible causes of apparent sex differences in physical health: An empirical investigation. *American Sociological Review, 44,* 126-146.

Greenberg, J., Pyszczynski, T., & Solomon, S. (1986). A terror management theory of the role of the need for self-esteem in social behavior. In R. F. Baumeister (Ed.), *Public self and private self* (pp. 189-212). New York: Springer.

Greenberg, J., Solomon, S., Veeder, M., Pyszczynski, T., Rosenblatt, A., Kirkland, S., & Lyon, D. (1990). Evidence for terror management II: The effects of mortality salience on reactions to those who threaten or bolster the cultural worldview. *Journal of Personality and Social Psychology, 58,* 308-318.

Greer, G. (1992). *The change: Women, aging, and the menopause.* New York: Knopf.

Guilford, J. P. (1950). Creativity. *American Psychologist, 5,* 444-454.

Guilford, J. P. (1967). *The nature of human intelligence.* New York: McGraw-Hill.

Gunderson, E. (1987, May 19). Fear and facts often don't match. *USA Today,* p. 6D.

Gunn, J. V. (1982). *Autobiography: Toward a poetics of experience.* Philadelphia: University of Pennsylvania Press.

Gunter, B. G., & Gunter, N. C. (1991). Inequities in household labor: Sex role orientation and the need for cleanliness and responsibility as predictors. *Journal of Social Behavior and Personality, 6,* 559-572.

Gutek, B. A. (1989). A review of the women's careers literature. *Contemporary Psychology, 34,* 272-273.

Hackett, G., & Betz, N. (1981). A self-efficacy approach to the career development of women. *Journal of Vocational Behavior, 18,* 326-339.

Hall, D. T. (1986). Breaking career routines: Midcareer choice and identity development. In D. T. Hall & Associates (Eds.), *Career development in organizations* (pp. 120-159). San Francisco: Jossey-Bass.

Hall, D. T., & Richter, J. (1985). *The baby boom and management: Is there room in the middle?* Unpublished paper, School of Management, Boston University.

Hamburg, D. A., & Lunde, D. R. (1966). Sex hormones in the development of sex differences in human behavior. In E. E. Maccoby (Ed.), *The development of sex differences* (pp. 1-24). Stanford, CA: Stanford University Press.

Hamer, D. H., Hu, S., Magnuson, V. L., Hu, N., & Pattanucci, A. M. L. (1993). A linkage between DNA markers on the X chromosome and male sexual orientation. *Science, 261,* 321-327.

Haney, D. Q. (1990, February 19). Sex survey reveals "typical" Americans not exactly libertines. *Lawrence Journal-World,* p. 12B.

Hansen, J.-I. C. (1989). Researching the career of women. *Contemporary Psychology, 34,* 759-760.

Hansson, R. O. (1986). Relational competence, relationships, and adjustment in old age. *Journal of Personality and Social Psychology, 50,* 1050-1058.

Hare-Mustin, R., & Marecek, J. (1988). The meaning of difference: Gender theory, postmodernism, and psychology. *American Psychologist, 43,* 455-464.

Harrison, A. A., & Saeed, L. (1977). Let's make a deal: An analysis of revelations and stipulations in lonely hearts advertisements. *Journal of Personality and Social Psychology, 35,* 257-264.

Harrison, J. (1978). Warning: The male sex role may be dangerous to your health. *Journal of Social Issues, 34,* 65-86.

Hebb, D. O. (1978). On watching myself grow old. *Psychology Today, 15*(12), 20-23.

Heider, F. (1958). *The psychology of interpersonal relations.* New York: John Wiley.

Heilbrun, A. B., Jr. (1976). Measurement of masculine and feminine sex role identities as independent dimensions. *Journal of Consulting and Clinical Psychology, 44,* 183-190.

Heilbrun, C. G. (1992, October 4). How girls become wimps. *The New York Times Book Review,* pp. 13-14.

Hermann, M. G. (1980). Assessing the personalities of Soviet Politburo members. *Personality and Social Psychology, 6,* 332-352.

Hess, B. (1972). Friendship. In M. W. Riley, M. Johnson, & A. Foner (Eds.), *Aging and society: Vol. 3. A sociology of age stratification.* New York: Russell Sage.

Heyman, D. K., & Gianturco, D. T. (1973). Long-term adaptation by the elderly to bereavement. *Journal of Gerontology, 28,* 359-362.

Heyn, D. (1992). *The erotic silence of the American wife.* New York: Turtle Bay Books.

Himmelweit, H. T., Humphreys, P., Jaeger, M., & Katz, M. (1981). *How voters decide: A longitudinal study of political attitudes and voting extending over fifteen years.* London: Academic Press.

Hite, S. (1987). *Women and love: A cultural revolution in progress.* New York: Knopf.

Hoffman, R. G., & Nelson, K. S. (1990, August). *Memory and cognitive change in normal aging.* Paper presented at meetings of the American Psychological Association, Boston.

Holahan, C. K., & Holahan, C. J. (1987). Life stress, hassles, and self-efficacy in aging: A replication and extension. *Journal of Applied Social Psychology, 17,* 574-592.

Holland, J. L. (1963). Explorations of a theory of a vocational choice and achievement. *Psychological Reports, 12,* 547-594.

Holland, J. L. (1966). *The psychology of vocational choice.* Waltham, MA: Blaisdell.

Holland, J. L. (1985). *Making vocational choices* (2nd ed.). Englewood Cliffs, NJ: Prentice Hall.

Holland, J. L. (1987). Current status of Holland's theory of careers: Another perspective. *Career Development Quarterly, 36,* 31-44.

Holmes, R. (1985). *Footsteps: Adventures of a romantic biographer.* London: Hodder & Stoughton.

Holroyd, M. (1988). How I fell into biography. In E. Homberger & J. Charmley (Eds.), *The troubled face of biography* (pp. 94-103). New York: St. Martin's.

Holtzworth-Munroe, A., & Jacobson, N. S. (1985). Causal attributions of married couples: When do they search for causes? What do they conclude when they do? *Journal of Personality and Social Psychology, 48,* 1398-1412.

Homberger, E., & Charmley, J. (1988). Introduction. In E. Homberger & J. Charmley (Eds.), *The troubled face of biography* (pp. ix-xv). New York: St. Martin's.

Hoopes, J. (1979). *Oral history: An introduction for students.* Chapel Hill: University of North Carolina Press.

Horn, J. L. (1970). Organization of data on life-span development of human abilities. In L. R. Goulet & P. B. Baltes (Eds.), *Life span developmental psychology: Research and theory* (pp. 423-466). San Diego, CA: Academic Press.

Horn, J. L. (1982). The aging of human abilities. In B. B. Wolman (Eds.), *Handbook of developmental psychology* (pp. 847-870). Englewood Cliffs, NJ: Prentice Hall.

Horn, J. L., & Cattell, R. B. (1967). Age differences in fluid and crystallized intelligence. *Acta Psychologica, 31,* 701-709.

Houseknecht, S., & Macke, A. (1981). Combining marriages and career: The marital adjustment of professional women. *Journal of Marriage and the Family, 43,* 651-661.

Howard, A., & Bray, D. W. (1988). *Managerial lives in transition: Advancing age and changing times.* New York: Guilford.

Howell, D. (1987, Spring). Clause and effect. *Teacher to Teacher,* p. 2.

Hultsch, D. (1969). Adult age differences in the organization of free recall. *Developmental Psychology, 1,* 673-678.

Hultsch, D. (1971). Adult age differences in free classification and free recall. *Developmental Psychology, 4,* 338-342.

Hultsch, D. (1974). Learning to learn in adulthood. *Journal of Gerontology, 29,* 302-308.

Hunt, D. (1966). A conceptual systems change model and its applications to education. In O. J. Harvey (Ed.), *Experience, structure, and adaptability.* New York: Springer.

Huston, T. L., Robins, E., Atkinson, J., & McHale, S. M. (1987). Surveying the landscape of marital behavior: A behavioral self-report to studying marriage. In S. Oskamp (Ed.), *Family processes and problems: Social psychological aspects* (pp. 45-72). Newbury Park, CA: Sage.

Ickes, W. (1981). Sex-role influence in dyadic interaction: A theoretical model. In C. Mayo & N. Henley (Eds.), *Gender and non-verbal behavior.* New York: Springer.

Ickes, W., & Barnes, R. D. (1977). The role of sex and self-monitoring in unstructured dyadic interactions. *Journal of Personality and Social Psychology, 35,* 315-330.

Ickes, W., & Barnes, R. D. (1978). Boys and girls together—and alienated: On enacting stereotyped sex-roles in mixed-sex dyads. *Journal of Personality and Social Psychology, 36,* 669-683.

Jacobs, B. (1986, July 18). Modern love: Share pad, tie knot. *USA Today*, p. 1D.

Jaffe, D. T., & Allman, L. R. (1982). Adaptation and development. In L. R. Allman & D. T. Jaffe (Eds.), *Readings in adult psychology: Contemporary perspectives* (2nd ed., pp. 3-12). New York: Harper & Row.

James, W. (1902). *Varieties of religious experience.* New York: New American Library.

Janus, S., & Janus, C. (1993). *Janus report on sexual behavior.* New York: John Wiley.

Jaques, E. (1965). Death and the mid-life crisis. *International Journal of Psychoanalysis, 46,* 502-514.

Jaquish, G. A., & Ripple, R. E. (1980). Divergent thinking and self-esteem in preadolescents and adolescents. *Journal of Youth and Adolescence, 9*(2), 143-152.

Jeffers, F., Nichols, C., & Eisdorfer, C. (1961). Attitudes of older persons toward death: A preliminary study. *Journal of Gerontology, 16,* 34-43.

John, O. P., & Robins, R. W. (1993). Gordon Allport: Father and critic of the five-factor model. In K. H. Craik, R. Hogan, & R. N. Wolfe (Eds.), *Fifty years of personality psychology* (pp. 215-236). New York: Plenum.

Jones, E. E., & Davis, K. E. (1965). From acts to dispositions: The attribution process in person perception. In L. Berkowitz (Ed.), *Advances in experimental social psychology* (Vol. 2, pp. 219-266). San Diego, CA: Academic Press.

Joy, S., Fein, D., & Kaplan, E. (1992, August). *The Digit Symbol Test of the WAIS-R as a neuropsychological instrument among healthy older adults.* Paper presented at the meetings of the American Psychological Association, Washington, D.C.

Joyner, C. (1984). *Down by the riverside.* Urbana: University of Illinois Press.

Kagan, J., & Snidman, N. (1991). Temperamental factors in human development. *American Psychologist, 46,* 856-862.

Kalish, R. A. (1963). An approach to the study of death attitudes. *American Behavioral Scientist, 6*(9), 68-71.

Kalish, R. A. (1976). Death and dying in a social context. In R. Binstock & E. Shanas (Eds.), *Handbook of aging and the social sciences* (pp. 483-507). New York: Van Nostrand Reinhold.

Kaminer, W. (1991, December). Put the blame on Mame. *Atlantic Monthly,* pp. 123-126.

Kaminer, W. (1992, April). Backlash. *Atlantic Monthly,* p. 17.

Kangas, J., & Bradway, K. (1971). Intelligence at middle-age: A thirty-eight year follow-up. *Developmental Psychology, 5,* 333-337.

Kaplan, D. A. (1991, September 16). Supreme mystery. *Newsweek,* pp. 18-31.

Kastenbaum, R. (1977). Death and development through the life span. In H. Feifel (Ed.), *New meanings of death* (pp. 17-45). New York: McGraw-Hill.

Kastenbaum, R. (1977). *Death, society, and human experience.* St. Louis: C. V. Mosby.

Kastenbaum, R., & Aisenberg, R. (1972). *The psychology of death.* New York: Springer.

Kastenbaum, R., & Costa, P. T., Jr. (1977). Psychological perspectives on death. *Annual Review of Psychology, 28,* 225-249.

Kausler, D. H. (1982). *Experimental psychology and human aging.* New York: John Wiley.

Kazin, A. (1979). The self as history: Reflections on autobiography. In M. Pachter (Ed.), *Telling lives: The biographer's art* (pp. 74-89). Washington, DC: New Republic Books/National Portrait Gallery.

Kazin, A. (1987, December 14). Apologia pro vita sua. *The New Yorker,* pp. 150-154.

Kearns, D. (1979). Angles of vision. In M. Pachter (Ed.), *Telling lives: The biographer's art* (pp. 90-103). Washington, DC: New Republic Books/National Portrait Gallery.

Kekes, J. (1983). Wisdom. *American Philosophical Quarterly, 20,* 277-286.

Kellas, G., Simpson, G., & Ferraro, F. R. (1988). Aging and performance: A mental workload analysis. In P. Whitney & R. Ochsman (Eds.), *Psychology and productivity* (pp. 35-50). New York: Plenum.

Kelley, H. H. (1967). Attribution theory in social psychology. In D. Levine (Ed.), *Nebraska Symposium on Motivation, 1967* (Vol. 15, pp. 192-238). Lincoln: University of Nebraska Press.

Kelley, J. (1985, November 20). Live-ins drop out of style; marriage in. *USA Today,* p. 1D.

Kelly, G. A. (1955). *The psychology of personal constructs.* New York: Norton.

Kemper, S. (1987). Life-span changes in syntactic complexity. *Journal of Gerontology, 42,* 323-328.

Kemper, S. (1990). Adults' diaries: Changes to written narratives across the life span. *Discourse Processes, 13,* 207-224.

Kiecolt-Glaser, J. K., Fisher, L. D., Ogrocki, P., Stout, J. C., Speicher, C. E., & Glaser, R. (1987). Marital quality, marital disruption, and immune function. *Psychosomatic Medicine, 49,* 13-34.

Kiell, N. (1964). *The universal experience of adolescence.* New York: International Universities Press.

Kim, M. P., & Rosenberg, S. (1980). Comparison of two structural models of implicit personality theory. *Journal of Personality and Social Psychology, 38,* 375-389.

Kinsey, A., Pomeroy, W., Martin, C., & Gebhard, P. (1953). *Sexual behavior in the human female.* Philadelphia: J. B. Saunders.

Kinsley, M. (1990, August 20). You must be very busy. *Time,* p. 82.

Kite, M. E., & Deaux, K. (1986). Gender versus category clustering in free recall: A test of gender schema theory. *Representative Research in Social Psychology, 16,* 38-43.

Knight-Ridder News Service. (1989, January 20). Study says 1 in 5 men has had homosexual encounter. *Lawrence Journal-World,* p. 5D.

Kohlberg, L. (1958). *The development of modes of thinking and choices in the years 10 to 16.* Unpublished doctoral dissertation, University of Chicago.

Kohlberg, L. (1963). The development of children's orientations to a moral order: Vol. I. Sequence in the development of moral thought. *Vita Humana, 6,* 11-33.

Kohlberg, L. (1971). From is to ought: How to commit the naturalistic fallacy and get away with it in the study of moral development. In T. Mischel (Ed.), *Cognitive development and epistemology* (pp. 151-235). San Diego, CA: Academic Press.

Kohlberg, L. (1973). Continuities in childhood and adult moral development revisited. In P. Baltes & K. W. Schaie (Eds.), *Lifespan developmental psychology* (pp. 179-204). San Diego, CA: Academic Press.

Kohlberg, L. (1980). The future of liberalism as the dominant ideology of the west. In R. W. Wilson & G. J. Schochet (Eds.), *Moral development and politics* (pp. 55-68). New York: Praeger.

Kohlberg, L. (1981). *Essays on moral development* (Vol. 1). New York: Harper & Row.

Koocher, G. (1973). Childhood, death, and cognitive development. *Developmental Psychology, 9,* 369-375.

Kramer, P. D. (1993). *Listening to Prozac.* New York: Viking.

Krantz, D. L. (1977). The Santa Fe experience. In S. B. Sarason (Ed.), *Work, aging, and social change: Professionals and the one-life, one-career imperative* (pp. 165-188). New York: Free Press.

Krawiec, T. S. (Ed.). (1972). *The psychologists* (Vol. 1). New York: Oxford University Press.

Krawiec, T. S. (Ed.). (1974). *The psychologists* (Vol. 2). New York: Oxford University Press.

Krueger, E. T., & Reckless, W. C. (1931). *Social psychology.* New York: Longmans.

Kübler-Ross, E. (1969). *On death and dying.* New York: Macmillan.

Kuhn, D., Langer, J., Kohlberg, L., & Haan, N. (1977). The development of formal operations in logical and moral judgment. *Genetic Psychology Monographs, 95,* 97-188.

Kurtines, W. M., & Gewirtz, J. L. (Eds.). (1984). *Morality, moral behavior, and moral development.* New York: John Wiley.

Kurtines, W. M., & Gewirtz, J. L. (Eds.). (1987). *Moral development through social interaction.* New York: John Wiley.

Kurtines, W. M., & Gerwirtz, J. L. (Eds.). (1991). *Handbook of moral behavior and development.* Hillsdale, NJ: Lawrence Erlbaum.

Lachman, M. E. (1991). Perceived control over memory aging: Developmental and intervention perspectives. *Journal of Social Issues, 47*(4), 159-175.

Landers, A. (1989a, January 22). Readers sketch disturbing picture of their marriages. *Kansas City Star,* p. 3G.

Landers, A. (1989b, January 23). More reports on sex after marriage. *Lawrence Journal-World,* p. 5A.

Langdale, C. J. (1986). A re-vision of structural-developmental theory. In G. L. Sapp (Ed.), *Handbook of moral development* (pp. 15-54). Birmingham, AL: Religious Education Press.

Langer, L. L. (1991). *Holocaust testimonies: The ruins of memory.* New Haven, CT: Yale University Press.

Larwood, L., & Gattiker, U. (1987). A comparison of the career paths used by successful women and men. In B. A. Gutek & L. Larwood (Eds.), *Women's career development* (pp. 129-156). Newbury Park, CA: Sage.

Laudenslager, M. L. (1988). The psychobiology of loss: Lessons from humans and nonhuman primates. *Journal of Social Issues, 49*(3), 19-36.

Lawrence, B. S. (1980, Summer). The myth of the midlife crisis. *Sloan Management Review, 21*(4), 35-49.

Lawson, C. (1991, April 4). When reluctant parents allow dating to extend to the bedroom. *The New York Times,* pp. B1, B2.

Lederberg, J. (1990). *Autobiographical memoirs of eminent scientists* (Vol. 3). Palo Alto, CA: Annual Reviews.

Lehman, D. (1988, June 13). Seeking the existential sleuth. *Newsweek*, p. 75.

Lehman, H. C. (1953). *Age and achievement*. Princeton, NJ: Princeton University Press.

Leonard, W. E. (1927). *The locomotive god*. New York: Century.

Lester, D. (1967). Experimental and correlational studies of the fear of death. *Psychological Bulletin, 67*, 27-36.

Lester, D. (1970). The fear of death. *Omega: Journal of Death and Dying, 1*, 181-188.

Levinger, G. (1979). A social psychological perspective on marriage dissolution. In G. Levinger & O. C. Moles (Eds.), *Divorce and separation*. New York: Basic Books.

Levinson, D. J. (1978). *The seasons of a man's life*. New York: Knopf.

Levinson, D. J. (1980). Toward a conception of the adult life course. In N. J. Smelser & E. H. Erikson (Eds.), *Themes of work and love in adulthood* (pp. 265-290). Cambridge, MA: Harvard University Press.

Levinson, D. J., Darrow, C. N., Klein, E. B., Levinson, M. H., & McKee, B. (1977). Periods in the adult development of men: Ages 18 to 45. In N. K. Schlossberg & A. D. Entine (Eds.), *Counseling adults* (pp. 47-59). Pacific Grove, CA: Brooks/Cole.

Lieberman, M. A., & Caplan, A. S. (1970). Distance from death as a variable in the study of aging. *Developmental Psychology, 2*, 71-84.

Lief, H. (1978). Unpublished research, cited by C. B. Broderick (1982): Adult sexual development. In B. B. Wolman & G. Stricker (Eds.), *Handbook of developmental psychology* (pp. 726-733). Englewood Cliffs, NJ: Prentice Hall.

Lifton, P. D. (1986). Personological and psychodynamic explanations of moral development. In G. L. Sapp (Ed.), *Handbook of moral development* (pp. 55-73). Birmingham, AL: Religious Education Press.

Lifton, R. J. (1979). *The broken connection*. New York: Simon & Schuster.

Lifton, R. J., & Olson, E. (1982). Death and the life cycle. In L. R. Allman & D. T. Jaffe (Eds.), *Readings in adult psychology: Contemporary perspectives* (2nd ed., pp. 73-79). New York: Harper & Row.

Light, L. L. (1991). Memory and aging: Four hypotheses in search of data. *Annual Review of Psychology, 42*, 333-376.

Light, L. L., Singh, A., & Capps, J. L. (1986). Dissociation of memory and awareness in young and older adults. *Journal of Clinical and Experimental Neuropsychology, 8*, 62-74.

Lindzey, G. (Ed.). (1974). *A history of psychology in autobiography* (Vol. 6). Englewood Cliffs, NJ: Prentice Hall.

Lindzey, G. (Ed.). (1980). *A history of psychology in autobiography* (Vol. 7). San Francisco: Freeman.

Lindzey, G. (Ed.). (1989). *A history of psychology in autobiography* (Vol. 8). San Francisco: Freeman.

Locksley, A., & Colten, M. E. (1979). Psychological androgyny: A case of mistaken identity? *Journal of Personality and Social Psychology, 37*, 1017-1031.

Loehlin, J. C. (1992). *Genetics and environment in personality development*. Newbury Park, CA: Sage.

Lonetto, R., & Templer, D. I. (1986). *Death anxiety*. Washington, DC: Hemisphere.

Lopata, H. Z. (1988). Support systems of American urban widowhood. *Journal of Social Issues, 44*(3), 113-128.

Lowenthal, M. F., Thurnher, M., Chiriboga, D., & Associates. (1975). *Four stages of life: A comparative study of women and men facing transitions.* San Francisco: Jossey-Bass.

Luck, J. M. (Ed.). (1965). *Autobiographical memoirs of eminent scientists* (Vol. 1). Palo Alto, CA: Annual Reviews.

Lykken, D. T. (1982). Research with twins: The concept of emergenesis. *Psychophysiology, 19,* 361-373.

Lykken, D. T., McGue, M., Tellegen, A., & Bouchard, T. J., Jr. (1992). Emergenesis: Genetic traits that may not run in families. *American Psychologist, 47,* 1565-1577.

Lyons, N. (1982). *Conceptions of self and morality and modes of moral choice: Identifying justice and care in judgments of actual dilemmas.* Unpublished doctoral dissertation, Harvard University.

Lyons, N. (1983). Two perspectives: On self, relationship, and morality. *Harvard Educational Review, 53*(1), 125-145.

Lytton, H., & Hunter, W. (1992). Morality play, part three: Acts 1-3. *Contemporary Psychology, 37,* 1159-1161.

Maas, H., & Kuypers, J. (1974). *From thirty to seventy.* San Francisco: Jossey-Bass.

Maciel, A. G., Sowarka, D., Smith, J., & Baltes, P. B. (1992, August). *Features of wisdom: Prototypical attributes of wise people.* Paper presented at the meetings of the American Psychological Association, Washington, D.C.

Maciel, A. G., Staudinger, U. M, Smith, J., & Baltes, P. B. (1991, August). *Which factors contribute to wisdom: Age, intelligence, or personality?* Paper presented at the meetings of the American Psychological Association, San Francisco.

MacMahon, B., & Pugh, T. F. (1965). Suicide in the widowed. *American Journal of Epidemiology, 81,* 23-31.

Magni, K. (1970). Reactions to death stimuli among theology students. *Journal for the Scientific Study of Religion, 9,* 247-248.

Malcolm, J. (1990). *The journalist and the murderer.* New York: Knopf.

Mallon, T. (1984). *A book of one's own: People and their diaries.* New York: Ticknor & Fields.

Malveaux, J. (1991, September 12). The Thomas view of "women's work." *USA Today,* p. 13 A.

Mandel, B. J. (1980). Full of life now. In J. Olney (Ed.), *Autobiography: Essays theoretical and critical* (pp. 49-72). Princeton, NJ: Princeton University Press.

Mangione, L. (1984). Artist and artistry: A representative case study. (Doctoral dissertation, University of Kansas, Lawrence). *Dissertation Abstracts International, 45,* 2659B.

Mangione, L. (1993). Life themes manifest though artistic creativity. In J. Demick & P. Miller (Eds.), *Development in the workplace* (pp. 109-128). Hillsdale, NJ: Lawrence Erlbaum.

Manniche, E., & Falk, G. (1957). Age and the Nobel prize. *Behavioral Science, 2,* 301-307.

Manning, A. (1991, June 7). Marrying age higher than ever before. *USA Today,* p. D1.

Manning, A. (1993, March 30). Women tell the stories of their lives. *USA Today,* p. 4D.

Markides, K. S., & Cooper, C. L. (Eds.). (1989). *Aging, stress and health.* New York: John Wiley.

Marshall, V. (1975). Age and awareness of finitude in developmental gerontology. *Omega: Journal of Death and Dying, 6*(2), 113-127.

Martin, D., & Wrightsman, L. S. (1965). The relationship between religious behavior and concern about death. *Journal of Social Psychology, 65,* 317-323.

Masters, W., & Johnson, V. (1966). *Human sexual response.* Boston: Little, Brown.

Matthews, K. A., Wing, R., Kuller, L., Meilahn, E. N., Kelsey, S. F., Costello, E. J., & Caggiula, A. W. (1990). Influences of natural menopause on psychological characteristics and symptoms of middle-aged healthy women. *Journal of Consulting and Clinical Psychology, 58,* 345-351.

May, W. (1973). Attitudes toward the newly dead. *Hastings Center Studies, 1*(1), 3-13.

McAdams, D. P. (1990). *The person: An introduction to personality psychology.* New York: Harcourt Brace Jovanovich.

McAdams, D. P., & Bryant, F. B. (1985, August). *Intimacy motivation and subjective mental health in a nationwide sample.* Paper presented at the meetings of the American Psychological Association, Los Angeles.

McCartney, K., Harris, M. J., & Bernieri, F. (1990). Growing up and growing apart: A developmental meta-analysis of twin studies. *Psychological Bulletin, 107,* 226-237.

McClelland, D. C. (1964). French national character and the life and works of André Gide. In D. C. McClelland, *The roots of consciousness* (pp. 93-116). New York: D. Van Nostrand.

McCrae, R. R., & Costa, P. T., Jr. (1988). Psychological resilience among widowed men and women: A 10-year follow-up of a national sample. *Journal of Social Issues, 44*(3), 129-142.

McCullough, D. (1992, July 19). Interview on "Book Notes," C-SPAN Television Network.

McFarlane, J. (1987, August 17). The meaning of marriage. *Newsweek,* p. 8.

Mednick, S. A. (1962). The associative basis of the creative process. *Psychological Review, 69,* 220-232.

Mednick, S. (1963). Research creativity in psychology graduate students. *Journal of Consulting Psychology, 27,* 265-266.

Metzler, K. (1977). *Creative interviewing.* Englewood Cliffs, NJ: Prentice Hall.

Meyers, J. (1985). Introduction. In J. Meyers (Ed.), *The craft of literary biography* (pp. 1-8). New York: Schocken.

Midler, B. (1980). *A view from a broad.* New York: Simon & Schuster.

Milgram, R. M. (1990). Creativity: An idea whose time has come and gone? In M. A. Runco & R. S. Albert (Eds.), *Theories of creativity* (pp. 215-233). Newbury Park, CA: Sage.

Miller, A. (1987). *Timebends: A life.* New York: Grove.

Minton, B., & Spilka, B. (1976). Perspectives on death in relation to powerlessness and form of personal religion. *Omega: Journal of Death and Dying, 7,* 261-267.

Mitchell, D. B. (1989). How many memory systems? Evidence from aging. *Journal of Experimental Psychology: Learning, Memory and Cognition, 15,* 31-49.

Moffitt, P. (1986, December). Cooling out. *Esquire,* pp. 47-48.

Morawski, J. G. (1987). The troubled quest for masculinity, femininity, and androgyny. In P. Shaver & C. Hendrick (Eds.), *Sex and Gender* (pp. 44-69). Newbury Park, CA: Sage.

Morin, R. (1993, June 7-13). What's fair in love and fights? *The Washington Post National Weekly Edition*, p. 37.

Moss, W. (1985). Oral history or literary impressionism? *The Oral History Review, 13*, 131-135.

Mulvey, M. (1963). Psychological and sociological factors in prediction of career patterns for women. *Genetic Psychology Monographs, 68*, 313-386.

Munnichs, J. M. (1961). Comments. In R. Havighurst (Ed.), Attitudes toward death in older persons: A symposium. *Journal of Gerontology, 16*, 44-56.

Munnichs, J. M. (1966). *Old age and finitude*. New York: Karger.

Murchison, C. (Ed.). (1930). *A history of psychology in autobiography* (Vol. 1). Worcester, MA: Clark University Press.

Murchison, C. (Ed.). (1932). *A history of psychology in autobiography* (Vol. 2). Worcester, MA: Clark University Press.

Murchison, C. (Ed.). (1936). *A history of psychology in autobiography* (Vol. 3). Worcester, MA: Clark University Press.

Murray, H. A. (1938). *Explorations in personality*. New York: Oxford University Press.

Murray, H. A. (1967). The case of Murr. In E. G. Boring & G. Lindzey (Eds.), *A history of psychology in autobiography* (Vol. 5, pp. 285-310). New York: Appleton-Century-Crofts.

Nadel, I. B. (1984). *Biography: Fiction, fact and form*. New York: Saint Martin's.

Nagy, M. H. (1948). The child's theories concerning death. *Journal of Genetic Psychology, 73*, 3-27.

Nassi, A. J., Abramowitz, S. I., & Youmans, J. E. (1983). Moral development and politics a decade later: A replication and extension. *Journal of Personality and Social Psychology, 45*, 1127-1135.

Neugarten, B. L. (1968). The awareness of middle age. In B. L. Neugarten (Ed.), *Middle age and aging: A reader in social psychology* (pp. 93-98). Chicago: University of Chicago Press.

Nevins, A. (1966). Oral history: How and why it was born. In D. J. Dunaway & W. K. Baum (Eds.), *Oral history* (pp. 27-36). Nashville, TN: American Association for State and Local History.

Nieva, V. F., & Gutek, B. A. (1981). *Women and work: A psychological perspective*. New York: Praeger.

O'Connell, A. N., & Russo, N. F. (Eds.). (1983). *Models of achievement: Reflections of eminent women in psychology*. New York: Columbia University Press.

O'Leary, A. (1989). Effects of a broken heart: Health consequences for survivors. *Contemporary Psychology, 34*, 553-554.

Olivier, L. (1982). *Confessions of an actor: An autobiography*. New York: Simon & Schuster.

Olney, J. (1972). *Metaphors of self: The meaning of autobiography*. Princeton, NJ: Princeton University Press.

Olney, J. (1980). Autobiography and the cultural moment: A thematic, historical, and bibliographical introduction. In J. Olney (Ed.), *Autobiography: Essays theoretical and critical* (pp. 3-27). Princeton, NJ: Princeton University Press.

O'Neil, J. M. (1981a). Male sex role conflicts, sexism and masculinity: Psychological implications for men, women, and the counseling psychologist. *Counseling Psychologist, 9*, 61-80.

O'Neil, J. M. (1981b). Patterns of gender role conflict and strain: Sexism and fear of femininity in men's lives. *Personnel and Guidance Journal, 60,* 203-210.

O'Neil, J. M., & Egan, J. (1992). Men's gender role transitions over the life span: Transformations and fears of femininity. *Journal of Mental Health Counseling, 14,* 305-324.

O'Neil, J. M., & Fishman, D. M. (1986). Adult men's career transitions and gender-role themes. In Z. B. Leibowitz & H. D. Lea (Eds.), *Adult career development: Concepts, issues, and practices.* Alexandria, VA: AACD.

O'Neil, J. M., Fishman, D. M., & Kinsella-Shaw, M. (1987). Dual-career couples' career transitions and normative dilemmas: A preliminary assessment model. *Counseling Psychologist, 15,* 50-96.

O'Neil, J. M., Helms, B. J., Gable, R. K., David, L., & Wrightsman, L. S. (1986). Gender-role conflict scale: College men's fear of femininity. *Sex Roles, 14,* 335-350.

O'Reilly, J. (1989, November 26). Any woman is an outsider. *The New York Times Book Review,* pp. 7-8.

Oromaner, M. (1981). The quality of scientific scholarship and the "growing" of the academic profession: A skeptical view. *Research in Higher Education, 15,* 231-239.

Orwoll, L., & Perlmutter, M. (1990). The study of wise persons: Integrating a personality perspective. In R. J. Sternberg (Ed.), *Wisdom: Its nature, origins, and development* (pp. 160-177). New York: Cambridge University Press.

Osarchuk, M., & Tatz, S. J. (1973). Effect of induced fear of death on belief in after life. *Journal of Personality and Social Psychology, 27,* 256-260.

Osherson, S. D. (1980). *Holding on or letting go: Men and career change at midlife.* New York: Free Press.

Owens, W. (1953). Age and mental abilities: A longitudinal study. *Genetic Psychology Monographs, 48,* 3-54.

Owens, W. (1959). Is age kinder to the initially more able? *Journal of Gerontology, 14,* 334-337.

Pachter, M. (1979). The biographer himself: An introduction. In M. Pachter (Ed.), *Telling lives: The biographer's art* (pp. 2-15). Washington, DC: New Republic Books/National Portrait Gallery.

Painter, K. (1991, March 5). Fewer kids save sex for adulthood. *USA Today,* pp. 1D, 2D.

Painton, P. (1993, April 26). The shrinking ten percent. *Time,* pp. 27-29.

Papadatou, D., & Papadatos, C. (Eds.). (1991). *Children and death.* New York: Hemisphere.

Parkes, C. M. (1972). *Bereavement: Studies of grief in adult life.* London: Tavistock.

Parkes, C. M. (1988). Bereavement as a psychosocial transition: Processes of adaptation to change. *Journal of Social Issues, 44,* 53-65.

Parkes, C. M., & Brown, R. (1972). Health after bereavement: A controlled study of young Boston widows and widowers. *Psychosomatic Medicine, 34,* 449-461.

Parron, E. (1979). *Relationship of Black and White golden wedding couples.* Unpublished doctoral dissertation, Rutgers: The State University of New Jersey.

Pauker, S. L., & Arond, M. (1989). *The first year of marriage: What to expect, what to accept and what you can change.* New York: Warner Books.

References 219

Pearlman, C. (1972, November). Frequency of intercourse in males at different ages. *Medical Aspects of Sexuality,* 92-113.

Pedersen, N. L., Plomin, R., McClearn, G. E., & Friberg, L. (1988). Neuroticism, extraversion, and related traits in adult twins reared apart and reared together. *Journal of Personality and Social Psychology, 55,* 950-957.

Pedhazur, E., & Tetenbaum, T. J. (1979). Bem Sex-Role Inventory: A theoretical and methodological critique. *Journal of Personality and Social Psychology, 37,* 996-1016.

Pellman, J. (1991, May). *Widowhood in elderly women: Exploring its relationship to community integration, hassles, and stress.* Paper presented at the meetings of the Midwestern Psychological Association, Chicago.

Pellman, J. (1992). Widowhood in elderly women: Exploring its relationship to community integration, hassles, stress, social support, and social support seeking. *International Journal of Aging and Human Development, 35,* 253-264.

Perun, P. J., & Bielby, D. D. (1981). Toward a model of female occupational behavior: A human development approach. *Psychology of Women Quarterly, 6,* 234-250.

Peters, R. G. (1971). Moral development: A plea for pluralism. In T. Mischel (Ed.), *Cognitive development and epistemology* (pp. 237-267). San Diego, CA: Academic Press.

Peterson, R. D. (1988, August). *Oral history: The issues surrounding its practice.* Unpublished paper, University of Kansas.

Petzel, T. P. (1988). Unraveling death anxiety. *Contemporary Psychology, 33,* 807.

Piaget, J. (1965). *The moral judgment of the child.* New York: Free Press. (Original work published 1932)

Pietropinto, A., & Simenauer, J. (1979). *Husbands and wives.* New York: Times Books.

Pineo, P. (1961). Disenchantment in the later years of marriage. *Marriage and Family Living, 23,* 1-12.

Pines, A., & Aronson, E. (1988). *Career burnout: Causes and cures.* New York: Free Press.

Pleck, J. H. (1981, September). Prisoners of manliness. *Psychology Today,* pp. 69-83.

Pleck, J. H. (1982). The male sex role: Definitions, problems, and sources of change. In L. R. Allman & D. T. Jaffe (Eds.), *Readings in adult psychology: Contemporary perspectives* (2nd ed., pp. 153-159). New York: Harper & Row.

Plomin, R. (1990). *Nature and nurture: An introduction to human behavior genetics.* Pacific Grove, CA: Brooks/Cole.

Plutarch. (1935). *Lives of the noble Grecians and Romans.* New York: Modern Library. (First published about A.D. 100)

Pocs, O., & Godow, A. G. (1977). Can students view parents as sexual beings? In D. Byrne & L. Byrne (Eds.), *Exploring human sexuality.* New York: Crowell.

Power, F. C., Higgins, A., & Kohlberg, L. (1989). *Lawrence Kohlberg's approach to moral education.* New York: Columbia University Press.

Pratt, M. W., & Royer, J. M. (1982). When rights and responsibilities don't mix: Sex and sex-role patterns in moral judgment orientation. *Canadian Journal of Behavioural Science, 14,* 190-214.

Pruyser, P. W. (1987). *Creativity without noted talent in aging persons.* Unpublished paper, Menninger Foundation, Topeka, KS.

Radloff, L. S. (1975). Sex differences in depression. The effects of occupation and marital status. *Sex Roles, 1,* 249-265.

Ralph, N. (1973). Stages of faculty development. In M. Freedman (Ed.), *Facilitating faculty development.* San Francisco: Jossey-Bass.

Ramey, E. (1987, June). *Hormones, stress, and aging.* Address to the National Press Club, Washington, D.C.

Raphael, B. (1983). *The anatomy of bereavement.* New York: Basic Books.

Rapoport, R., & Rapoport, R. N. (1969). The dual-career family: A variant pattern and social change. *Human Relations, 22,* 3-29.

Rawls, J. (1971). *Theory of justice.* Cambridge, MA: Harvard University Press.

Rebecca, M., & Hefner, R. (1982). The future of sex roles. In L. R. Allman & D. T. Jaffe (Eds.), *Readings in adult psychology: Contemporary perspectives* (pp. 160-170). New York: Harper & Row.

Rebok, G. W., & Balcerak, L. J. (1989). Memory self-efficacy and performance differences in young and old adults: The effect of mnemonic training. *Developmental Psychology, 25,* 714-721.

Reefer, M. M. (1990, November/December). Expecting an exposé. *American Book Review, 12*(5), 14.

Reicher, S., & Emler, N. (1984). Moral orientation as a cue to political identity. *Political Psychology, 5,* 543-551.

Reid, H. G., & Yanarella, E. J. (1980). The tyranny of the categorical: On Kohlberg and the politics of moral judgment. In R. W. Wilson & G. J. Schochet (Eds.), *Moral development and politics* (pp. 107-132). New York: Praeger.

Renner, V. J., Alpaugh, P. K., & Birren, J. E. (1978, November). *Divergent thinking over the life span.* Paper presented at the annual meetings of the Gerontological Society, Dallas.

Rest, J. R. (1975). Longitudinal study of the Defining Issues Test of moral judgment: A strategy for analyzing developmental change. *Developmental Psychology, 11,* 738-748.

Rest, J. R. (1983). Morality. In P. Mussen (Ed.), *Carmichael's manual of child psychology* (Vol. 3, pp. 556-629). New York: John Wiley.

Richardson, L. (1992, September 2). Cookie-cutter roles for mothers are gone. *The New York Times,* p. A18.

Richardson-Klavehn, A., & Bjork, R. A. (1988). Measures of memory. *Annual Review of Psychology, 39,* 475-543.

Roberts, R. F. (1971). *The new communes: Coming together in America.* Englewood Cliffs, NJ: Prentice Hall.

Robinson, J. P., & Shaver, P. R. (1969). *Measures of social psychological attitudes.* Ann Arbor: University of Michigan, Institute for Social Research.

Rokeach, M. (1968). *Beliefs, attitudes, and values.* San Francisco: Jossey-Bass.

Rose, R. J., Koskenvuo, M., Kaprio, J., Sarna, S., & Langinvainio, H. (1988). Shared genes, shared experiences, and similarity of personality: Data from 14,188 adult Finnish co-twins. *Journal of Personality and Social Psychology, 54,* 161-171.

Rosenberg, S., & Jones, R. A. (1972). A method for investigating and representing a person's implicit theory of personality: Theodore Drieser's view of people. *Journal of Personality and Social Psychology, 22,* 372-386.

Rosenblatt, P. C. (1983). *Bitter bitter tears: Nineteenth century diarists and twentieth century grief theories.* Minneapolis: University of Minnesota Press.

Rosenwald, G. C. (1988). A theory of multiple-case research. In D. P. McAdams & R. L. Ochberg (Eds.), *Psychobiography and life narratives* (pp. 239-264). Durham, NC: Duke University Press.

Rossi, A. (1965). Barriers to the career choice of engineering, medicine, or science among American women. In J. A. Mattfield & C. Van Aken (Eds.), *Women and the scientific professions* (pp. 51-127). Cambridge: MIT Press.

Rubin, D. C. (Ed.). (1986). *Autobiographical memory*. Cambridge: Cambridge University Press.

Rubin, I. (1965). Transition in sex values: Implications for the evaluation of adolescents. *Journal of Marriage and the Family, 27,* 185-189.

Runyan, W. M. (1982). *Life histories and psychobiography*. New York: Oxford University Press.

Runyan, W. M. (1988). A historical and conceptual background to psychohistory. In W. M. Runyan (Ed.), *Psychology and historical interpretation* (pp. 3-60). New York: Oxford University Press.

Safier, G. (1964). A study of relationships between the life and death concepts of children. *Journal of Genetic Psychology, 105,* 283-294.

Sales, E. (1978). Women's adult development. In I. Frieze, J. E. Parsons, P. B. Johnson, D. N. Ruble, & G. L. Zellman (Eds.), *Women and sex roles: A social psychological perspective* (pp. 157-190). New York: Norton.

Sampson, E. E. (1977). Psychology and the American ideal. *Journal of Personality and Social Psychology, 35,* 767-782.

Sanders, C. M. (1988). Risk factors in bereavement outcome. *Journal of Social Issues, 44*(3), 97-111.

Sanford, N. (1971). Academic culture and the teacher's development. *Soundings, 54,* 357-371.

Sapiro, V. (1990, July). *What do we know about socialization during adulthood?* Paper presented at the meetings of the International Society for Political Psychology, Washington, D.C.

Sarason, S. B. (1977). *Work, aging, and social change: Professionals and the one life-one career imperative*. New York: Free Press.

Sarnoff, I., & Corwin, S. (1959). Castration anxiety and the fear of death. *Journal of Personality, 27,* 374-385.

Sarnoff, I., & Sarnoff, S. (1989, October). The dialectic of marriage. *Psychology Today*, pp. 54-57.

Schaie, K. W. (1983). Age differences in adult intelligence. In D. S. Woodruff & J. E. Birren (Eds.), *Aging: Scientific perspectives and social issues* (2nd ed., pp. 137-148). Pacific Grove, CA: Brooks/Cole.

Schmalz, J. (1993, April 16). Survey stirs debate on number of gay men in U.S. *The New York Times*, p. A10.

Schmid, R. E. (1985, November 20). Census says fewer unmarried couples living together. *Lawrence Journal-World*, p. 34.

Schmid, R. E. (1987, June 12). America's marriages setting records high and low. *Lawrence Journal-World*, p. 8D.

Schochet, G. J. (1980). From household to polity. In R. W. Wilson & G. J. Schochet (Eds.), *Moral development and politics* (pp. 206-215). New York: Praeger.

Schoenrade, P. A. (1986). *Belief in afterlife as a response to awareness of individual mortality*. Unpublished doctoral dissertation, University of Kansas.

Schoenrade, P. A. (1989). When I die . . . Belief in afterlife as a response to mortality. *Personality and Social Psychology Bulletin, 15,* 91-100.

Sears, D. O. (1990). Whither political socialization research? The question of persistence. In O. Ichilov (Ed.), *Political socialization, citizenship education, and democracy* (pp. 69-97). New York: Teachers College Press.

Sears, R. R. (1979, June). Mark Twain's separation anxiety. *Psychology Today,* pp. 100-104.

Seldon, A., & Pappworth, J. (1983). *By word of mouth: "Elite" oral history.* London: Methuen.

Sharpe, M. J., & Heppner, P. (1991). Gender role, gender role conflict, and psychological well being in men. *Journal of Counseling Psychology, 38,* 323-330.

Sheehy, G. (1976). *Passages: Predictable crises of adult life.* New York: E. P. Dutton.

Sheehy, G. (1992). *The silent passage: Menopause.* New York: Random House.

Shneidman, E., & Farberow, N. (1957). *Clues to suicide.* New York: McGraw-Hill.

Shuchter, S. R. (1986). *Dimensions of grief: Adjusting to the death of a spouse.* San Francisco: Jossey-Bass.

Siegman, A. W. (1961). *The relationships between religion, personality variables, and attitudes and feelings about death.* Paper presented at the meetings of the Society for the Scientific Study of Religion, New York City.

Sigel, R. S. (1989). Introduction: Persistence and change. In R. S. Sigel (Ed.), *Political learning during adulthood* (pp. vii-xvi). Chicago: University of Chicago Press.

Silver, A. (1981, November 8). Writing the good life. *The New York Times Book Review,* pp. 11, 22.

Silverman, P. R., & Cooperband, A. (1975). On widowhood: Mutual help and the elderly widow. *Journal of Geriatric Psychiatry, 8,* 9-27.

Simonton, D. K. (1977). Creative productivity, age, and stress: A biographical time-series analysis of 10 classical composers. *Journal of Personality and Social Psychology, 35,* 791-804.

Simonton, D. K. (1984). *Genius, creativity, and leadership: Historiometric inquiries.* Cambridge, MA: Harvard University Press.

Simonton, D. K. (1985). Quality, quantity, and age: The careers of 10 distinguished psychologists. *International Journal of Aging and Human Development, 21,* 241-254.

Simonton, D. K. (1988). Age and outstanding achievement: What do we know after a century of research? *Psychological Bulletin, 104,* 251-267.

Simonton, D. K. (1989). The swan-song phenomenon: Last-work effects for 172 classical composers. *Psychology and Aging, 4,* 42-47.

Simonton, D. K. (1990). Creativity in the later years: Optimistic prospects for achievement. *The Gerontologist, 30,* 626-631.

Simonton, D. K. (1993, February 19). *Gifted child—genius adult: Three life-span developmental perspectives.* Paper presented at the Third Annual Esther Katz Rosen Symposium on the Psychological Development of Gifted Children, Lawrence, KS.

Sinnott, J. D., & Guttman, D. (1978). Dialectics of decision-making in older adults. *Human Development, 21,* 190-200.

Skidelsky, R. (1988). Only connect: Biography and truth. In E. Homberger & J. Charmley (Eds.), *The troubled face of biography* (pp. 1-16). New York: St. Martin's.

Skinner, B. F. (1973). *A matter of consequences.* New York: Knopf.

Skinner, B. F. (1976). *Particulars of my life.* New York: Knopf.

Skinner, B. F. (1979). *The shaping of a behaviorist.* New York: Knopf.

Smart, N. (1968). Attitudes toward death in eastern religions. In A. Toynbee, A. K. Mant, N. Smart, J. Hinton, C. Yudkin, E. Rhode, R. Heywood, & H. H. Price (Eds.), *Man's concern with death* (pp. 95-115). London: Hodder & Stroughton.

Smelser, N. J. (1980). Issues in the study of work and love in adulthood. In N. J. Smelser & E. H. Erikson (Eds.), *Themes of work and love in adulthood* (pp. 1-26). Cambridge, MA: Harvard University Press.

Smetana, J. G. (1981). Reasoning in the personal and moral domains: Adolescent and young adult women's decision-making regarding abortion. *Journal of Applied Developmental Psychology, 2,* 211-226.

Smith, M. B., Bruner, J. S., & White, R. W. (1956). *Opinions and personality.* New York: John Wiley.

Smolowe, J. (1992, June 22). Revenge of Donna Reed. *Time,* pp. 74-76.

Snarey, J. R. (1985). Cross-cultural universality of social-moral development: A critical review of Kohlbergian research. *Psychological Bulletin, 97,* 202-232.

Snider, M. (1991, September 16). More elderly turn to suicide. *USA Today,* p. 1A.

Solomon, S., Greenberg, J., & Pyszczynski, T. (1991). A terror management theory of social behavior: The psychological functions of self-esteem and cultural worldviews. In M. P. Zanna (Ed.), *Advances in experimental social psychology* (Vol. 24, pp. 93-159). San Diego, CA: Academic Press.

Sommers, D., & Eck, A. (1977). Occupational mobility in the American labor force. *Monthly Labor Review, 100*(1), 3-19.

Spence, J. T., & Helmreich, R. (1978). *Masculinity and femininity: Their psychological dimensions, correlates and antecedents.* Austin: University of Texas Press.

Spence, J. T., Helmreich, R., & Stapp, J. (1974). The Personal Attributes Questionnaire: A measure of sex-role stereotypes and masculinity-femininity. *JSAS Catalog of Selected Documents in Psychology, 4,* 127.

Spilka, B., Stout, L., Minton, B., & Sizemore, D. (1977). Death and personal faith: A psychometric investigation. *Journal for the Scientific Study of Religion, 16,* 169-178.

Spotts, J. V., & Shontz, F. C. (1980). *Cocaine users: A representative case approach.* New York: Free Press.

Spotts, J. V., & Shontz, F. C. (1987). Drug-induced ego states: A trajectory theory of drug experience. *Social Pharmacology, 1,* 19-51.

Spranger, E. (1928). *Types of men* (P. J. Pigors, Trans.). New York: Stechert-Hafner.

Squires, P. C. (1937). Fyodor Dostoevsky: A psychopathological sketch. *Psychoanalytic Review, 24,* 365-385.

Stambrook, M., & Parker, K. C. (1987). The development of the concept of death in childhood. *Merrill-Palmer Quarterly, 33,* 133-157.

Stanton, A. L., & Berger, B. A. (1987). Stresses and satisfactions of the two-pharmacist relationship. *American Journal of Hospital Pharmacy, 44,* 2729-2732.

Steel, R. (1986). Living with Walter Lippmann. In W. Zinsser (Ed.), *Extraordinary lives: The art and craft of American biography* (pp. 121-160). New York: Book-of-the-Month Club.

Stein, M. (1977). A psychoanalytic view of mental health: Samuel Pepys and his diary. *Psychoanalytic Quarterly, 46,* 82-115.

Stern, W. (1925). *Anfange der Reifezeit.* Leipzig: Quelle & Meyer.

Sternberg, R. J. (1986). A triangular story of love. *Psychological Review, 93,* 119-135.

Stewart, A., Franz, C., & Layton, L. (1988). The changing self: Using personal documents to study lives. In D. McAdams & R. Ochberg (Eds.), *Psychobiography and life narratives* (pp. 41-74). Durham, NC: Duke University Press.

Stewart, A. J., & Healy, J. M. (1985). Personality and adaptation to change. In R. Hogan & W. Jones (Eds.), *Perspectives on personality: Theory, measurement, and interpersonal dynamics* (pp. 117-144). Greenwich, CT: JAI Press.

Stewart, S. A. (1985, August 27). Affairs in our 30s: Both sexes sneak. *USA Today,* p. 1D.

Stewart, S. A. (1986, May 15). Sex is casual, despite new concerns. *USA Today,* p. 5D.

Stillson, R. W., O'Neil, J. M., & Owen, S. V. (1991). Predictions of adult men's gender-role conflict: Race, class, unemployment, age, instrumentality-expressiveness, and personal strain. *Journal of Counseling Psychology, 38,* 458-464.

Strachey, L. (1933). *Eminent Victorians.* New York: Modern Library.

Strasberg, S. (1980). *Bittersweet.* New York: Putnam.

Strasser, F., & Coyle, M. (1991, September 30). Still searching for the real Clarence Thomas. *National Law Journal,* p. 26.

Stroebe, M. S., Gergen, M. M., Gergen, K. J., & Stroebe, W. (1992). Broken hearts or broken bonds: Love and death in historical perspective. *American Psychologist, 47,* 1205-1212.

Stroebe, M. S., & Stroebe, W. (1983). Who suffers more? Sex differences in health risks of the widowed. *Psychological Bulletin, 93,* 279-301.

Stroebe, M. S., Stroebe, W., & Hansson, R. O. (1988). Bereavement research: An historical introduction. *Journal of Social Issues, 44,*(3), 1-18.

Stroebe, W., & Stroebe, M. S. (1987). *Bereavement and health: The psychological and physical consequences of partner loss.* New York: Cambridge University Press.

Stroebe, W., Stroebe, M. S., Gergen, K. J., & Gergen, M. (1982). The effects of bereavement on mortality: A social psychological analysis. In J. R. Eiser (Ed.), *Social psychology and behavioral medicine* (pp. 527-560). Chichester, England: John Wiley.

Strouse, J. (1986). The real reasons. In W. Zinsser (Ed.), *Extraordinary lives: The art and craft of literary biography* (pp. 161-195). New York: Book-of-the-Month Club.

Suedfeld, P., & Rank, A. D. (1976). Revolutionary leaders: Long-term success as a function of cognitive complexity. *Journal of Personality and Social Psychology, 34,* 169-178.

Sullivan, A. (1988, May 2). Oh my God. *New Republic,* pp. 23-25.

Super, D. E. (1957). *The psychology of careers.* New York: Harper & Row.

Super, D. E. (1971). A theory of vocational development. In H. J. Peters & J. C. Hansen (Eds.), *Vocational guidance and career development* (2nd ed., pp. 111-122). New York: Macmillan.

Super, D. E. (1986). Life career roles: Self-realization in work and leisure. In D. T. Hall & Associates (Eds.), *Career development in organizations* (pp. 95-119). San Francisco: Jossey-Bass.

Super, D. E. (1990). A life-span, life-space approach to career development. In D. Brown, L. Brooks, & Associates, *Career choice and development* (2nd ed., pp. 197-261). San Francisco: Jossey-Bass.

Surtees, P. G. (1980). Social support, residual adversity, and depressive outcome. *Social Psychiatry, 15,* 71-80.

Swede, S. W., & Tetlock, P. E. (1986). Henry Kissinger's implicit theory of personality: A quantitative case study. *Journal of Personality, 54,* 617-646.

Swenson, W. (1961). Attitudes toward death in an aged population. *Journal of Gerontology, 16,* 56-66.

Swogger, G. (1984, October). *Notes on "The Turning Key."* Paper presented at the meetings of the Mid-America Psychological Study Group, Topeka, KS.

Szuchman, L. T. (1991, August). *The wisdom of personal experience: Adult age differences in advice-giving.* Paper presented at the meetings of the American Psychological Association, San Francisco.

Tannen, D. (1992, October 2). The real Hillary Clinton factor. *The New York Times,* p. A17.

Taylor, M. C., & Hall, J. A. (1992). Psychological androgyny: Theories, methods, and conclusions. *Psychological Bulletin, 92,* 347-366.

Tellegen, A., Lykken, D. T., Bouchard, T. J., Wilcox, K., Segal, N. L., & Rich, S. (1988). Personality similarity in twins reared apart and together. *Journal of Personality and Social Psychology, 54,* 1031-1039.

Templer, D. I. (1971). The relationship between verbalized and nonverbalized death anxiety. *Journal of Genetic Psychology, 119,* 211-214.

Templer, D. I. (1972). Death anxiety in religiously very involved persons. *Psychological Reports, 31,* 361-362.

Templer, D. I., & Dotson, E. (1970). Religious correlates of death anxiety. *Psychological Reports, 26,* 895-897.

Templer, D. I., Ruff, C., & Franks, C. (1971). Death anxiety: Age, sex, and parental resemblance in diverse populations. *Developmental Psychology, 4,* 108.

Terkel, S. (1970). *Hard times: An oral history of the Great Depression.* New York: Pantheon.

Terkel, S. (1974). *Working: People talk about what they do all day and how they feel about what they do.* New York: Pantheon.

Terkel, S. (1980). *American dreams: Lost and found.* New York: Pantheon.

Terkel, S. (1984). *"The good war": An oral history of World War II.* New York: Pantheon.

Terkel, S. (1988). *The great divide: Second thoughts on the American dream.* New York: Pantheon.

Terman, L. M. (1925). *Genetic studies of genius.* Stanford, CA: Stanford University Press.

Tetlock, P. E. (1981). Pre- and post-election shifts in presidential rhetoric: Impression management or cognitive adjustment? *Journal of Personality and Social Psychology, 41,* 207-212.

The uses of personal testimony. (1981, June). *Items, 35*(1/2), 20-21.

Thomas, W. I., & Znaniecki, F. (1918). *The Polish peasant in Europe and America.* Boston: Gorham Press.

Thompson, J. (1988). *Gumshoe: Reflections in a private eye.* Boston: Little, Brown.

Thwaite, A. (1988). Writing lives. In E. Homberger & J. Charmley (Eds.), *The troubled face of biography* (pp. 17-32). New York: St. Martin's.

Torrance, E. P. (1963). *Education and the creative potential.* Minneapolis: University of Minnesota Press.

Torrance, E. P. (1974). *The Torrance Tests of Creative Thinking: Technical-norms manual.* Bensenville, IL: Scholastic Testing Services.

Torrance, E. P. (1987). *The blazing drive: The creative personality.* Buffalo, NY: Bearly Limited.

Torrance, E. P. (1988). The nature of creativity as manifest in its testing. In R. J. Sternberg (Ed.), *The nature of creativity* (pp. 43-75). New York: Cambridge University Press.

Tozzer, A. M. (1953). Biography and biology. In C. Kluckhohn, H. A. Murray, & D. M. Schneider (Eds.), *Personality in nature, society, and culture* (pp. 226-239). New York: Knopf.

Troll, L. E. (1982). *Continuations: Adult development and aging.* Pacific Grove, CA: Brooks/Cole.

Trudeau, M. (1979). *Beyond reason.* New York: Beekman.

Trump, D. J. (with C. Leerhsen). (1990). *Trump: Surviving at the top.* New York: Random House.

Tuchman, B. W. (1979). Biography as a prism of history. In M. Pachter (Ed.), *Telling lives: The biographer's art* (pp. 132-147). Washington, DC: New Republic Books/National Portrait Gallery.

Tulving, E. (1972). Episodic and semantic memory. In E. Tulving & W. Donaldson (Eds.), *Organization of memory* (pp. 382-403). Orlando, FL: Academic Press.

Tulving, E. (1985). How many memory systems are there? *American Psychologist, 40,* 385-398.

Tyler, L. (1977). The encounter with poverty—its effects on vocational psychology. In H. J. Peters & J. C. Hansen (Eds.), *Vocational guidance and career development* (3rd ed.). New York: Macmillan.

Uhlenhuth, K. (1987, September 5). A matter of conscience. *Kansas City Times,* pp. E-1, E-2.

Usdansky, M. L. (1992, December 9). 1990's wedding bell blues. *USA Today,* p. 12A.

Vaillant, G. E. (1977). *Adaptation to life.* Boston: Little, Brown.

Vansina, J. (1985). *Oral tradition as history.* Madison: University of Wisconsin Press.

Veroff, J., & Feld, S. (1971). *Marriage and work in America: A study of motives and roles.* New York: Van Nostrand.

Voda, A. M. (1982). Menopausal hot flash. In A. M. Voda, M. Dinnerstein, & S. R. O'Donnell (Eds.), *Changing perspectives on menopause* (pp. 126-159). Austin: University of Texas Press.

Vondracek, F. W., Lerner, R. M., & Schulenberg, J. E. (1986). *Career development: A life-span developmental approach.* Hillsdale, NJ: Lawrence Erlbaum.

Wachs, T. D. (1992). *The nature of nurture.* Newbury Park, CA: Sage.

Walker, L. J. (1984). Sex differences in the development of moral reasoning: A critical review. *Child Development, 55,* 677-691.

Walker, L. J. (1986). Cognitive processes in moral development. In G. L. Sapp (Ed.), *Handbook of moral development* (pp. 109-145). Birmingham, AL: Religious Education Press.

Walker, L. J. (1989). A longitudinal study of moral reasoning. *Child Development,* *60,* 157-166.

Walker, L. S., & Wallston, B. S. (1985). Social adaptation: A review of dual-career family literature. In L. L'Abate (Ed.), *The handbook of family psychology and family therapy* (pp. 698-740). Hillsdale, NJ: Lawrence Erlbaum.

Wallis, C. (1980, September 8). People and things. *Time,* p. 57.

Walsh, D. A. (1983). Age differences in learning and memory. In D. S. Woodruff & J. E. Birren (Eds.), *Aging: Scientific perspectives and social issues* (2nd ed., pp. 149-177). Pacific Grove, CA: Brooks/Cole.

Watts, K. F. (1989, Winter). A voice for Central America. *SMU Magazine,* pp. 23-24.

Weaver, S. L., & Lachman, M. E. (1990, August). *When memory fails: Adulthood age differences in attributions for memory.* Paper presented at the meetings of the American Psychological Association, Boston.

Wechsler, D. (1958). *The measurement and appraisal of adult intelligence* (4th ed.). Baltimore, MD: Williams & Wilkins.

Weg, R. B. (1989). Sensuality/sexuality of the middle years. In S. Hunter & M. Sundel (Eds.), *Midlife myths: Issues, findings, and practice implications* (pp. 31-50). Newbury Park, CA: Sage.

Weinberg, S. (1992). *Telling the untold story: How investigative reporters are changing the craft of biography.* Columbia: University of Missouri Press.

Weinrach, S. G., & Srebalus, D. J. (1990). Holland's theory of careers. In D. Brown, L. Brooks, & Associates, *Career choice and development* (2nd ed., pp. 37-67). San Francisco: Jossey-Bass.

Weintraub, K. J. (1978). *The value of the individual.* Chicago: University of Chicago Press.

Weisbard, K. (1988, August). *Parent-child relationships and the development of autonomy in women.* Paper presented at the meetings of the American Psychological Association, New Orleans, LA.

Weisman, L. (1992, September 2). Kelly gives book more than just a passing interest. *USA Today,* p. 3C.

Wells, H. G. (1934). *Experiment in autobiography.* New York: Macmillan.

West, M. (1959). *Goodness had nothing to do with it.* New York: Woodhill.

Whitbourne, S. K., & Weinstock, C. S. (1979). *Adult development: The differentiation of experience.* New York: Holt, Rinehart & Winston.

White, J. E. (1991, September 16). The pain of being Black. *Time,* pp. 24-27.

White, P. (1982). *Flaws in the glass: A self-portrait.* New York: Viking.

White, R. W. (1975). *Lives in progress: A study of the natural growth of personality* (3rd ed.). New York: Holt, Rinehart & Winston.

White, R. W. (1981). Exploring personality the long way: The study of lives. In A. I. Rubin, J. Arnoff, A. M. Barclay, & R. A. Zucker (Eds.), *Further explorations in personality* (pp. 3-19). New York: John Wiley.

Whittemore, R. (1988). *Pure lives: The early biographers.* Baltimore, MD: Johns Hopkins University Press.

Wiener, W. J., & Rosenwald, G. C. (1993). A moment's monument: The psychology of keeping a diary. In R. Josselson & A. Lieblich (Eds.), *The narrative study of lives* (pp. 30-58). Newbury Park, CA: Sage.

Wiersma, U. J., & van den Berg, P. (1991). Work-home role conflict, family climate, and domestic responsibilities among men and women in dual-career families. *Journal of Applied Social Psychology, 21,* 1207-1217.

Winkler, K. J. (1980, October 14). Oral history: Coming of age in the 1980's. *Chronicle of Higher Education,* p. 3.

Winters, S. (1980). *Shelley, also known as Shirley.* New York: William Morrow.

Wolff, G. (1979). Minor lives. In M. Pachter (Ed.), *Telling lives: The biographer's art* (pp. 56-72). Washington, DC: New Republic Books/National Portrait Gallery.

Woolf, V. (1973). *A writer's diary.* New York: Harcourt Brace Jovanovich. (Original work published 1916)

Wrightsman, L. S. (1993). Allport's personal documents: Then and now. In K. H. Craik, R. Hogan, & R. N. Wolfe (Eds.), *Fifty years of personality psychology* (pp. 165-175). New York: Plenum.

Wyman, D. S. (1991, April 21). You won't understand. You must understand. *The New York Times Book Review,* p. 7.

Yuasa, M. (1974). The shifting center of scientific activity in the West: From the 16th to the 20th century. In N. Shigeru, D. L. Swain, & Y. Eri (Eds.), *Science and society in modern Japan* (pp. 81-103). Tokyo: University of Tokyo Press.

Yin, R. K. (1989). *Case study research: Design and methods* (Rev. ed.). Newbury Park, CA: Sage.

Zawadski, B., & Lazarsfeld, P. (1935). The psychological consequences of unemployment. *Journal of Social Psychology, 6,* 224-251.

Zimmerman, P. D. (1976, April 5). Writer into scientist. *Newsweek,* pp. 83-84.

Zinsser, W. (1986). Introduction. In W. Zinsser (Ed.), *Extraordinary lives: The art and craft of American biography* (pp. 9-21). New York: Book-of-the-Month Club.

Author Index

Subject Index

About the Author

Lawrence S. Wrightsman (Ph.D., University of Minnesota, 1959) is Professor of Psychology at the University of Kansas, Lawrence. Trained as a social psychologist, he has maintained a career-long interest in individual differences in personality and social behavior. He is one of the editors (with John P. Robinson and Phillip R. Shaver) of *Measures of Personality and Social Psychological Attitudes.* His presidential address to the Society of Personality and Social Psychology dealt with the use of personal documents in testing theories of personality development in adulthood. He is the author or editor of 18 books.